MONEY FOR NOTHING

A History of the Music Video
from the Beatles to the White Stripes

Saul Austerlitz

continuum

NEW YORK • LONDON

2007

The Continuum International Publishing Group Inc
80 Maiden Lane, New York, NY 10038

The Continuum International Publishing Group Ltd
The Tower Building, 11 York Road, London SE1 7NX

www.continuumbooks.com

Printed in the United States of America

Library of Congress Cataloging-in-Publication Data

Austerlitz, Saul.
  Money for nothing : a history of the music video, from the Beatles to the White Stripes / Saul Austerlitz.
    p. cm.
  Includes videography (p.   ).
  ISBN-13: 978-0-8264-2958-2 (hardcover : alk. paper)
  ISBN-10: 0-8264-1818-X (hardcover : alk. paper)
  1. Music videos--History and criticism. I. Title.

PN1992.8.M87A97 2006
780.26'7--dc22

                                                          2006029185

Contents

Foreword & Acknowledgments

Back in the early 1990s, when I was a music-mad teenager, anxiously rifling through the latest issue of *Spin* for cultural guidance, I had a ritual. Every Sunday evening at 9 PM, I tuned in the East Coast feed of MTV, pen and notebook in hand, and watched the latest installation of the alternative-rock video showcase *120 Minutes*. While hosts Lewis Largent and Matt Pinfield chatted with that week's musical guests, I jotted down notes: artists, song titles, directors' names. I suppose I should have known then.

In a way, this book has been in gestation since then. Not having been a part of that initial MTV generation, I always felt like a latecomer to the music-video party, continually hoping to catch up on what I had missed. In fact, I was doubly impeded, lapped repeatedly by my schoolmates and friends in my knowledge of music-video arcana by virtue of not having had steady access to MTV until age fourteen. Seeking to make up for lost time, I became an amateur music-video scholar of sorts, hunting down unfamiliar videos on their rare onscreen appearances, tracking the arc of video directors' careers, and, always, making sure to watch *120 Minutes* every Sunday. After a number of years, I put music videos to the side, but my interest never abated entirely, only receded temporarily.

In writing this book, I have sought to use this sensation of tardiness I once felt in regard to music videos profitably, writing what I hope will be an accessible, readable introduction to the music video as a genre, and approaching the topic without preconceived notions about what music-video history looked like. I've discovered that writing a history of the music video is as hopelessly ludicrous an enterprise as penning a two-hundred-fifty-page history of film, or of pop music; there is an ocean of material out there, and any writer, in tackling the music video, can only watch a tiny fraction of the videos that are available. The subtitle of my book is "A History of Music Video from the Beatles to the White Stripes," not "The History . . ."; *Money for Nothing* follows one thread of music-video history, but there are dozens, if not hundreds, of others, all equally valid.

In that vein, some limitations had to be put on the scope of the book. As much as I had wanted to include them, this book almost entirely ignores the voluminous contributions of the non-English-speaking world to the music video. Between the near-impossible task of tracking down non-American videos, and my admittedly poor language skills, any attempt at briefly summarizing the vast scope of foreign-language music video would have been more farcical than informative. I do hope, though, that someone else takes the lead and writes that book—I, for one, would be eager to read it. I am also, of course, unable to escape the prison house of my own biases and experiences. Having been born in the late 1970s, the years between 1991 and 1996 were my formative video years, and if I pay undue attention to the videos of that era in these pages, it is only because they are the ones that first awoke my interest in the subject.

With MTV and the other music-video channels having mostly ditched the music video in favor of a twenty-four-hour celebration of celebrity and wealth, it has grown exceedingly difficult to track down old music videos. The good news for me, and for anyone interested in seeing the great music videos of the past (see my personal top one hundred videos list, page 225), is that the Internet has blossomed into a superb music-video resource. MTV's Overdrive and VH1's VSpot offer streaming video of many of the clips in those channels' archives, and Yahoo, Google, and AOL have also begun to offer music videos among their video content. Idiosyncratic noncorporate sites like Another Brick in the Wall, Video-C, and Antville offer a wide array of videos, and the indispensable Music Video Database provided a plethora of music-video-related information. As this book was nearing completion, YouTube began to offer a huge amount of previously near-impossible-to-find videos, making my life immensely easier in the process.

Many people assisted in ways large and small in making this process more manageable. I would like to thank Barbara London, Charles Silver, and Paul Power at the Museum of Modern Art and David Schwartz and Livia Bloom at the Museum of the Moving Image for generously allowing me to view some of their music videos. Jim McDonnell was exceedingly gracious in giving me a tour of his fantastic collection of early music videos.

My editor, David Barker, has been unfailingly enthusiastic and supportive from the first moment I approached him with the idea for this book. His willingness to believe in this book was a major factor in its coming to fruition. Wendy Raffel, Gabriella Page-Fort, and Emma Cook at Continuum have also been wondrously helpful in navigating this book to its completion.

I would like to thank the following people for their assistance in editing parts of this book at various stages of its writing: Aaron Zamost, Reuben Silberman, Rabbi Daniel Smokler, Kate Lee, and Margaret Miller. Josh Olken provided crucial help during the research process.

My parents, Michael and Sarah Austerlitz, have been miraculously supportive of my pursuits, from as early as I can remember. Without them, it is highly doubtful this book could ever have been written. My sisters Annie and Ali have been willing to put up with my distracted telephone conversations over the past year. My wonderful in-laws, Carla and Dan Silber, and my sister-in-law Abby Silber, have been like a second family to me. My wife, Becky Silber, has been a tireless fount of ideas, support, and encouragement at every step of the way. Her belief in me, and my work, has meant the world to me.

Introduction

Coming at the intersection of art and commerce, somewhere between avant-garde film and television advertisement, appears that ignored artifact of contemporary culture—the music video. Uniting the two most influential media of post-World War II culture, popular music and filmmaking, the music video straddles genres, typologies, functions: Is it an ad for the song? Is it its own discrete work of art? Is it a work of art, period?

The music video is a medium that appears to have mostly run its course, or at least hit a momentary rut in its evolution. MTV and VH1 have morphed into lifestyle channels, the musical component of their programming reduced to a mere blip on their schedule. BET, Fuse, and other music channels are still dedicated to showing music videos regularly, but they are niche channels for particular audiences. And the Internet, the new home of the music video, has not fully emerged as a replacement video nexus. The video's shining moment as part disposable crap, part momentary, fleeting genius, the exact cinematic/televisual equivalent of the pop song, may have passed, but its triumphs render it a subject worthy of deeper study and attention.

The history of the music video is that of an underappreciated, critically unnoticed subgenre of filmmaking. Its uncataloged depths, though, contain a panoply of the brilliant, fascinating, and simply odd, shedding enormous light on pop music, mythmaking, and the enduring, limitless possibility of the music video as short film, liberated from the feature-length narrative's requirements to proceed in logical order, follow an easily gleaned plot, etc. The music video marks the triumph of the visual over the oral, eschewing dialogue in favor of style, aura, and, occasionally, plot, propelled forward by a dependence on the cinematic language of montage as a necessary means of communication. In short, the music video is a fascinating oddity, capable of packing great wit, emotion, and insight into its brief span. A compelling marker of cultural history, the video emerges onto television screens nationwide, shining for a brief moment before disappearing into the remembrance of television past.

1

Before proceeding any further, we must clarify exactly what music videos are. Having played so omnipresent a role in the cultural landscape of the past quarter-century, music videos sometimes seem to have emerged from the womb fully formed, but a significant part of their development has been a gradual hardening of form. Music videos are short films intended to serve as accompaniment to their musical soundtracks. They are intended to sell the music, and so the song comes first in a number of ways. Reversing the working method of most filmmaking, the music is composed first, then joined by its accompanying image. As a result, the length of the song in most cases determines the length of the clip, and the action is secondary to the musical soundtrack. Videos are also almost always silent (other than the music, of course). There may be an occasional scrap of dialogue, there may be a prologue or postscript, there may be subtitles (or intertitles), but videos mostly rely on image, and acting, to get their scenarios across.

Emphasizing sensation over information, the music video strives for deliberate ambiguousness rather than straightforward exposition. Most videos take place in fantasy worlds, whether elaborate depictions of other realms, or more mundane fantasies of sexual gratification and musical pleasure. These are often less about a coherent narrative, one easily translatable into words, than an effect. Music videos seek to create atmosphere, above all—a mood, and a space, that viewers could slip into time and again. It is crucial to the project of the music video that they not be used up too quickly. Music-video outlets had to keep viewers returning for another fix, or another chance to crack the code, and with the necessity of repeat viewings built into the business model of MTV and its companions, it was necessary that the videos they played be ever-so-slightly beyond reach of total, immediate comprehension.

In the music video, where acting and narrative, and, most important, the passage of time, are effectively neutralized by the sheer brevity of the work, film-school stylists and advertising gurus become rulers of the realm. As a genre of filmmaking, the music video does not lend itself well to austerity or transcendentalism; its pleasures are immediate and of the moment. The music video demands such triviality, much the same as its source material, the pop song, leans toward the ephemeral and disposable rather than the lasting or durable. In the same way that classic Top 40 preferred the Bee Gees' catchy fluff to Bob Dylan, the music video demanded immediately arresting imagery over subtler, slower to develop material. While there would be many exceptions (the Replacements' "Bastards of Young" and Johnny Cash's "Hurt," to name just two), they would only serve to prove the rule by standing out so thoroughly from their MTV compatriots.

The music video has traditionally been divided into two main categories: the performance video and the concept video. A performance video consists primarily of the musicians' performance of the song, often in a concert hall, performance space, or some other narrative-justified locale; it rarely embraces the everybody-bursts-into-song tone of certain musicals. The concept video spices up the song with an accompanying visual track, one that tells a story or emphasizes a mood. While this division stands as the primary distinction among music videos, the form's stylistic proclivities hold true across all boundaries. The music video is dependent on such elements of mise-en-scène as rapid-fire editing, jump cuts, and distinctive lighting to set its tone. Above all, music videos are intended to be immediate, their impulse to speed, color, and light intimately related to their overarching quest for hipness.

As a product of youth culture, the music video stakes all on its claim to coolness, and its embrace of stylistic extremity is a direct result. Even more so than its desire for perpetual motion, the music video craves spectacle. The biggest, the loudest, the sexiest, the most colorful—even the longest—music videos aimed for a consistent renewal, and amplification, of the initial scopophilic thrill of such grandiosity. In its brashness, in its desire, so typically American, to forever top the magnificence of what came before it, lurked the seeds of its polar opposite. As such, integrated within the bigger-louder-faster impulse of music-video history is a braking motion, cutting back in the opposite direction toward slower edits, less glamour, and less spectacle. Groundbreaking videos like Sinead O'Connor's "Nothing Compares 2 U," Sarah McLachlan's "World on Fire," and New Order's "Perfect Kiss" make consistent appearances in the history of the music video, their relative austerity an implicit rebuke to the form's Kubla Khan–like dreams of endless video Xanadus.

Music videos are consumer products. They are simultaneously the casing for an agglomeration of consumerist lifestyle choices, and themselves the commodity which they advertise. Having come of age during the early 1980s, the music video internalized the ethos of commodity fetishization—a perpetual hankering for the next product over the horizon, that idealized, imaginary solution to all of its consumers' real problems. The music video offered the prospect of goods that could not readily be purchased. Like any good ad man, the music video channeled these wants into specific goods—the song, and artist, being cast into the marketplace.

Having borrowed so heavily from the rituals of the ad's hard sell, the music video found its formalized techniques borrowed back by the advertising industry and, eventually, by mainstream filmmakers as well. The restless aesthetic of the music video became the primary mode of communication of American visual life, its stylistic foundation serving as a code for all the things the music video audience possessed or dreamt of—youth, sexiness, and wealth. The already hazy boundary between music video and advertisement grew even hazier, with superstars like Madonna and Michael Jackson shooting video-like advertisements for Fortune 500 corporations. Similarly, the rise to Hollywood prominence of ad- and video-trained directors like Ridley and Tony Scott, David Fincher, and Brett Ratner, and the arrival of a new generation of MTV-damaged film school graduates, meant that the music video's once-edgy aesthetic became fully integrated into the mainstream. Films like *Top Gun* and *Seven* took the video's advances and made them their own, with particular emphasis on the form's ADD-friendly editing techniques.

At the same time, and largely as a result of its influences, music videos are also the province of the clichéd and the hackneyed. More so even than its older brother, the Hollywood film, the average music video is intended not to rock the boat, to blend in amidst its neighbors. The cliché of clichés, the elephant in the screening room, must be the objectification of women as fantasy objects of desire. The presence of half-nude women in the background (and foreground) of practically every music video ever made has grown so commonplace that it appears almost unworthy of mention. Music videos, for the most part, are intended for men's eyes, providing them with endless opportunities to delectate in the spectacle of beautiful women performing for their pleasure. Videos are male fantasies of controlling and possessing women, and to avoid this subject is to miss one of the most fundamental aspects of music video. These conditions will be very familiar to any movie buff, *Maxim* subscriber, or reader of Laura Mulvey's essay "Visual Pleasure and Narrative Cinema." As Mulvey writes in her famous essay, "The magic of the Hollywood style at its best . . . arose . . . from its skilled and satisfying manipulation of visual pleasure." This visual pleasure was to be found in the female body, and videos, like their older brothers on the silver screen, made the act of looking, and the complex transference of gazes, its primary task: "Going far beyond highlighting a woman's to-be-looked-at-ness, cinema builds the way she is to be looked at into the spectacle itself. . . . Cinematic codes create a gaze, a world, and an object, thereby producing an illusion cut to the measure of desire." Men were onscreen to look at the women, and by looking both excuse the audience's ogling and provide a worthwhile stand-in who ogles both with us and for us. The difference between film and music video is just that the corpus of music video is so shamelessly forthright about its lechery, not even deigning to cloak it in the finery of celebrity profile or cinematic narrative. In music video, the primary role of women is to serve as eye candy, and any deviation is seen as a variation from the norm.

Even when women are the performers, their videos often merely conflate two roles: instead of the male performer as audience stand-in, ogling the scenery, the performer is the body to be ogled (see any Madonna video for further proof). It is too easy to excuse all this apologetically as "boys will be boys," but it is also far too simple to dismiss music videos wholesale. To fully appreciate their impact, music videos require both responses: disgust at the endless commodification of women, turning their bodies into yet another retail product, and also appreciation of the moments when the medium's inherent prurience is spun into art (Chris Isaak's "Wicked Game," Madonna's "Justify My Love"). And to deny that music video is a highly effective turn-on mechanism is to pretend to be more than human. One may resent the forced emotion, but much like contemporary advertising, one must be impressed at how consistently and skillfully the button is pushed. Music video is not any different from the bulk of American popular culture at the end of the twentieth century, and the beginning of the twenty-first, merely more shameless.

No matter how many different ways the button is pushed, though, it still remains the same button. For proof, compare the relative presence of the female body in the music video with that of its male counterpart, whether as lust object or otherwise. With a few exceptions, the male body is wholly absent from the music video, other than a token handful of flipping-the-script scenarios by female artists (Salt-N-Pepa, Toni Braxton). Videos live and die on the presentation of women as ready, luscious, and able, always unclothed, often nubile, and unquestioningly present as objects of male desire. Just flip on any hip-hop video from the mid-1990s forward and watch for the backup dancers. Almost always dressed in short shorts and halter tops, vigorously shaking what their mama gave them, they are unremarkable in their ubiquity. This is merely another aspect of selling the rock-and-roll fantasy, of which a crucial part has always been the promise of sex's easy availability. The parade of women is also evidence of music videomakers catering to their core audience: hormonal, sex-starved teenage boys. Sometimes, though, it feels like music videos are not just made *for* teenage boys, but *by* teenage boys; witness the juvenile sexual innuendo of Warrant's "Cherry Pie," or the Ying Yang Twins' "Wait (The Whisper Song)."

As Mim Udovitch once noted, "The predominant fantasy narrative of the [music-video] genre involves the stalking, restraint, conquest, or flat-out extinction of women." This is not a new trend, nor was it started by MTV; the Soundie video for Eppy Pearson's "Tabby the Cat," a finger-snapper from World War II, has its jiving singers surrounded by backup dancers in skimpy outfits. Videos invest feminine beauty with physical powers, as in ZZ Top's "Legs," where a posse of beauties who look like they've just left their aerobics class stomp into a strip mall to save the video's heroine in distress. Videos also worship beauty, especially the silent type. Hence their persistent affection for putting models on display, as in Isaak's "Wicked Game," Robert Palmer's "Addicted to Love," George Michael's "Freedom 90," and the White Stripes' "Just Don't

Know What to Do with Myself." Similarly, their love for porn stars, who spice things up with a frisson of the forbidden (Metallica's "Turn the Page," Everclear's "Boys Are Back in Town," and Eminem's "Superman," for example). With some notable exceptions, videos are boys' clubs, celebrating masculinity by imposing a severely limited range of roles on women as a condition of joining in the fun. If much of contemporary mainstream American popular culture feels like a celebration of delayed adolescence, music video is without doubt the sixteen-year-old doomed to endlessly repeat the ninth grade.

Even more crucially, though, music video is about the foregrounding of image. It is an inherent rebuke to the obstinacy of rock snobs who insist on the primacy of the music itself, to the exclusion of marketing, image, and hype. Instead of seeing everything music-related as a sideline to the main attraction of the music, the music video evens out the playing field. Music videos have always been intimately tied up with advertising, serving as the most sophisticated kind of marketing push to sell CDs, cassettes, 8-tracks, or LPs. They are both advertisements for a product (the music) and ads for themselves. In many ways, music videos are the very products they are shilling for. Music videos may be mere commerce, far more sullied by the touch of capitalism than music's ethereal purity, but they are no more commercialized than Hollywood films, and far more honest about their essential purpose. Hollywood is also present to sell us on a way of living, whether in the grubby, immediate meaning of pitching Coke over Pepsi, or in the larger sense of American filmmaking being a grandiose ad for an increasingly unreachable lifestyle, but films consistently deflect attention away from their materialist aims with chatter about love, satisfaction, and other such nonmaterial objects. Videos, however, do no such thing; they are open about their desire to sell, and like hucksters shilling their latest wonder drug, each video is an unfulfilled promise of unimaginable pleasures. Music videos are pure consumption—all they ask is to be swallowed gratefully.

Academics like Jody Berlan have often seen music video as a triumph of image over sound, with Berlan arguing in her essay "Sound Image, and Social Space: Music Video and Media Reconstruction" that the video "present[s] a particular mode of cultural cannibalization, in which the soundtrack has been digested lifetimes ago, in fact consumed by the image, which appears to be singing." This analysis fails to acknowledge the basic economic principles regarding the music video. The music video's purpose for existence is to advertise and accompany its soundtrack, and without the supposedly secondary songs, nary a music video would ever have been made. Music videos are first, last, and always about commerce: they are engines meant to drive consumers to stores to pick up their favorite band's new CD and to keep them from changing the channel.

In fact, image does not triumph over sound nearly enough; just take a look at all the hit videos of the past twenty years that would be utterly unwatchable without the catchy songs they are attached to. If the music video is the triumph of disposable image's empty calories over the genuine feeling of music, what the form needs is more fat. Much like film, videos are at their best when they embrace their own nature and become what they already are, rather than attempt to march to the beat of another art form's drummer. This is not to say that only the shlockiest videos, with the most lowbrow content, are worthwhile; on the contrary, some of video's classics are attempts to imitate the highbrow intellectuality of the avant-garde (R.E.M.'s "Losing My Religion," the Replacements' "Bastards of Young"). Rather, it is that music video is an inherently visual art form, and it is sheer fallacy to think that some types of image (concert footage and its brothers) are "natural" to the video, while other types are foreign interlopers, disrupting music's inherent drive toward genuine feeling. If all images are equally created, equally artificial, then why not create something of interest? If music video is the collision of two of the twentieth century's greatest cultural breakthroughs, pop music and the recorded image, shouldn't we hold the latter to the same standards of ingenuity and formal innovation that we hold the former? In that vein, it becomes useful to treat music videos as short films, but only to a point. Music videos have the ability to be every bit the equal of their feature-length siblings, and demand to be measured against the same yardstick; but to lose sight of music videos' essential function as outgrowths of the *music* industry is to treat them as found objects, leaching them of their rightful place in the capitalist structure and their very reason for existence.

Postmodernists had good cause for their interest in music videos. In trying to suss out the stylistic rules of the music video, it rapidly becomes apparent that, above all, videos are intended to serve as clashes of sensibility, a textural mash-up. Theorists like Fredric Jameson would return time and again to the notion of pastiche as an essential component of postmodernism, where the cultural particulars of another era or milieu are grafted onto the present for the sake of authenticity, titillation, or a sense of stylistic daring. The music video is a riot of competing textures, embracing pastiche and the clash of styles in the name of maintaining the steady flow of excitement. Pastiche is also crucial to videos' role within the music industry's commodification of image. Artists maintain their stranglehold on fame, and record sales, by continually tweaking, updating, and varying their image. Thus, we have videos that swipe their imagery from avant-garde photography (Janet Jackson's "Love Will Never Do," Nine Inch Nails' "Closer"), commercials (Foo Fighters' "Big Me"), game shows (Dandy Warhols' "Not If You Were the Last Junkie on Earth"), or even other videos (Bowling for Soup's "1985," Weird Al Yankovic's "Smells Like Nirvana").

The list of video's borrowings from the movies is the most voluminous of all, ranging from obvious targets like *Casino* (Nas' "Street Dreams") and *Reservoir Dogs* (Cool Breeze's "Watch for the Hook") to more eclectic fare like Georges Melies' 1902 *A Trip to the Moon* (Smashing Pumpkins' "Tonight, Tonight") and the German Expressionist classic *The Cabinet of Dr. Caligari* (Marilyn Manson's "The Beautiful People"). The relentless borrowing is sometimes a sign of laziness, to be sure, but it is also, like sampling in hip-hop, an opportunity to align oneself within the pop-culture continuum. It is a shorthand revealing of sensibility and taste, an opportunity to speak clearly to an audience with a minimum of explanation. Like hip-hop sampling, music video's dependence on pastiche made it a prototypically postmodern affair, a fractured hall of mirrors in which each video cast its reflection elsewhere.

Luckily, musicians and directors understood the possibilities of video for opening up a world of experimentation and innovation. Primary among these were the capabilities of video to emphasize its role-playing capabilities. In the same way that rock stars are essentially playing a character of their own creation, video became a showcase for "the mutability of identity," in Jim Farber's phrase. Many of the great manipulators of the video form used it to flip through permutations of their complex personae, with each video an opportunity to present a new snapshot of themselves, or a new fantasy role to play.

Three key elements go into the making of a video: performer, director, and concept. To make a video, the performer and director enter into a symbiotic relationship, one best compared to that between an architect and his or her client. One supplies the need and the money, one supplies the technical know-how, and either or both provide the germ of the idea. The architect has the expertise, but it is only through working with the client, grasping their vision, and melding two diverging dreams together, that a compelling final product emerges. The architect may have an idea for what type of house he would like to build, but it is ultimately the client who must live there. So too with the video, where the client (the musician) hires the architect (the filmmaker) to craft a unique and distinctive home for the performer's song to live in.

The performer-director relationship, like the dynamic between architect and client, must exhibit flexibility and open-mindedness on both sides to allow for the free flow of ideas. The performer is rarely a blank slate, having imprinted themselves with the personae of videos past, and the director often has a specific aesthetic that carries over, auteurlike, from video to video. It is the successful video that harmoniously marries performer and videomaker, and crafts a final product that satisfies both their needs. The performer, being the primary name associated with the video, often exerts a larger, more noticeable role in its formation than their closest cinematic equivalent, actors, adopting at least a portion of the auteur function traditionally ceded to a film's director. Artists like Missy Elliott may not direct their own videos, but their idiosyncratic stamp appears in every frame of their clips nonetheless. It is this relation that will serve as a guide through the sometimes murky waters of music-video history, and provide a framework to appropriately parcel out credit for the work of video-making. In this endeavor, great clients must be saluted as much as (if not more than) their architectural enablers.

In addition to individual performers looking to meet certain needs in their work, music videos also tend to abide by the rules established by genre. Rock videos, for example, tend to exhibit a similar look, sticking to a set of guide-lines about lighting, camera movement, and style, especially when placed in contrast with the body of hip-hop videos, which follow an entirely different (although equally binding) set of core standards. Watch enough music videos, and the odd unfamiliar clip will be easily pegged into a genre and era, even with the sound off. For the most part, musical genre creates music video genre, a rule of thumb best proven by the video oeuvre of genre converts like Mariah Carey. Carey's early videos, when she was marketed as a whitebread pop princess, are remarkably different in plotline, directorial style, clothing, and aura from later videos like "Heartbreaker," where Mariah is on display as a post-ethnic R&B diva. Rock videos, hip-hop videos, pop videos, country videos—each exist on their own timeline, with their own clichés and their own techniques. In the history of video, there are many moments of interaction, but music video is as rigorously divided by genre as the music itself, and any history of music video demands an acknowledgment of genre's outsize influence on the videos themselves.

Music videos live or die on their timing. Making a music video is like beginning a film by writing its soundtrack and then building the visuals to relate to the sound, rather than vice versa. A music video is a challenge for its director, who is like a poet adopting a specific (and arbitrary) set of rules in which to confine his verse. A director comes to a music video, handed an exact length for their film, and seeks to pin key moments in the clip to the moments of greatest musical urgency in the accompanying song. Radiohead's "Just" is perhaps the ultimate example of a director using the emotional peaks and valleys of the song as markers for the corresponding moments in the video, but the practice of synchronizing key moments in the song with similarly dazzling visual sequences is a bedrock practice of the music video director.

From the very outset, music videos sought to entertain, to stimulate, and to shock. Less concerned with lasting artistry than immediate gratification, the music video began as a series of disparate lines of inquiry, ranging from the musical numbers of Hollywood films to Oskar Fischinger's animated works to the proto-videos played on video jukeboxes and as shorts preceding feature-length films. It was only with the passage of time, and the steady growth of interest in the form as cultural effluvium and market force, that the diverse lines of inquiry banded together to create what we now know as the music video.

CHAPTER 1

Music Video in Fugue

For as long as music had been a fundamental aspect of human cultural expression, its enjoyment had been inextricably intertwined with the experience of watching a performer physically produce musical sound. Whether strumming a guitar, beating drums, bowing a violin, or using the vocal chords to turn out sound, the means of musical production had always been immediately present and immediately visible. A performer's body language, the way he stood, danced, held his instrument—these were fundamental aspects of the musical experience, every bit as important as the sounds themselves. Until the twentieth century, and the rise of technologies of reproduction that allowed music to emerge, as if disembodied, from the belly of machines, rather than from the hands and throats of human beings, the notion of separating music and the musician was a nonsensical one. With few exceptions (the player piano springs to mind), it was illogical to think of music as existing separately from the people and the instruments that created it.

The rise of radio in the early twentieth century, and of recordings made available for commercial purchase, changed the equation drastically. For the first time, music could be enjoyed alone, in the privacy of one's home, or out in public without the mediating presence of musicians. Music, like so much else, became a commodity, a formerly ephemeral, fleeting object of momentary pleasure now available for commercial purchase.

Concomitant with the rise of this technology, efforts were made to reunite the separated segments of the musical experience, seeking to mechanistically realize nineteenth-century German composer Richard Wagner's dream of the *gesamtkunstwerk*, the total artwork, combining the heretofore disparate strands of artistic endeavor. By this logic, if technical know-how could take the work of musicians in a studio, or onstage, and preserve it for posterity, then perhaps a visual record could be preserved as well. Beyond mere mechanical reproduction, the hope was to organically reunite sound and image, creating a new art form that activated, and heightened, all the senses. The problem of reuniting sound and image, of capturing the musical experience in its entirety, led to a wide range of experiments with what would eventually come to be music video. While none of these experiments reached the critical mass that propelled the music video in its current MTV incarnation, short-lived unions of image and sound, like Soundies, Snader Telescriptions, and the Scopitone, are worthy of attention, if only as reminders of roads ultimately not traveled.

From the outset, the notion of bringing sound and image together was a musically grounded experiment. It was no accident that the very first talking picture, in 1927, was a musical—Al Jolson's *The Jazz Singer*. For the film industry, the burgeoning musical format was a means of demonstrating the quality of its technology, able to capture the tonal nuance of song. Musicals also became the financial and emotional cornerstones of the burgeoning sound film, their exuberant frivolity a balm for Depression-scarred audiences. Musicals' juggling of imaginative musical numbers and (sometimes only slightly) more realistic intermediary sequences meant that a space had been carved out, inside Hollywood's most treasured products, for the expression of unfettered fantasy. Musical sequences were discrete short films in and of themselves, often possessed of unique sets, costumes, camera angles, and performers distinct from the prosaic, nonmusical scenes of the film.

The Hollywood musical's influence on the music video cannot be overlooked, its innovations written into the DNA of the medium. Look at a musical number like those in the Fred Astaire-Ginger Rogers film *Top Hat* (1935), and you will see the prototype for dance videos to come; elongated sequences like the "Girl Hunt" from *The Band Wagon* (1953), or the closing ballet of *An American in Paris* (1951), were hints of what epic videos like "Thriller" would soon attempt. More broadly speaking, the movie musical's emphasis on the musical number as discrete performance would inexorably lead to the music video, by process of a winnowing down to essences. If audiences flocked to movies for the delights found in their musical numbers, then short films composed entirely of musical numbers were sure to be a smash success. With that rationale in mind, Paramount and other studios made a large number of musical shorts, starring major performers like Billie Holiday, Bing Crosby, and Duke Ellington, intended to be shown before features. The logic was sound—it merely took another fifty or so years to come due.

The Hollywood musical was not the only hotspot where music and image could mingle. Animation was another preferred medium for innovators kicking the tires of the new sound film, investigating its capabilities, with none more influential, or unique, than German filmmaker Oskar Fischinger. Originally trained as an architect, Fischinger's motion-experiment short films of the 1930s brought a builder's mentality to his scored short films. Tightly synchronizing his films' movement to their accompanying music (usually new recordings of short classical pieces like Paul Dukas' "Sorcerer's Apprentice," for which Fischinger's films were intended as advertisements), Fischinger shorts like "Study 8" (1931) and "Composition in Blue" (1935) featured dancing geometrical shapes—whizzing circles, squares, and diamonds, and wiggling lines. Fischinger was a gifted painter, and at times his films resemble live-action versions of the geometric abstraction of Mondrian or Kandinsky. At other times, their simplicity, and the elegance of their motion, make them precursors to the intricate movie credit sequences of Saul Bass. Fischinger was convinced he was inventing a new, scientific, nonverbal film language through his forms, and while that never came to fruition, his films are remarkable as proto-music videos. Fischinger's drawings in his motion studies are so perfectly synchronized to their chosen music that what appears onscreen seems to be summoned by the very musical notes themselves. Looking by turns like archery targets, voltage meters, cylinders, and Kenneth Noland circles, the figures of "Composition in Blue" dance across the screen in unerring harmony with their musical accompaniment.

Fischinger had sought for years to collaborate with composer Leopold Stokowski on a hybrid project. Stokowski would provide the music, Fischinger would furnish animation to accompany it, and the union of two such kindred souls would create a film greater than the sum of its illustrious parts. Stokowski liked the idea, but ended up taking it to Walt Disney, who laid the groundwork for what would come to be *Fantasia* (1940). Stokowski convinced Disney to hire Fischinger to animate the opening sequence of the film, set to Bach's "Toccata in Fugue." In what would become a wearyingly familiar routine in Fischinger's abortive Hollywood career, his work was tampered with by the Disney design committee, who voted to alter nearly all of it.

Bits and pieces of Fischinger can still be seen in the final version of *Fantasia*, described by Jim Farber as "the first unintentional long-form music video." "Toccata in Fugue" bears witness to the influence of Fischinger's dancing geometric shapes and taste for abstract design. *Fantasia* is a grab bag of visual styles, one for each segment of the film, with some considerably more successful than others. The Mickey Mouse–starring "Sorcerer's Apprentice" is charming, with sound and image superbly coordinated, while the playful romping of lovestruck animals to Beethoven's "Pastoral Symphony" is downright tedious. Broken up into discrete segments, with each introduced by famed composer Deems Taylor, *Fantasia* was an avatar of the coming music-video genre in more ways than one. Not only did the film create a visual world to accompany its musical selections, its placement of a sequence of unrelated short films in close quarters, linked by a smooth, unbroken link of introductory and intermediary material, presaged the format of music-video channels to come.

Life During Wartime

With new technology allowing for the projection of moving images onto a small screen, the stage was set for a new class of jukebox that combined music with short movie clips. The Soundie, child of World War II, was thus born, making its way into bars, restaurants, and nightclubs across the United States in the early 1940s. Between 1941 and 1946, when the Soundie boom began to wane, soon to be made entirely obsolete by television, thousands of short-form music videos were produced—mostly of blues and jazz acts, novelty performers, and comedians. Soundies were played back on the Panarom Sound, a tall, squat apparatus paneled in dark wood that resembled an audio jukebox, with its screen positioned where the carousel of records would normally be visible. The Soundies used celluloid for playback, a medium not intended for continuous play. When combined with the technologically advanced but very maintenance-heavy Panarom, the Soundie was not a form designed for the long haul. (In the 1980s, when the video jukebox made a brief resurgence with the Startime Video Muzzikboxx, the machines experienced similar durability problems).

Appearing mostly in nightspots, and charging ten cents a throw, Soundies were delightfully low-class, simultaneously able to imitate their cultural superiors (like the movies) while also, as nontheatrical releases, exempt from the Hays Code, free from the shackles of overly aggressive supervision. Soundies reflected the passing trends and fads of the moment, ranging from the zoot suits and tight slit skirts of jazz-happy hepcats to the aquatic hijinks popularized by cinematic swimming stars Esther Williams and Johnny Weissmuller.

As commercial products, Soundies advertised their performers, but they were also themselves for sale, subject to the approval or disapproval of customers able to vote with their dimes. Often shot by the same handful of directors (including Josef Berne and William Forest Crouch), the bulk of Soundies, much like their MTV grandchildren, sought to dazzle. Be it comic pratfalls (famed silent comic Harry Langdon makes a guest appearance in "Beautiful Clothes (Make Beautiful Girls)"), exhibitions of dancing skill, or the sight of chorus girls' long legs, Soundies were desperate to capture their viewers' attention. Like slimmed-down versions of the musical numbers from Hollywood, Soundies featured the same Art Deco sets, tuxedo-clad musicians, and Busby Berkeley–

inspired geometric dance patterns familiar from countless musicals. Regrettably, they also feature much the same brand of racial prejudice so wearyingly familiar from feature filmmaking of the 1940s: in Raymond Duke's "Solid Jive," a phenomenal African-American dancer performs a solo routine whose frenzied roboticism presages the tightly controlled popping and locking of hip-hop breakdancing. The unstated rules of humiliation regarding the presence of African-Americans onscreen, though, demanded that he appear dressed as a bellhop, taking away with one hand the measure of dignity it had granted with the other.

In a manner that would be eminently familiar to any contemporary MTV watcher, Soundies were primarily concerned with selling sex. Leggy chorus girls and bashful bobbysoxers in short skirts are regular presences in Soundies, often every bit as blatant in their role as eye candy as any contemporary hit video's backup dancers. Soundies promised the caress of beautiful women, for everyone from Langdon in "Beautiful Clothes," to the cop on the beat in Eppy Pearson's "Tabby the Cat," to the old codger of "Hoosier Hot Shots."

There were other kinds of videos, too, ones that emphasized Soundies' small part as a cog in the vast entertainment apparatus of a country desperate to get its mind off the war raging overseas. Roller skaters, winter-sports shenanigans, and animated frogs all served as diversions, but occasionally even Soundies were required to approach the unapproachable: "Hands" is a solemn reminder to weary laborers of the crucial work of hands in the war effort—typing, praying, dialing telephones, and the like. "Hands" includes surprisingly explicit footage of wounded soldiers, their mangled hands reaching heavenward in supplication, before ending with one final hand, this one closed into a fist to knock back the Japanese soldier hell-bent on killing Americans. In "A Good Man Is Hard to Find," weary American soldiers march with an extra spring in their step, knowing that their women are knitting much-needed clothing for them back at home. Never quite as successfully escapist as they professed to be, Soundies were the soundtrack to a nation at war, depicting a carefree youth culture that could not, by virtue of world war, fully exist. Its occasional forays into strained seriousness were reminders that Soundies were, for better or for worse, fantasies of a carefree American life that did not yet exist.

Rock the Jukebox

Snader Telescriptions, named after their director, George Snader, were filmed musical performances sold in blocks to television stations to fill gaps in their programming. Making their biggest splash between 1950 and 1954, by which time television had grown entrenched enough to schedule a full day of programming, eliminating the need for filler material, the Snaders (shot on 35mm

film with live audio) were for the most part visually unremarkable live performances constricted to a single set. Adding to the blandness, multiple Snaders were
usually shot at the same time, only distinguished, at best, by a change of costume. Snaders did feature a wide variety of white, African-American, and Latin
artists, violating the unwritten rules that stipulated strict separation of the races
onscreen. Artists like Nat King Cole, the Ink Spots, Peggy Lee, and Bob Willis all
made Snaders, as did more offbeat acts like Herb Jeffries (a Latin crooner with a
bird perched on his shoulder, singing from the heart of a tropical forest) and the
Bob Mitchell Choirboys (a group of ten-year-olds in Huck Finn straw hats performing "Old MacDonald Had a Farm"). The Snaders were notable for their
lack of T&A; in comparison with Soundies, they are remarkably prim, and
remarkably staid.

Most Scopitones, by contrast, seemed to take place at parties, where well-
scrubbed boys and fresh-faced girls gathered and frolicked. These videos were
primarily concerned with the nature of young people at play—dancing, making
music, making out, and, above all, enjoying their vigorous bodies. The videos
themselves enjoyed the vigorous bodies, too, marking an unabashed return to
the sensual abandon and lustful eye of the Soundies. Nonetheless, there was a
certain awkwardness to some of the videos produced, as if they had not quite
figured out the nature of the endeavor just yet.

Scopitones were the invention of a French division of Philips, which sought
to bring short-form music clips to a youth audience in France via placement in
bars, cafés, and restaurants. Unlike the prudish Snaders, Scopitones never
intended to be about much else other than beautiful flesh, their awakening to
youth culture cohabitating with an awakening to sex as cultural revolution and
marketing opportunity. One can sense the influence of the American youth-
rebellion films of the 1950s on the French Scopitones (which later made a brief
foray into the United States)—their inclination to rebellion, their romance with
outlaws, their bodice-bursting sexuality. And yet, the French-produced Scopitones are delightfully charming and weightless, a Gallic variation on *Rebel Without a Cause* that owe more to Jacques Demy than James Dean. Freddie Bell and
Roberta Linn's "For You" is a Wild West hoedown with girls in Daisy Dukes
unabashedly shaking their moneymakers, while Johnny Hallyday's "Noir C'est
Noir" features leotard-clad backup dancers doing ballet pirouettes. Joi Lansing's
"The Web of Love" has Lansing living out the drama of her song's lyrics in literal fashion—trapped in a giant spider web, roasted under a low flame by hungry cannibals, and mauled by a distinctly human slithering snake—all this while
appearing in an array of skimpy, seductive costumes. The delightfully unhinged
scenario for "Mother Nature, Father Time," from R&B singer Brook Benton, is
seemingly at odds with Benton's lovelorn ballad. Like a team of Vanna Whites to

Benton's Pat Sajak, a series of women outfitted in skimpy costumes helpfully point out signs illustrating the song's lyrics. Benton, emoting manfully, performs in a realm entirely disconnected from the campy, perky women, only occasionally deigning to acknowledge, with a wink and a nod for the audience, the surreal silliness of "Mother Nature, Father Time's" scenario.

Scopitones' initial success in France prompted a slew of imitators, including the Italian and British Cinebox and the American Colorsonics. Neither of these were particularly successful, and even the original Scopitones were out of business by 1967. In the U.S., Scopitones were allegedly a Mafia-run business, an intentional money loser intended to tighten the mob's grip on nightclubs, restaurants, and other urban establishments.

The Scopitone shorts echoed a similar, prior flowering of youth culture across the ocean in the United States. Early-1950s films like *The Wild One* (1953), with Marlon Brando, and *Rebel Without a Cause* (1955), with James Dean, had established the nature of the burgeoning teenage rebelliousness, rock and roll films before rock and roll. Youth-culture films like *Blackboard Jungle* (1955), *The Girl Can't Help It* (1956), and *Jailhouse Rock* (1957) marked rock and roll's newly central place at the nexus of youthful energy, musical innovation, and antiauthoritarian impulse. These movies celebrated rock and roll as something vigorous, dangerous, and quintessentially now. *Blackboard Jungle*, the first film to feature rock and roll on its soundtrack, only had a rock song (Bill Haley & the Comets' "Rock Around the Clock") over its credits, but *The Girl Can't Help It* (featuring a raucous Little Richard) and *Jailhouse Rock* integrated performance into the body of the films themselves. Elvis Presley's performance of the title song in *Jailhouse Rock* looks now, to our eyes, like a proto-video, with Presley and his pals dancing on a jail set—swinging on cell doors, dancing on mess-hall tables, and playing on swings. The film codes the performance as part of the narrative itself (in which Presley plays an up-and-coming singer), but the inventiveness and energy of "Jailhouse Rock" overwhelm its ostensible intentions, becoming the most electric aspect of this otherwise staid film.

I'm Looking Through You

As with so many other things, the Beatles were innovators in the music video. Intended as a quick cash-in on their overnight success, the Beatles' first film, *A Hard Day's Night* (1964), directed by Richard Lester, was an accidental comic classic and a key precursor to the music video. Beatles songs provide a wall-to-wall sonic carpet for the film, and Lester artfully moves the music from background to foreground and back again. Lester turns the musical numbers into discrete short films, less about the stately strumming of guitars than dazzling, unhinged expressions of male camaraderie, clever hijinks, and Marxian physical humor. "Can't Buy Me Love" is the most brilliant of all, a series of crane shots swooping over the four Beatles running, jumping, and leaping through a field. The Beatles' performances in *A Hard Day's Night*, even the ones that are studio-bound, are remarkably loose—in part because of Lester's roving, impetuous camera work, and in part because he sets the Beatles' cheeky personalities free. "Can't Buy Me Love" and the rest of the songs from *A Hard Day's Night* take a substantial step forward in the formation of the music video by virtue of their anarchic illogic. Feeling no need to justify themselves, Lester's proto-videos run amok in the fields of the silly, the surreal, and the comic. Needless to say, these qualities, in many ways, made Lester the godfather of the music video.

Burned out by the endless touring and television commitments that were a requisite of mid-60s rock stardom, the Beatles sought to promote their latest singles without facing screaming teenagers, inane interviewers, and insipid countdown shows, and hit on the idea of shooting promotional films and sending them out to television in their stead. Compared to Lester's work in *A Hard Day's Night* and *Help!* (1965), these clips lack visual panache; however, when placed side by side with the uninspired video work of their late-60s peers, videos like "Penny Lane" and "Strawberry Fields Forever" manage to capture some of the group's chaotic cheeriness, taste for comic non sequitur, and, above all, their understanding that videos, like any other outgrowth of popular culture, sell themselves on the basis of strong, clearly defined personae.

Working with director Michael Lindsay-Hogg (who would later direct an intriguing pair of videos for the Beatles' rivals the Rolling Stones), the four Beatles gathered in a West London sculpture garden in May 1966 and shot clips for their two latest singles. "Paperback Writer" and "Rain" (the two videos are essentially halves of the same whole) seek to capture something of the Beatles' flair for zany humor side by side their newfound gravitas as rock statesmen. "Paperback Writer" emphasizes the caught-on-the-fly quality of its footage, with clappers and other technical equipment intruding into the frame. There are also self-consciously artsy touches, like the close-ups of each Beatle's sunglasses, but "Paperback Writer" and "Rain" are among the first true music videos because of their underlying logic, one that would serve as the unspoken underpinning of music videos to come: each shot of the videos was an independent contractor, providing its own dose of cool, rather than playing a part of a larger whole. By later standards, "Paperback Writer" and "Rain" are very slow, with long, sustained shots of the Beatles lost in thought; nonetheless, they established the groundwork for what was to come.

Among later Beatles videos, both "Penny Lane" (1967) and "Strawberry Fields Forever" (1967) assemble an array of clever ideas, but they leave their designs unbuilt, the final products little more than a tangled heap of good intentions. In the former, Lennon, walking down the street as a Penny Lane bus cruises by, runs into his bandmates and the quartet leap onto awaiting white horses. They ride through the streets and into the forest, where they sit down to a meal, waited on by eighteenth-century noblemen. The bewigged gentlemen bring the band their instruments, and they play their song in the great outdoors. "Penny Lane" is speckled with clever touches, from the unexplained presence of the noble waiters to Paul McCartney's odd, threadbare-royalty coat, but the pieces never quite fuse into a full picture.

The same part-versus-whole dichotomy plagues "Strawberry Fields Forever." Taking place in the same woods from "Penny Lane," "Strawberry Fields" arranges the band around a peculiar musical instrument seemingly growing out of an aged oak tree. This odd instrument, whose strings extend like a spider's web from its casing into the lowest branches of the tree, becomes the centerpiece of "Strawberry Fields'" surrealist vision, in which John Lennon leaps into the tree to tighten the strings and the band dribble paint along its trunk-body. Nature and technology fuse together in the video, forming an unclassifiable new hybrid, but the overarching significance of such an improvement on God's design is left unstated, swallowed up by "Strawberry Fields'" tendencies toward enthusiastic meaninglessness. The Beatles' videos laid the table for future music-video experiments in symbolism, but their own symbols were, for the most part, muddled and unclear.

The influence of A Hard Day's Night spread beyond the Beatles and into the work of their imitators. Turn on any episode of the Beatles-biting rock and roll sitcom The Monkees, which ran on American television from 1966 to 1968, and, almost inevitably, there would be a montage set to one of their songs, in which the band horsed around on the beach, rode dune buggies, or battled baddies. These interludes are music videos of a sort, rarely advancing the plot in any significant way. Instead, they channeled the spirit of the Beatles and Lester to invest their prefab, television-created band with some of the effortless hip and charm of their legendary older brothers. In taking Lester and the Beatles' innovations from A Hard Day's Night and bringing them to a mass television audience, The Monkees (and the band's drug-addled 1968 film Head, directed by Bob Rafelson) laid the foundation for the future intersection of television and music video. In fact, one of the original Monkees, Michael Nesmith, would become a music-video pioneer in his own right.

The Beatles were far from the only major act of the 1960s to shoot promotional videos. Between 1968 and 1970, the musical promotional film came into being in a form similar to the contemporary music video, with the Doors, the Animals, the Byrds, and others making mostly utilitarian clips that chose not to engage, as the Beatles had, with the artistic potentialities of the form. Seeing the videos as filmed stand-ins intended for use on countdown shows, the bands (and more often, their labels) made videos that themselves literalized their function, being little more than taped performances. Often, these clips were taken from performances on American television shows and were meant to be played on countdown and rock-and-roll shows around the world. There being little outlet for them in the U.S., these proto-videos were almost never seen stateside. Other videos were shot by record labels for promotional reels intended to be broadcast in record stores, marketing meetings, or at music conferences. A third brand of music video was put together by European television networks for broadcast on countdown programs, occasionally making their way back to the U.S. These often involved uniting the music with completely unrelated footage, in the interest of limited time and limited funds. Some hesitant attempts at breaking out of the live-performance box were quite enjoyable; the Exciters' "Tell Him" (1962) has the R&B group singing to the animals at the local zoo, serenading the polar bears, swans, and gorillas, and the wildlife seem to enjoy it—the video ends with a bear standing up and applauding the show.

Pink Floyd chose to imitate the absurdist, anarchic humor of *A Hard Day's Night*, while appearing slightly more unhinged and less telegenically good-natured than the Beatles. In "Arnold Layne" (1967), the band lugs a mannequin up a hill, watching in dismay as its body steadily falls apart over the course of the journey. Its head pops off, but the mannequin nonetheless manages to tip its cap to the audience. Apparently enjoying the company of inanimate, near-human objects, Pink Floyd pals around with a scarecrow in "The Scarecrow" (1967), treating it as their newfound mascot on a meandering tour of the English countryside. "See Emily Play" (1968) also finds the band out of doors, horsing around in a public park, playing imaginary drums, and batting an imaginary cricket ball. It was oddly endearing, albeit bizarre, to see so reclusive a band do their best to make like the Beatles. As the announcer at the beginning of "The Scarecrow" said, "Pink Floyd . . . have taken their improbable psychedelic colors into the open air."

The Who and the Kinks made the Lester-esque collapse of genre the primary subtext of their forays into the music video, borrowing heavily from the loose charm of *A Hard Day's Night*, with both the former's "Happy Jack" (1966) and the latter's "Dead End Street" (1966) beginning as one thing and ending up something entirely different. "Happy Jack" opens as a tense heist film, with the Who a team of safecrackers racing the clock to pull off a dazzling theft. In the middle of the action, with the outcome hanging in the balance, lead singer Roger Daltrey is distracted by a cream pie on a side table and the band winds up rubbing pie in each other's faces, hair, and clothes. Caught unawares by a police officer on the beat, they pie the cop and dash off into the night. "Dead End Street" stars the Kinks as top-hatted pallbearers lugging a coffin through the streets of London. Pausing momentarily to rest their weary arms, the band are shocked to see the coffin's lid pop off and the supposed corpse dash off down the street. For the remainder of "Dead End Street," the band chases after their former burden as he flees into the urban maze. For both the Who and the Kinks, the music video was an opportunity to illustrate how well they had studied the lessons of *A Hard Day's Night*.

Underground

Also initially appearing as part of a feature film, similarly using the services of a top-flight director, Bob Dylan's "Subterranean Homesick Blues" (1967) (directed by D.A. Pennebaker) was the first music video to build on, rather than imitate, Lester and the Beatles' triumphs. Appearing in the midst of Pennebaker's Dylan documentary *Don't Look Back*, "Subterranean Homesick Blues" is a bracing dose of fresh air, made up of equal parts avant-garde New York filmmaking and trademark Dylan detachment, as he literally and figuratively tosses away the words to his song. (Beginning a trend that would bear much fruit in later years, "Subterranean Homesick Blues" also inaugurates the celebrity cameo, with Beat poet Allen Ginsberg lurking at the video's edges for no discernible purpose.)

Dylan stands in a New York City alley, holding a large stack of oversized flashcards on which the song's lyrics are written. In time with his singing, Dylan pulls the relevant card off the pile, holding it up to the camera before throwing it to the ground. The video's drama revolves around the way Dylan rides the song's beat, running ahead and falling behind in his dispersal of the cards. Dylan coyly looks away from the camera, only occasionally meeting its glance. Insouciantly beyond caring whether this miniature drama is of any interest to viewers, Dylan automatically renders it fascinating by way of his devil-may-care attitude. Black-and-white and grainy, "Subterranean Homesick Blues" looks and feels like an emanation from the world of underground film, worlds away from Dylan's contemporaries' overpolished performance clips.

If Lester's Beatles videos would come to define the highest early realization of music video's capacity to charm and salesmanship, "Subterranean Homesick Blues" is its avant-garde counterpart, unabashedly intellectual and cool where "A Hard Day's Night" was physical and warm. Dylan and the Beatles' early video work established the twin poles from which later music videos stemmed, but each also contained traces of its opposite. Never a pure medium to begin with, the music video, in years to come, would oscillate between the example set by its two most immediate forebears, but would also grow to realize that it was all part of the same game of salesmanship. Frosty or inviting, Ph.D or GED, the music video's ultimate purpose was to advertise, and in advertising, no approach was superior to another, unless it was a more successful seller.

Sons of the Silent Age

The music video henceforth grew in two very different fields, with the interests of two diverse groups dovetailing in the eventual format of MTV and its siblings. Major corporations, having invested in the burgeoning cable-television industry, found themselves starved, above all, for content. In a rapidly growing television universe, niche programming was the order of the day, and where niches did not yet exist, they had to be created. Music, still an overwhelmingly non-television-friendly medium, had to be shoehorned into cable TV, and promotional music videos were the safest bet. It was television, and not the music industry, that made the initial push for a music-video channel; the labels, cautiously conservative to the point of financial blindness, refused to believe that the music video could be anything other than a money loser and a passing fad. The music industry were followers, not leaders, in music video, and skeptical followers at that. Hesitant to commit serious money to a medium they believed was of dubious commercial or aesthetic value, and which they were required to provide free of charge, the record labels adopted a wait-and-see attitude to the music video, refusing to invest heavily at the outset. It was the cable-television owners, they of the gaping holes in their station lineups, who believed most strongly in music videos as a potential windfall in attracting young, upwardly mobile viewers.

Besides the corporate investors (who included Warner Brothers and American Express, the initial investors in MTV), the other group of dreamers who believed in the music video were the artists themselves. Musical groups of the mid-to-late-1970s, emboldened by the success of the previous decade's acts in crafting short films as promotional tools, and means of artistic expression, sought to harness music and film together even more closely. In addition to its functional use as a second-unit band, making the rounds of the countdown shows, the promotional video also served as yet another canvas for performers to paint on. Musicians had never been limited to music alone as a means of expression; album covers, photo sessions, live shows, costumes, and even interviews had been opportunities for performers to design a look, or shape an aura, for themselves. Standing at the nexus of film, television, and advertising, the music video was, at times, each one, and as combination album cover, photo shoot, and promotional appearance, also something fundamentally new: a form of visual art equally dedicated to the huckster's come-on and the artist's sincere appeal.

Not quite commodities themselves, music videos were short films in the service of other commodities, made not to be sold themselves (for the most part), but to sell other products: albums, T-shirts, posters, and the like. The music video, therefore, was merely the latest in a long line of recording industry promotional techniques, all designed to increase the labels' bottom line. For the musical acts themselves, however, the video was about more than money. While there had been many precedents as promotional tools, there had been few in the realm of artistic enterprise; for performers like Dylan and the Beatles, the music video had been not merely a fill-in for the latest *Top of the Pops*, but an exciting, challenging, wholly new art form to tackle.

Taking off from the advances of "Subterranean Homesick Blues," some later videos borrowed the Dylan clip's charming sense of humor, while others adopted its avant-garde detachment. Captain Beefheart's "Lick My Decals Off, Baby" (1970) took the tone of a late-night television commercial, its offscreen announcer's orotund pronouncements providing a sonic overlay for the barrage of eccentric images onscreen—disembodied hands, masked terrorist types silently playing their instruments, a foot nudging white goo onto an empty stretch of macadam. "New on Reprise, it's 'Lick My Decals Off, Baby'"—the very title of the song belying the strained seriousness of the announcer's efforts at shilling. Masked Bay Area oddballs the Residents also viewed the short film set to music as an opportunity to engage with their inner freak. "Land of 1000 Dances" (1975) is a deranged amusement-park ride through their brains, crammed full of deviant imagery. Giant lasers careen around a polka-dotted floor, KKK aliens in papier-mâché masks bang drums and dance like stereotypical African savages, and a woman and a skeleton dressed all in black dance on a stage dominated by a giant swastika. The band's "One Minute Movies" (1980), codirected by the group and Graeme Whifler, are similarly absurdist, a set of four conjoined sixty-second shorts: "The Act of Being Polite," "Perfect Love," "Moisture," and "Simple Song." In "The Act of Being Polite," tuxedoed eyeball-men and women cuddle in bed and a heart is smashed by a metal pole; in "Perfect Love," a zhlubby guy lies on his bed watching the Residents on a television with staticky, jumpy reception; and in "Simple Song," the Residents dance around with a pig's head. The "One Minute Movies" are casually, deliriously avant-garde in much the same way "Subterranean Homesick Blues" had been, choosing not to make a big fuss about its aliens, eyeballs, or masked dancers, or about its complete and utter strangeness.

In between the two Residents videos, a growing number of late-70s punk and New Wave performers, along with non-American acts already accustomed to the idea of making videos, got into the game. Barnes and Barnes' "Fish Heads" (1980) is every bit as unhinged as "Land of 1000 Dances," its protagonist unnaturally attached to his pet fish heads—taking them to the movies (where the fish wears a miniature green fedora), planting them in his front yard, bringing them to the beach. Commander Cody's "Two Triple Cheese, Side Order of Fries" (1979) takes place in a fast-food phantasmagoria, its hamburgers a lurid shade of purplish pink and all manner of culinary perversions taking place in the establishment's back rooms. Commander Cody's left-field anthem leads the oppressed burger-flippers of the world to rocking out, and its dancing French fries evinced an interest in anthropomorphism it shared with the near-schizophrenic enthusiasm of "Fish Heads."

Devo were the Residents' best students, their videos a riotous jumble of found footage, masked freaks, and sci-fi mash-ups. The band, whose videos were directed by bassist Gerald Casale, and assisted by Chuck Statler (who would later work with Elvis Costello, Madness, and Nick Lowe), were the first to release a long-form video album and the first to include extramusical sound in their video (in "Whip It"). Taking Luis Buñuel, Russ Meyer, and Stanley Kubrick as their inspiration, clips like "Satisfaction" (1978), "A Worried Man" (1979), and "Beautiful World" (1981) star the band as blue-collar workers adrift in a nightmare world of sexual frustration, geopolitical insanity, and topsy-turvy cultural dislocation. Devo were the house band for the end of the world, reveling in the chaos and fragmentation of a planet adrift. "Beautiful World" gradually spins out of control, its nostalgic 1950s futurism steadily poisoned by images of death and destruction: World War I trench fighters, bridge collapses, Ku Klux Klan rallies, Southern police beating civil-rights demonstrators. "It's a beautiful world for you—not me," the song determined, and the video ends with the ultimate punch line to the cruel joke of the civilized world's ceaseless brutality—a nuclear explosion's slowly spreading mushroom cloud. "A Worried Man" appears to take place in the same five-minutes-to-midnight world, with the band as radioactive-waste workers whose bodies take on an unnatural nuclear glow. It was not merely the world of geopolitics that had gone off the rails; life at home was no more comforting. Adults chase off adolescent lovebirds with rolling pins in "Satisfaction," consumerist ambitions turn yuppies into mindless uniformed drones in "Freedom of Choice" (1980), and in "Love Without Anger" (1981), married dolls have a knock-down, drag-out fight that culminate in a headless Barbie and legless Ken. Devo were the masked court jesters of the nascent punk-rock movement, their videos jocular affirmations of the Sex Pistols' motto—"No Future." Casale's videos are capable of turning their satiric guns on the band's relative obscurity as well; the purple-tint "Girl U Want" (1980) celebrates a wholly imaginary Devo-mania, with hordes of screaming teenage girls freaking out at the band's every move. "Whip It" (1980) is the band's best video of all, a delirious homage to the movie Western and sadomasochism, and a testimonial to their skills with a lash.

Elvis Costello's "Accidents Will Happen" (1978) is low-rent Pop Art, dropping the singer into a series of line drawings sketched on graph paper fleshing out the theme of accidents: lurking banana peels, crushed sunglasses, spilled ketchup, and the like. Directors Annabel Jankel and Rocky Morton (who would later make the superb videos for Miles Davis' "Decoy" and Tom Tom Club's "Genius of Love") divide the screen into boxes, each possessed of its own funky energy; delicately sculpted ink lines in motion indicated the sweat flying off the singing Costello and out of the boxes, liberated to the frame at large. Blondie's videos were never as high-concept or artsy, concentrating mostly on keeping sexpot lead singer Debbie Harry front and center. Along with Devo and the Residents, though, Blondie were one of the first American groups to fully embrace the art of the music video, even before MTV came along and made it worth their while to do so. Blondie's late-70s videos were low-budget goofs, a series of raging parties punctuated by Harry's posing and flouncing. Mostly directed by David Mallet and Keef, Blondie's videos were the flipside to Suicide's dour, menacing "Frankie Teardrop" (1978); for them, life in "Ford to New York: Drop Dead" Manhattan was one nonstop bash.

Five Minutes to MTV

British stadium rockers Queen made what would become one of the most famous clips of the 70s, and the video often incorrectly referred to as the first music video, for "Bohemian Rhapsody" (1975), directed by Bruce Gowers. The misconception was understandable, for "Bohemian Rhapsody" was one of the first promotional clips to truly look like a music video. This was partially a product of attitude, but it was also a reflection of its aesthetic choices. Neither an imitation performance clip, meant to fool audiences into thinking they were watching a live performance, nor a self-consciously artsy project, "Bohemian Rhapsody" (its mise-en-scène inspired by the cover of the band's Queen II album) is simultaneously glorious and silly in a manner that would soon grow very familiar. "Bohemian Rhapsody" was also one of the very first examples of a music video playing a major part in the promotion of a pop single.

Gowers' video begins with Queen silhouetted against a gray-sky background, each member of the quartet filmed from a low angle as the lights come up and they sing in unison. There is something unquestionably silly about these images, some combination of poofy rock-star hair and unbridled theatrics that add up to hilarity, but the showmanship of lead singer Freddie Mercury rescues the video from any accidental resemblance to a Monty Python skit. "Bohemian Rhapsody" favors the lap dissolve as its means of transport, appropriate for a song that bounces restlessly from one musical style to another over the course of its six-plus minutes. The video serves to explain the song, rendering its convoluted aural density intelligible for the television audience. Turning each voice into a physical presence, the video establishes "Bohemian Rhapsody" as a dueling song for voices. The band's four members appear onscreen for the more vocally intricate sections, then multiply to infinity as the production grows yet denser. Voices appear and disappear onscreen in an extended dramatization of the song's call-and-response, eventually overlapping into one unified whole. At the heart of the video is the relatively straightforward footage of the band in concert, with Mercury prowling the stage like a caged tiger, rubbing the mike stand between the legs of his silver lamé jumpsuit. The infinity of faces from the song's interlude wash away, replaced by the simple, powerful footage of the live band. "Bohemian Rhapsody" teaches its viewers how to hear the song, sifting out each element of its complex mix and making the entire process of its assembly a visually stimulating event.

Later Queen videos built off the innovations of "Bohemian Rhapsody," with "Bicycle Race" (1978) employing tints and multiplying effects familiar from the earlier video, mixing concert footage with cheesy insert shots. "I Want to Break Free" (1984) turned the band into a crew of desperate housewives, straining at the bars of their tastefully appointed shared home. All four members of the band dressed in drag for the video, but it was clear that only Mercury truly loved the opportunity to play dress-up, and his hirsute drag queen in a leather miniskirt, simultaneously thrusting her vacuum across the carpet and winking at the camera, is the comic highlight of the video.

As always, Queen were masters of the widescreen emotion, and their kitchen-sink drama of mundane middle-class drudgery fireballs into a mass demonstration, with a quasi-mythical nude warrior blowing a clarion call on his trumpet and thousands of flashing lights heeding Mercury's impassioned cry in concert. "Radio Ga Ga" (1984) begins large, using then-cutting-edge technology to insert the band into the backdrops of Fritz Lang's *Metropolis* (a music-video touchstone; see Madonna's "Express Yourself," chapter 4). The glowing, otherworldly radios in most every scene of the video were symbols of both totalitarian dystopia and the slumbering potential for rebellion, with the trudging workers below summoned by the sound of Queen's anthem (itself a complaint about the sad state of contemporary rock radio). Eventually, the band's white-clad fans thrust their fists into the air in unison, their spirits raised by yet another Queen call to arms. In Queen's videos, the band always managed to triumph over grubby, unpleasant reality.

AC/DC, even more so than Queen, dedicated their videos to celebrating the joys of raucous, unhinged, anarchic performance. In videos like "Jailbreak" (1976), "Highway to Hell" (1979), and "You Shook Me All Night Long" (1980), the Australian hard-rockers were lascivious rebels loosed on their guitars, attacking authority with the same panache and brute force with which they attacked their instruments. "Jailbreak" and "You Shook Me All Night Long" took the impetus to include mini-narratives within their frames, opening the door a bit wider toward the full flowering of the music video as independent art form.

Taking things one critical step further, David Bowie realized that video could become an opportunity for rock stars to put on (and remove) a dizzying variety of masks. Musicians had formerly turned to acting in feature films to express the multiplicity of beings trapped inside them, struggling to emerge, but now that same role-playing could be a vital aspect of the musicmaking process itself. The Beatles had gotten the game started, but they had stopped halfway, playing cartoonish versions of themselves in their videos, for the most part. Refusing to be so easily essentialized, Bowie took on a profusion of roles, leaving even his most ardent fans a bit confused as to who, precisely, he might be. Video became an indispensable aspect of Bowie's profusion of quicksilver changes, documenting and preserving each incarnation for a potential galaxy of television viewers unable to catch his elaborate, theatrical live performances.

An ambiguousness regarding gender and sexuality lies at the heart of these 70s Bowie videos, with multiple clips emphasizing the homoerotic intensity of his persona. The tint-heavy "Jean Genie" (1972), directed by Mick Rock, had Bowie shirtless, in a gold dog collar, while "Life on Mars?" (1973) emphasizes his androgynous, entrancing charm with close-ups of his mascara-painted eyes. "Be My Wife" (1977), directed by Stanley Dorfman, presents a "natural," unencumbered Bowie, his guitar swung around behind his back when not being played, as if to appear before us entirely naked. Bowie toys with the camera—meeting our gaze and then mock-coyly turning away from it. "Heroes" (1977) changes the script slightly, with Bowie in profile gazing piercingly, swooningly, at some offscreen presence, making the dangerous passion of the song's lyrics, with lovers embracing at the Berlin Wall, into the unstated drama of the video.

The gay undertones of these videos never came right out and announced themselves, but they were to be seen everywhere, from the prominent use of makeup to the flamboyantly androgynous clothing to the hints dropped by Bowie's sexually ambiguous lyrics. "Boys Keep Swinging" (1979), directed by David Mallet, brings the subtext substantially closer to the surface. The video takes place at a transvestite's fashion show, where flashing fluorescent lights illuminate cross-dressers taking off their wigs and wiping off their lipstick, and a trio of trannies (including one church-lady type) serve as Bowie's backup singers. At least some of the women appeared to be played by Bowie himself, only adding to the video's gender-bending confusion.

In "D.J." (1979), directed by David Mallet, Bowie messes around with the turntables and headphones in his psychedelically washed-out study, then hits the streets, where he saunters with some newfound friends, makes out with a male well-wisher, and does a quick two-step with a middle-aged female passerby before returning to his lair and letting loose some destruction on a wayward mirror and amplifier. Throughout, Bowie makes love to the camera with unrelenting zeal—embracing its gaze and demanding its undivided attention.

"Ashes to Ashes" (1980), the most distinctive clip of Bowie's career, casts him as a medieval jester drifting helplessly between the past and the present, lost somewhere between the earth and his home. Shot in bleached reds and pinks, like a damaged photo negative, this clip, codirected by Bowie and Mallet, is structured around surprising juxtapositions of character and mise-en-scène: the jester, along with his queen and noblemen, walks along an empty beach, while a bulldozer rumbles behind them; a space traveler in a suburban kitchen; a medieval nobleman and prom queen providing backup vocals to Bowie, dressed in heroic fashion, with flowing hair and white robes. "Ashes to Ashes" has a lonesome Bowie trapped between personae like a time traveler trapped between stars. Looking out of place wherever he was, his forlorn mien and heavy, ashy makeup tell us that having played so many parts, he found that the tragic clown, doomed to endless, joyless performance, might be the one closest to his heart.

The Residents, and later Devo, had made the music video a storage unit for glorious non sequiturs, taking Bowie's advice not to neglect the visual aspect of rock stardom. With music videos emerging at the same moment that video art was making its first forays into museums and galleries, the boundary between the two subgenres grew blurred. Groups like Suicide, existing at the fringes of the New York music scene that would spawn punk rock and New Wave, made videos that themselves could have been on display at the Museum of Modern Art alongside Nam June Paik and Jonas Mekas films. Their "Frankie Teardrop," shot on Super 8 in the streets of New York City, directed by Paul Dougherty and Walter Robinson, and running more than ten minutes, was willfully obscure in intention, choosing aura over narrative. It also owed a clear debt to the avant-garde films that were its near-contemporaries, looking more like Hollis Frampton or Michael Snow than "Bohemian Rhapsody."

Water imagery abounded in "Frankie Teardrop," but far from being soothing, its surfaces seemed to augur impending violent death, conjoined as they were with shots of James Dean, Nixon masks, yellow and red lights splattering across the frame, and pulsing waves of static. Images of dolls and babies swarmed the screen, but the ceaselessly throbbing water coursed over them as well, erasing their faces in the process. The song itself was a fractured urban nightmare about the deranged Frankie, who is "gonna kill his wife and kids." The video functions as a series of abstract images intended as a gloss on the lyrics' explicit narrative. Each image adds another piece to the puzzle, from statues of saints to caged rats to figurines depicting the crucified Christ. The water, simultaneously veiling and revealing all, is the liquid in which the video's angst and unfettered trauma swims, a slowly building tidal wave soon to break over land. If the imagery itself only hints at the nature of the violence soon to occur, it was unstinting in its implications for us, its spectators: "We're all Frankie," the song told us, and the video ends with shots of industrial New York, followed by herds of Manhattan pedestrians streaming along a midtown sidewalk. There was a dark, ugly side to the city, yes; but even worse, there was an unseen brutal side to ourselves, hidden in the false placidity of daily life. "Frankie Teardrop" ends with a freeze-frame on a man's face, one that had already been seen earlier, and marked as a likely Frankie. In the freeze-frame, the light and dark halves of his face are in perfect balance. Looking a little closer, it becomes clear that we are looking at not one image, but two; two shots of this man's face superimposed on each other, as if to give us a double look at the same face. The evil lurking inside the city had burrowed its way inside Frankie, and it would burrow its way inside the rest of us as well, if we were not careful.

Having been in on some of the earliest music-video experiments as a founding member of the Monkees, it was no surprise that Michael Nesmith would take to the form as a solo artist as well. Nesmith had orchestrated the video show *Popclips* for the Nickelodeon cable channel in 1977 (the latest in a line of music-video shows that included Manhattan cable's *Nightclubbing*, USA's *Night Flight*, PBS' *Soundstage from Chicago* and *Austin City Limits*, NBC's *The Midnight Special*, the British *Kenny Everett Video Show*, which was directed by future video auteur David Mallet, and the syndicated *Don Kirshner's Rock Concert*), and had sought unsuccessfully to begin a full-fledged music-video channel of his own. Nesmith had initially been included in Warner Amex's plans for their cable channel, but he was rapidly cut out once it became clear that Nesmith's idiosyncratic aesthetic tastes would never jibe with his corporate masters' bottom line. His 1977 video "Rio" (directed by William Dear) is a riot of competing textures, ranging from garish color to black-and-white to rudimentary special effects. Its Brazil-love crammed dancers in Carmen Miranda headdresses, fruity-looking mixed drinks, and oceanfront love into one overstuffed frame. "Rio's" kooky good humor has Nesmith awkwardly dropping mike stands, desperately searching for his lost shoe while winging around the dance floor with his lady friend, and flying into outer space like an absurdist Superman. Along with "Bohemian Rhapsody," "Rio" was one of the first harbingers of a commercially accessible, middlebrow video style, one that looked back to the Beatles, and even Soundies, and forward to twenty-four-hour music video channels to come, as well as video shows like *Night Tracks* (TBS), *Friday Night Videos* (NBC), and *Nick Rocks* (Nickelodeon).

It would be MTV, though, that would revolutionize the music industry, creating a new wave of video-driven superstars and permanently changing the rules for performers and labels alike. The twenty-four-hour music-video channel created demand where none had previously existed and, in the process, perfectly encapsulated the essence of an era. The desire for endless visual stimulation that MTV satisfied would be lambasted by the conservative gatekeepers of culture, but the music video was an emblem of a culture in hyperdrive, constantly in search of its next fix—for better and for worse.

CHAPTER 2

Television Vaudeville

In the early years of its ascendance, when MTV was the cable channel du jour, and teenagers and academics alike buzzed about the form's revolutionary potential, the music video grew at an ever-increasing clip. This growth came both in the overall footprint of music videos within pop culture, and in the size and scope of individual videos. In the early 1980s, the music video had its era of possibility, going from perennial also-ran to linchpin of the music industry, surging in cost, production values, star quality, and skillfulness.

During the 80s, performers lived and died on the strength of their videos, and it is no coincidence that many of the era's biggest stars were also its savviest videomakers. Madonna, Michael Jackson, Bruce Springsteen, U2—these artists were among the first to grasp the nature of the new medium, harnessing its power for their own benefit. Those who were unable to do so, for the most part, were left behind. The rise of the music video was a key turning point in the history of pop music mythmaking, moving the heretofore secondary quality of image-making to front-and-center position. This image-centrality was a godsend for performers like Madonna, who were selling themselves as much as their music, and a one-way ticket to oblivion for musicians who failed to wrap their heads around the music video's demands.

When MTV debuted in 1981, its goals were relatively modest. The channel was intended as a visual equivalent to the album-rock radio stations then flourishing in almost every American market. Like those radio stations, MTV was designed to serve an almost exclusively white audience, with its musical selection determined, and limited, by genre. In its earliest incarnation, MTV conceived of itself as a national radio network on television, exposing its audience to singles lurking just below the heavy-rotation playlists of album rock stations. It is essential to understanding the rise of MTV to realize that the impetus for the channel came, not from the music industry but through the growth of cable television, and that its success owed less to the marketing genius of the major record labels and more to the vagaries of the then-fledgling cable business. Where earlier attempts to meld television and music had been doomed to failure because teenage males, the primary purchasers of recorded music at the time, were underrepresented in the TV audience, MTV attracted a female-heavy audience at its start, and later bridged the gender gap through its emphasis on heavy metal—a bastion of male fans in the music industry.

In the initial era of MTV, which lasted from 1981 until its debut in New York and Los Angeles in 1983, the channel was, more than anything, starved for product to fill the gaping holes in its schedule, and turned to Britain (and, to a lesser extent, Australia), where bands had been making videos for a number of years to be played on popular countdown shows like *Top of the Pops*. The imported British videos, with their emphasis on artificiality, both in image and musical content, imposed a wrenching, 180-degree shift on the American music industry, and meant that, contrary to its intentions, MTV was a space profoundly different from the meat-and-potatoes world of rock radio. That said, it was also devoid of the great majority of groundbreaking music from the era— no rap, no punk, no disco, mostly just fey British trios with synthesizer solos. As MTV learned to crawl, it featured no programs and no schedule; only an uninterrupted flow of imagery, broken up by commercials and VJ chatter alone. It was not until after MTV's national launch that the channel began to divide its programming schedule into genre-themed blocks and to feature the heavy metal clips that would be a staple throughout the 1980s. MTV leapfrogged the moribund music industry, crowning its own stars and leaving the mainstream scrambling to catch up. Thus, in this early phase, and continuing on into the mid-1980s, videos went from trifles to blockbusters, with more money, more effort, and greater professionalism marking the music video's graduation to pop culture's major leagues.

Cable television was not the only venue for music video in the early 1980s. In addition to MTV and other video-related cable programming, music videos were also shown on NBC's *Friday Night Videos*, which occasionally trumped MTV by agreeing to pay record labels for showing videos. They were also screened on second-wave video jukeboxes like the Startime Video Muzzikboxx; broadcast on satellite simulcasts as "video concerts"; played in rock and dance clubs as a diversion or break from live entertainment (many of the most risqué early videos, like "Girls on Film," were partially intended for rowdy clubgoers); and packaged onto cassette for playback on the new video cassette recorders then making headway into American consumers' homes.

Money for Nothing, and Chicks for Free

In its first phase, the music video sought to embrace more—more sex appeal, more excitement, more violence, more intellect—in short, more of anything that would enable it to spread its gospel. Music video branched out every which way, willing to take on any role, or swallow whole any artistic tradition, in its relentless surge forward. Sometimes this meant bigger budgets (Duran Duran's "Hungry Like the Wolf"); sometimes it meant better special effects (musician-directors Godley and Creme's "Cry"); sometimes it meant more sexual shame-lessness (Van Halen's "Hot for Teacher"); and sometimes it even meant slower edits and black-and-white film stock (the Police's "Every Breath You Take").

Frame by frame, shot by shot, video by video, a new film language was being crafted for the fledgling form. Often, this language developed into a lazy short-hand that replaced creativity with an onslaught of the familiar—exploding tele-visions, rain-slicked streets, motorcycles, urban alleyways, slow-motion shots, luxury cars, prison breaks, nightclub scenes, movie quotes, and extensive lifts from photography and art history, just to name a few. With the rise of the music video to cultural ubiquity, the free-form aesthetic exploration of the early videos was channeled into the repetitive charms of the MTV video. Video direc-tors became known for their ability to provide certain effects, or turn out a cer-tain brand of allure, and were hired on the basis of those skills. Directors like Russell Mulcahy, Godley and Creme, David Mallet, Don Letts, Tim Pope, and Bob Giraldi all formed their own unique directorial styles, but the music video as a whole became an immediately recognizable art form, its look (encompass-ing everything from rapid-fire edits to glossy film stock to a certain brand of captivating narrative senselessness) distinguishable at a glance from its counter-parts on the TV dial. This led some cultural critics and longtime video buffs to bemoan the death of an aesthetic only just arrived to prominence, but the increasing uniformity of the music video as a genre was the sign of an art form settling in for the long haul.

The inaugural video shown on MTV, famously, was the Buggles' "Video Killed the Radio Star" (1979)—a dart thrown in the direction of the fledgling form's then-rival—but the quintessential videomakers of this early era were New Wave stars Duran Duran. The quartet of easy-on-the-eyes British lads were among the first, along with David Bowie and Michael Jackson, to under-stand the extent to which music video could create and craft image. In their videos, the Durannies were musical playboys out for a good time, game for anything as long as it was glamorous. True children of the Reagan-Thatcher 80s, Duran Duran made videos that catered to their sense of chic grandiosity and leading-man sex appeal, creating clips that were prime examples of conspicuous-consumption-by-proxy. True to their status as the first larger-than-life stars of the music video, they released their biggest, brashest, sexiest video, "Girls on Film," in August 1981—just in time for the debut of MTV.

"Girls on Film," whose raunchiness and sexual explicitness has rarely been matched in the prurient but conservative history of the music video, is structured as a series of silly-sexy fashion shoot tableaux. True to the song's title, the video features photographers snapping away as a parade of models strutted their stuff. Directed by Godley and Creme (perhaps the most prominent directorial team of the early MTV era), "Girls on Film" is a grouping of small stories and miniature inspirations, none substantial enough to support an entire video. Most crucially, "Girls on Film" understands its audience, and it devoted itself to two primary goals that would help set the tone for a quarter-century of videos to come: titillation and amusement.

"Girls on Film" even begins with credits: "Duran Duran in Girls on Film," as if to assert the band's status as cinematic stars in the making. The video itself drew a parallel between the models getting primped and polished before their runway appearance and the band's own pre-show preparations—glamour-pusses-to-be. The models, once they appear, participate in a series of routines more akin to burlesque than a fashion show. The first group of models comes out in skimpy lingerie, marching across the catwalk (positioned precariously high above the ground) to a matching set of whipped-cream-covered poles. A referee hands them each a pillow, with which they proceed to beat each other silly as whipped cream flew in every direction. The next scene features a model dressed in a sumo wrestler's white loincloth, and little else. A genuine, behemoth (male) sumo appears with her, and she proceeds to flip him with ease as the camera lovingly caresses her diaper-clad posterior. The sumo wrestler receives a post-match rubdown, which begins fairly professionally, but soon has the masseuse straddling his back while providing a more vigorous massage. This is followed by a white model in cowgirl getup riding a black man with a horse mask over his face, and a swimsuit-clad beauty pretending to drown in a kiddie pool in order to be saved by, and make out with, the lifeguard on duty.

The campiness of each of these scenes clarifies just what this video is: a half-serious male fantasy of international fashion. As if to highlight the international aspect of that equation, the last segment of "Girls on Film" turns the Cold War into a lesbian mud-wrestling match, replacing President Ronald Reagan and Chairman Leonid Brezhnev with a Southern honey-blond and a Russian beauty in a fur coat. The pair pull at each other's swimsuits in slow motion, pouring mud where the sun doesn't shine, until the match comes to an end and the combatants both get hosed down. Communism or capitalism, it doesn't matter much, "Girls on Film" tells us; as long as we can all agree that there's nothing like watching two supermodels catfight in the mud. (Seemingly enamored with the notion of Cold War as wrestling match, Godley and Creme would return to it more explicitly in their video for Frankie Goes to Hollywood's "Two Tribes" [1984]. In the video for that anthem to superpower hostility, Ronald Reagan and then-Soviet leader Konstantin Chernenko face off in the ring, alternately posturing and fighting as the crowd of racetrack touts and *Guys and Dolls* rejects bet heavily on the match's outcome.)

Nothing could quite match the spectacular silliness of "Girls on Film," but "Hungry Like the Wolf" (1982), their next big video, cast Duran Duran in another brand of fantasy video. Here, the boys were neo-colonialist explorers in safari gear, searching for the other dark meat in an unspecified third-world metropolis. Simon LeBon and company wear sunglasses indoors, wander through bustling, dingy markets, and cause a ruckus in dive bars, all part of their prerogative as rock stars and white men. Director Russell Mulcahy meaningfully contrasts Simon in his explorer's kit, flipping a table over, with the object of his affection (a Nubian princess in full face paint) slinging him to the ground in a forest clearing. Sticking with the tried and true, "Hungry Like the Wolf" also ends with a wrestling match. This time, Simon and his beloved engage in some violent slow-motion foreplay, the pair brought together (according to the logic of the video) by their similarly animalistic natures. They are two sides of the same coin, united in an embrace of their roots in the animal kingdom. "Hungry Like the Wolf" took in a different milieu than "Girls on Film," but it intended to provide the same jet-setter-by-proxy glow to its TV audience. The glitz may have been in a slightly more exotic locale, but the intent was much the same.

Like its predecessors, Duran Duran's "Rio" (1982) (also directed by Mulcahy) felt like money, tingling with the sensation of easy living. The band plays on a yacht as bathing beauties in bikinis cavorted poolside and butlers scurried in the background. The video's ad-influenced aesthetic subscribes less to narrative than to overall sensation, seeking to indelibly associate the song with its wealthy, beautiful milieu. Like their big-screen equivalents of the early 1980s, these Duran Duran videos were affordable luxuries, with the price right for audiences to enjoy their high-life aura. Mulcahy, who had gotten his start making promotional videos for Australian acts in the early 1970s, became the first name director of the music-video era (appropriately enough, since he directed the first MTV video, "Video Killed the Radio Star") and the first video auteur to graduate to feature films, in part by doling out an affordable vision of the high life, accessible in three-minute chunks. Knowing just how to profitably ransack the vaults of pop culture past and present, Mulcahy's videos pilfered the stark lighting of 1940's *noir* films (the Motels' "Only the Lonely"), the creeping paranoia of Roman Polanski's classic chiller *Repulsion* (Ultravox's "The Thin Wall"), and the look and feel of romance-genre comic books (the Motels' "Take the L Out of Lover"). Mulcahy was the original videomaker as postmodernist, his clips cutting and pasting at will, borrowing as needed to create the necessary aura for his work. He is also, as Michael Shore described him in his *Rolling Stone Book of Rock Video*, "the prime source of most rock-video clichés."

One of the luxuries Duran Duran offered in their videos was that of male sexual swagger, a trait embraced full force by fellow Brit Billy Idol in his videos "White Wedding" (1982), "Dancing with Myself" (1983), and "Eyes Without a Face" (1984). Idol struts and sneers his way through these videos, themselves amalgams of B-grade horror and German Expressionist tropes meant to convey an aura of glamorously gloomy danger. Idol was the bare-chested purveyor of pop-punk for the masses, leading his army of goblins and spectral figures through a landscape of Gothic castles, underground caverns, and *film noir* sidewalks. In "Dancing with Myself," an army of the undead comes in search of their leader, Billy; while in "White Wedding," Idol memorably kisses off a female acquaintance from the comfort of his dungeon for choosing bland suburban safety. The settings in these videos were mere props, intended to associate Idol with a suitably ominous class of visual antecedents, but the focus always remained Idol himself, peacocking in full knowledge of his own allure.

Not all that far removed from Idol, Adam Ant made sure to always look prettier than any of the women in his videos, his face impeccably made up and his clothing artfully ripped. Ant's videos are a riotous jumble of eras, fashions, and attitudes held together by his uncanny ability to be the center of attention, and their time-traveler's leap from the eighteenth century ("Stand and Deliver") to the nineteenth ("Strip") to the future ("Apollo 9"). Working with director Danny Kleinman, Ant sneers and play-acts in "Antmusic" (1980) (inspiring some of Idol's later videos), and dresses like a space-age explorer in "Apollo 9" (1984), looking as if he had just removed his space helmet to perform in the latter video. Fascinated by himself (he repeatedly looked into a hand-mirror in "Stand and Deliver" [1981] and smiled, as if pleased with what God hath wrought), Ant saw no reason why the music-video audience should be any less so.

In using the music video as a role-playing mechanism, Idol, Ant, and Duran Duran were tilling the soil originally planted by that musical master of the quick change, David Bowie. In a series of late 70s clips, Bowie had perfected a certain brand of glam on the cheap that depended on the force of his chameleonic persona for the sell. The 80s successor to Bowie's throne as role-player extraordinaire was, surprisingly enough, Peter Gabriel. Bland where Bowie was thrilling, Gabriel looked more like a rock star's attorney than a rock star himself. Nonetheless, his "Shock the Monkey" (1982), directed by Brian Grant, combined "Hungry Like the Wolf's" civilization-versus-savagery dichotomy with Bowie's fondness for changing roles. Gabriel plays both a white-collar type in an undertaker's suit shuffling papers in a dank office and a noble savage in white face paint dashing through the forest. Over the course of the video, the bureaucrat and the savage take cautious steps in the other's direction, with the former slathering on face paint and cavorting with a monkey and the latter showing up in the bureaucrat's office, taking a nap at his desk. Extremes converge, and worlds bleed together, with a London office and a third-world jungle coming to look like parts of the same whole. "Shock the Monkey" is reminiscent of "Hungry Like the Wolf" in its dress-up otherness, but Gabriel's video goes for more than the tingle of fright, or sexual thrill. The savage is not to be found in some distant jungle; rather, it is located inside each and every sun-deprived Londoner, only waiting for the proper moment to emerge. The aborigines here and in "Hungry Like the Wolf" were symbols of music video flexing its muscles; by depicting, presumably, the last individuals on the planet left untouched by television, the medium managed to include them, too, within its embrace—a bear hug much like the nature footage of Talk Talk's "It's My Life" (1984), which briefly turned MTV into a wildlife channel each time it played. The music video had aspirations to the universal, and "Shock the Monkey" was merely the first salvo in its gunning for worldwide appeal.

Follow the Yellow Brick Road

With MTV sticking to its guns about its self-declared genre limitations, it took a force of nature to move the channel from its quasi-racist ban on African-American performers. It required the impact of Michael Jackson's twenty-nine-times platinum *Thriller*, perhaps the last album to attract so sizable a percentage of the American record-buying public, to pull the channel away from its whites-only policy. In Jackson's wake came Prince, Tina Turner, and all the black artists initially left out in the cold, soon to be MTV staples. Lurking just around the corner was the genre soon to become MTV's favorite son— hip-hop. "Billie Jean," "Thriller," and the rest of Jackson's videos from *Thriller* opened MTV to what would become the genius of its second phase of programming—its knocking down of genre walls, creating a broader-based, desegregated music mix in which "Beat It" was bookended by videos from the likes of Guns N' Roses and the Beastie Boys.

Jackson helped break down MTV's doors to let in African-American musicians by making videos viewers simply demanded to see. A big part of that, of course, was the enormous popularity of *Thriller*, but in his videomaking, Jackson continued down the path blazed by Bowie and Gabriel, casting himself as a dancing magic-man—tough and smooth, dark and light, threatening and reassuring. His videos looked to other genres for inspiration, with the aura of the Hollywood musical serving above all as a guiding light. Other genres were discernible as well—gangster films in "Beat It," 1970s urban-paranoia flicks like *Three Days of the Condor* in "Billie Jean," horror in "Thriller." It was appropriate for the videos that sought most to widen MTV's scope, to render the music video bigger and glitzier, that they borrowed so heavily from Hollywood's past. This was visible not only in horror star Vincent Price's voiceover in "Thriller," but also in the tough guy making like George Raft in *Scarface* and flipping a coin in "Billie Jean," or the *West Side Story*-esque gang war in "Beat It."

"Billie Jean" (1983), the first video from *Thriller*, is a parable of Reaganite urban abandonment, taking place as it did in a desolate, devastated, and mysteriously empty city. A more fanciful take on the tragedy of inner-city life than its contemporary, Grandmaster Flash and the Furious Five's "The Message," "Billie Jean" is a living portrait of life during Morning in America. The yellow brick road of *The Wizard of Oz* had been replaced here by a drab concrete path, and the magical metropolis takes on a disheveled, forlorn mien.

"Billie Jean," directed by Steve Barron, offers an imaginary solution to this very real problem: the King of Pop himself. Jackson's magic invigorates drab spaces, lighting up everything from trash cans to lampposts to sidewalks with his touch. A homeless man in rags, sleeping on the street, receives Michael's loving tap and wakes to find himself in a sparkling new tuxedo. Jackson's powers also extended to sleight-of-hand; pursued by a mysterious representative of The Man, he eludes capture through use of a handy Polaroid camera, disappearing as its flash goes off. Even with its paranoiac edge, "Billie Jean" looked like a sequence from a Gene Kelly musical, marked by its light-hearted glimmer and the effortless effervescence of Jackson's dancing.

"Beat It," released in April 1983, took the racial polarization of early MTV and made it literal, borrowing heavily from *West Side Story*, taking everything from the synchronized finger-snapping of the urban gang to the leaders' switchblade-fight duet. Two gangs, one black and one white, face off, its leaders armed with switchblades and ready to tangle to the death. Jackson, stepping between them, breaks up the fight and defuses the polarized, hostile environment through sheer force of personality. "Beat It," directed by Bob Giraldi, casts Jackson as the new cock of the walk, a superstar capable of breaking down all barriers. "Beat It" took the behind-the-scenes tangling over MTV's direction and made drama out of it, with Jackson reconciling the fighters, leading them in making beautifully choreographed dance, not war.

"Thriller," emerging at the end of 1983, took the ambiguity at the heart of these portrayals of Jackson and made them the centerpiece of what was then the largest, most expensive music video ever made. Helmed by feature-film director John Landis, the fourteen-minute video starred Jackson in his own horror film, one that played up the confusion inherent in his persona. Was he a bland nice guy—boyfriend material? Or was there a threatening wacko lurking within? In raising these doubts, Jackson was toying with a nation of white record buyers and MTV watchers, simultaneously telling them not to fear him as a black man and raising doubts about his own trustworthiness.

"Thriller" got to have it both ways, repeatedly turning over its established order to reveal the terror simmering below. In a setup straight out of a thousand horror films, the young lovers' car pulls up onto a deserted lane. Michael, aghast, protests against his girlfriend's raised eyebrow that "honestly, we're out of gas." No horndog he, Jackson sweetly asks her to be his steady and presents her with a ring, but soon enough, fears of another sort break to the surface. "I have something I want to tell you—I'm not like the other guys." Elmer Bernstein's ominous music, all swirling strings, creeps forward, and Landis cuts to a shot of the full moon coming out from behind a cloud. Jackson jerks and twitches, morphing into a clawed, hairy monster, with enormous fangs and beady yellow eyes—a werewolf in a letterman's jacket. Chasing his girlfriend into the forest, he knocks her down and the sounds of his ravaging her helpless body are heard as "Thriller" cuts to the interior of a movie theater where patrons scream in fright at the carnage onscreen.

Back to playing nice, Jackson is watching the movie along with his girlfriend (played by the same actress, Ola Ray), who, after digging her nails into his forearms, decides she cannot take any more of the film and storms out. Jackson good-naturedly chases after her, and the pair walk away from the theater down a smoke-filled urban street. It is at this point, four and a half minutes into the video, that the song finally begins to play. Jackson dances beside, behind, and in front of her, subtly paying homage to the familiar choreography of zombie films with his circular, shuffling steps. Michael puts his arms around her neck and does a stiff-jointed walk like a card-carrying member of the undead.

The zombie reference becomes relevant moments later when the duo pass a cemetery and the camera zooms in on one grave, where the ground is disturbed by the emergence of a horde of spooks (occurring during the song's horror-movie-homage voiceover by legendary actor Vincent Price). Like a "Video of the Dead" sequel to the George A. Romero series of horror classics, Michael and his girl find themselves surrounded by the undead, the song pausing so we can hear the ghouls' inhuman mewling. Jackson abruptly turns zombie as well and leads his minions in dance. Michael's girlfriend runs into an abandoned house and bars the door against the zombies, but they break in through the floor, walls, and windows. As the ghoulish Michael closes in on his prey and extends his bony finger toward her, she wakes to discover it is only the harmless real Michael waking her and offering to take her home. Horror once again has been proven to exist solely in the overworked imaginations of the skittish, and Jackson's character returned to his inoffensive, puppy-dog ways, but "Thriller" gets in one final, ghoulish joke, ending with a freeze-frame of Jackson's face, his eyes narrowed into the yellowish slits of a zombie.

Landis' video gets its kicks from pulling the rug out from under its viewers, refusing to allow them to settle comfortably into any sequence. "Thriller" is horror stripped of its power to genuinely unsettle, its tropes used here as a familiar set of genre standards to reference. Landis and Jackson's video is a lovingly crafted homage to the horror film, but it is not itself particularly frightening. Much like the elaborate "Girls on Film," Jackson and Landis took "Thriller" as an opportunity to make their own, somewhat abbreviated version of a Hollywood film. Not content with the three or four minutes of the average video, "Thriller" ballooned to a size where the song itself, whose selling was ostensibly the purpose of the video, became something of an afterthought. Nobody likes "Thriller" the song as much as "Thriller" the music video.

"Thriller" was the fullest realization to date of music video's enormous ambitions, but with few exceptions (Guns N' Roses' early-90s videos come to mind) its epic sprawl was rarely duplicated. First and foremost, it was simply too expensive. For the great majority of musicians, the budget assigned for shooting a music video would barely have sufficed to cover the catering for "Thriller." And even for superstars, the record labels were often hesitant to budget excessive amounts of money for video shoots. Having stumbled haphazardly into a world where video was king, the powers that be remained somewhat dubious about music video's staying powers, and they sought to get what it could out of the medium with as little investment as possible. Hence, "Thriller" proved to be the exception, rather than the benchmark, for videos to come.

For a superstar every bit the equal of Michael Jackson, Prince's videos were always a bit disappointing, lacking Jackson's blockbuster showmanship or Madonna's friskiness. They were often sexy and showy, but they felt cheap, cobbled together in a fashion unbecoming a figure of Prince's stature. "When Doves Cry" (1984), "Raspberry Beret" (1985), and "Kiss" (1986), the former two directed by Prince, are outlets for Prince's unembarrassed androgyny and taste for hokey graphics: psychedelia in "Raspberry Beret," artful silhouetting in "Kiss." Prince's gender-fuck occasionally trumped even Madonna's (witness the Little Richard impression of "Raspberry" or the role-reversal of male eye candy and inscrutable female musician in "Kiss"), but lacked Madonna's unerring eye for MTV gloss; his videos were surprisingly unsophisticated. Prince was often dancing at the center of his videos, the lasciviousness of his songs' lyrics finding expression in the movement of his hips. His later videos "Gett Off" (1991) and "Cream" (1991) both unabashedly substituted the dance for sex, with the former's X-rated contortionists imitating different sexual positions, and the latter's pair of auditioning dancers treated by Prince as his personal playthings, to be fiddled with and discarded at his will. Prince was far better off making live videos that emphasized his magnetic stage presence, as we shall see later.

Affordable Luxuries

As music videos grew respectable, the ranks of its directors expanded, and fashion photographers, filmmakers, and artists began to take up the video's reins. Major Hollywood filmmakers began to moonlight as videomakers, offering a touch of their sensibility to sympathetic artists. Joining Landis and John Sayles (who often collaborated with Bruce Springsteen) as occasional videomakers would be Spike Lee, George Lucas, Kevin Smith, Wong Kar-Wai, John Singleton, Sam Peckinpah, Bob Rafelson, and Martin Scorsese, among others. Some collaborations, like Lee and Public Enemy's "Fight the Power," were ideal unions of director and performer, sound and image. Other director-performer matchups were not as fortuitous; Sam Peckinpah, that poet of slow-motion violence, directed a strangely stagnant video for Julian Lennon's "Valotte" (1984) and Bob Rafelson, director of *Five Easy Pieces*, collaborated with Lionel Richie on his perky dance number "All Night Long" (1983). The aesthetic of choppy editing and emphasis on speed and surface allure penetrated Hollywood at around the same time, with films like *Flashdance*, *Top Gun*, *Breathless*, and the work of Ridley Scott coming to represent the MTV-ization of feature filmmaking. Television commercials also adopted the MTV look, further blurring the already-hazy line between art and ad, come-on and craftwork.

With most videos interested in effect, not plot, the influx of filmmaking talent was trumped by the fashion photographers who turned to videomaking: Herb Ritts, Jean-Baptiste Mondino, and David LaChappelle, among others. Bringing over their taste for glamour and distinctive mise-en-scène, and a well-trained eye for captivating (if not always logically motivated) imagery, the fashion photographers were a perfect fit for the thrill-a-minute world of the music video. Fashion photography was dedicated to the notion of crafting the most alluring, unusual, and sexually enthralling images possible, and photographers like Ritts and Mondino brought their sense of spectacle over to the music video. Flipping through a magazine like *Vogue* was meant to push a complex sequencing of buttons in its readers' minds, evoking a mingled brew of sexually tinged excitement, fantasy, and jealousy. Videos like Ritts' "Wicked Game" (1991) (for Chris Isaak) and Mondino's "Justify My Love" (1990) (for Madonna) were like music-video fashion shoots, almost tactile in their exquisiteness, erotically charged, and composed with an eye toward maximizing the beauty of each perfectly composed frame.

Under their tutelage, the music video grew into full-on spectacle, signifying little more than its own allure. The work of fashion-damaged directors exponentially increased the glamour levels of the average music video, turning the genre into an expression of breathtakingly lovely uselessness. These videos dispensed with the explanations, the justifications, and the half-hearted attempts at plot, offering in their stead a vision of unalloyed beauty. Whether or not a video by Ritts was to your liking, though, was probably dependent on how much aesthetic pleasure you could take away from a perfume ad.

Ritts' video for Madonna's "Cherish" (1989) was a perfect example of the thought process at work in his videos. Madonna lolled about in the surf, surrounded by a gaggle of shirtless male models and adorable children. Sopping-wet and sexy, she approached the camera, meeting its unblinking gaze with her own high-octane, come-hither look, pulling her dress open to show off some cleavage, making bodybuilder poses, and shaking her rump. The elegant black-and-white footage, the casual air of sexual omnivorousness—"Cherish" is like an Abercrombie & Fitch photo shoot gone live-action. As evidenced by "Wicked Game," "Cherish," and Janet Jackson's "Love Will Never Do (Without You)" (1990), Ritts' video work was unquestionably lovely, a celebration of youthful vigor and beauty bathed in glorious light. Much like the fashion photography from which it stemmed, all that beauty ultimately seemed too much of a good thing, only consumable in small doses. Take too big a bite, and you were liable to get a stomachache.

Kings of Rock

Opening the door for other black artists, Michael Jackson also let in a burgeoning genre whose initial growth spurt coincided with that of the music video. Hip-hop, having begun in the burned-out streets of the Bronx in the mid-1970s, had grown into a commercially promising genre by the early 1980s. With record labels unsure about the future of a brand of music they viewed as a passing fad, and still dubious about videos in general (illustrated most famously by Sugar Hill Records' rejecting a spec video for Grandmaster Flash's "White Lines" from a then-unknown Spike Lee), hip-hop videos remained rarities on American television screens until the multiplatinum prowess of the Beastie Boys and Run-D.M.C. blew the doors off hip-hop's ghettoization. Blondie's "Rapture" had crashed the rap party early, featuring the legendary hip-hop man-about-town Fab 5 Freddy, graffiti artists, and a faux Bronx streetscape, but

Grandmaster Flash and the Furious Five's "The Message" and Afrika Bambaataa's "Planet Rock," both debuting in 1982, were two of the earliest videos entirely devoted to hip-hop.

Taking place on stoops, outside housing projects, and along streets that rumbled with a never-ending stream of ambulances, taxis, and subway trains, "The Message" looks now like a time capsule from New York City's bad old days. Knowing that hip-hop videos required a solid sense of place, "The Message" was about little other than the city's relentless motion and the silent poetry of those places, like the rubble-filled lot where the group gathered, that had been left behind by progress. Lead MC Melle Mel dressed in a Michael Jackson-like leather jacket and glove, but he did so standing on an ugly, battle-scarred Bronx street corner, not some Hollywood simulacrum of urban squalor, like in "Billie Jean." Whodini were nowhere near as politically astute as Grandmaster Flash, but their videos were equally receptive to the look and feel of early-80s New York. Their best video, "Big Mouth" (1985) (directed by Adam Friedman), imagined a hip-hop party atop a Hudson River barge tricked out with a set of office cubicles, and their other clips (including "Magic's Wand") ventured the length and breadth of the metropolis—a visual counterpart to the group's city-centric lyrics.

A trickle of other videos, including Run-D.M.C.'s "Rock Box" and "King of Rock," followed, but it was not until 1986 that a pair of hip-hop clips fought their way into MTV rotation and national recognition. Cynics might point out that the uniting factor in the two videos was the comforting presence of white people, but hip-hop pushed forward, by whatever means necessary, and the prominence of Run-D.M.C. and Aerosmith's "Walk This Way" and the Beastie Boys' "Fight for Your Right to Party" (joined by the Fat Boys and the Beach Boys' "Wipeout") opened the doors to hip-hop on television, leading to *Yo! MTV Raps*, the Video Jukebox, and other tools of rap's ascent to cultural prominence.

"Walk This Way" has the boys from Queens literally breaking down the walls that separated them from their hard-rock cronies, and while the video was intended to be about rock and rap coming together, it was also symbolic of the scratching and clawing necessary for hip-hop to get its foot in the door of the wider pop world. Run-D.M.C. are swathed in darkness in their dingy chambers as Aerosmith rocked out, bathed in light. Tyler may use his mike stand to break the first hole in the wall, but it is clearly the rappers who are the stars of the video, bursting onstage at an Aerosmith concert and stealing the show. "Walk This Way" duplicated the party-crashing motif of "King of Rock" (1985), where the band bum-rushes the Museum of Rock & Roll, rapping amidst the Elvis, Buddy Holly, and Sex Pistols memorabilia, and spray-painting the museum's pristine white walls with a crude, and not unreasonable, message: "Run-D.M.C.—King of Rock."

Later videos chose to emphasize the cuddlier, more mainstream attributes of the group, even making a Christmas-themed video ("Christmas in Hollis," 1987) in which the boys from Queens palled around with St. Nick. For "It's Tricky" (1987), Run-D.M.C. helicoptered into Times Square, beating three-card monte hustlers Penn and Teller at their own game, and outfitting the comedians in the band's trademark Adidas shell-toe sneakers and black hats. "Mary Mary" (1988) took on Tipper Gore's antiprofanity crusade, with a Tipper manqué protesting a Run-D.M.C. concert, only to be seduced by the band's mellifluous craftsmanship into shedding a few inhibitions and boogieing onstage.

The Beastie Boys, themselves blurring the boundaries between hard rock and rap, staged an all-inclusive bash in "Fight for Your Right to Party," taking over a nerdy soiree and dramatically amping up the sleaze factor. The boys stole beers, spit in partygoers' faces, and made out with strange women. Dressed like urban scuzzballs in leather jackets, porkpie hats, and *Miami Vice* stubble, the Beasties brought their metalhead friends to crash a tame house party, initiating a memorable pie-throwing melee. It was significant that the Beastie Boys ushered in the metal fans, because "Fight for Your Right to Party" was an outbreak of metal video's party-hearty mentality within hip-hop.

Clearly lacking in the street cred of compatriots like Run-D.M.C., if for obvious, melanin-related reasons, the Beastie Boys chose to celebrate their outsiderdom by latching onto another genre's conventions. Directed by Rick Menello and Adam Dubin, "Fight" did not look much like "The Message," nor did it contain breakdancing, beatboxing, or any of the other skills that traditionally form the five elements of hip-hop. Instead, it was a hip-hop video that looked more like a metal band's MTV offering, a suburbia-friendly tale that would play nicely in Peoria. When compounded with the Beastie Boys' unthreatening Caucasian-ness, it came as no surprise that "Fight for Your Right to Party" would be one of the first major hip-hop videos on MTV. In its wake would follow Public Enemy, LL Cool J, and the rise of hip-hop to video glory.

Singing Cowboys

Another latecomer to the video game was country music, which did not begin seriously producing music videos until 1983—the year of the debut of Country Music Television (CMT). Even then, the bulk of country videos were ultra-low-budget affairs, most coming in around the $5,000 mark. Country video's late bloom was somewhat surprising, given its long tradition of combining sound and image. The genre's immersion in the proto-video dated back as far as the singing cowboy films of Gene Autry and Jimmie Rodgers' 1930 short film *The Singing Brakeman*, which featured Rodgers good-naturedly playing requests for a pair of women as they went about their morning housekeeping and he waited for his train to arrive. In its early-1980s incarnation, country was an occasional, if irregular, presence on noncountry music-video channels, with Hank Williams Jr. receiving airplay on MTV and artists like Alabama, Willie Nelson, and Kenny Rogers making appearances on its sister channel VH-1 (which had made its debut in 1985). Country videos borrowed heavily from the "traditional" playbook, making use of familiar rural iconography like cowboys, small towns, and juke joints without devoting significant energy to coherent narrative. Early country videos attempted to establish a foothold in the rock-dominated video world, almost comically overemphasizing their own down-home aesthetic as a means of distinguishing themselves. Nowhere was this more obvious than in the spate of videos that paid homage to country's own legendary past. These ran the gamut from George Jones' "Who's Gonna Fill Their Shoes?" (1986), which featured sentimental footage of old-time country stars, to Hank Williams Jr.'s "There's a Tear in My Beer" (1989), a virtual duet with his dead father, present in the video as a disembodied voice summoned from old film footage.

Country videos were dominated by nostalgia, whether for its own roots, or for the roots of its songs' protagonists—as in K.T. Oslin's "80s Ladies" (1987) and Rodney Crowell and Rosanne Cash's "It's Such a Small World" (1988), which both featured middle-aged characters watching home-movie footage of their younger selves. At the same time that country protected its legendary past, it also sought to tear it down and start afresh. Hank Williams Jr.'s video "Young Country" (1988) (a kinder, gentler "Fight for Your Right") epitomized this desire, with two old codgers nostalgic for the genre's past rudely surprised by the country scion's inclusive, open-minded, downright rock-and-roll party. Metalheads, surfers, and punks were all invited to join "Young Country," and whether the old folks liked it was a moot point to Hank Jr. Country's umbrella was now wide enough to include both Chicago Bears running back Walter Payton (making a cameo appearance) and Van Halen (lyrically namechecked, and referenced by the Eddie Van Halen–style ax wielded by Williams' guitarist).

Girls on Film

The King of Pop was followed in short order by a fresh face who provided a push to another underrepresented group on MTV: women. Madonna, at the start of her career just another pop upstart, was soon to become the Queen of Music Video to Michael Jackson's King, using the video as a marker of her ever-changing moods, phases, and modes. It was always easy to place Madonna's videos chronologically, because they served as a moving photo album of her stylistic restlessness. Working with director Mary Lambert, Madonna's early videos were by no means as opulent as Jackson's; at this early point in her career, she was not even remotely the star he was. But these early clips, of which "Borderline," "Like a Virgin," and "Material Girl" are the most significant, depict a rapid-fire ascent from just another girl from around the way to the glam queen of 80s opulence.

"Borderline" (1984) features Madonna as a working-class girl discovered by a yuppie photographer while dancing on the streets of downtown Los Angeles. Ushered away on the wings of eagles in his sports car, she gladly poses for him, but grows to miss her boyfriend from the old neighborhood. She struggles to choose between her working-class man's man and the ambitious upscale smoothie before ultimately deciding to stick to her roots. At the video's end, she goes back to the photographer's house to spray-paint its walls. In this early appearance, Madonna was ambivalent about the trappings of fame: wealth, success, and comfort. Never feeling fully comfortable in her new role, she embraces her roots as a means of staying true to herself.

Needless to say, this ambivalence was short-lived, to say the least, and by the time of "Like a Virgin," later that year, the backdrop had shifted considerably. No old neighborhoods were anywhere in sight; instead, Madonna cavorts on a gondola and inside a Venetian palazzo. All "Like a Virgin" was missing was a shot of the Piazza San Marco and it could have been an advertisement for the local tourist bureau. The video dresses her in two diametrically opposing outfits: a sporty-looking ensemble for exterior shots and a wedding dress in the palace. There was surely a message here about maintaining her virginal purity on the inside, but between the Venetian setting, and her pas-de-deux with a bemasked mysterious stranger, a more important message was being transmitted: that Madonna was a hood-rat no longer.

"Material Girl" (1985) switches genres entirely, casting Madonna in an updated 1950s' musical, a *Gentlemen Prefer Blondes* for the 1980s. Much like the song itself, the video simultaneously upheld and mocked a certain ethos of materialistic self-interest. Dressed in a pink taffeta gown, Madonna is pursued by tuxedoed suitors who shower her with gifts. These retro scenes alternate with contemporary sequences, in which the singer is chased by a single suitor through a more "realistic" landscape: a movie studio and her capacious dressing room. Madonna vamps for the camera, a fur coat over her shoulders as she collects her baubles, but at video's end, she goes off with the guy who brings her daisies and picks her up in a pickup truck. The video makes an express point of informing us that this suitor, too, was loaded, so any moral expressed here remained rather shallow. Once again, the explicit message remained secondary to the stylistic message, which was that Madonna was a superstar before whose feet the world's treasures fell, a Marilyn Monroe for the MTV era. By the time of "Dress You Up" (1985), Madonna could straight-facedly shoot a video whose opening sequence showed hundreds of her fans dressed up as their favorite singer. It was already a long way back to the "Borderline," and Madonna's stylistically adventurous, variegated videos of the late 80s and early 90s would further her status as one of the great manipulators of image of her time.

Madonna may not have been the first woman in music video, but her ascendance led to a spate of videos by women about being women. A wave of female video innovators would emerge along with Madonna, including Cyndi Lauper, Pat Benatar, Donna Summer (whose "She Works Hard for the Money" [1983] featured Summer as a struggling waitress), and Annie Lennox of the Eurythmics. In their videos, womanhood was a gift and a curse, a source of power and a terrible handicap. Above all, being a woman in these videos meant playing a role, shuffling through a dizzying array of masks in the hopes of finding one's true face.

The elaborate, Rube Goldberg contraption animating Annie Lennox's head in the video for "Missionary Man" (1986) only made explicit what almost all the Eurythmics' videos made their implicit theme: the constructed nature of personality, and by extension, femininity. In their videos for "Love Is a Stranger" (1982) and "Beethoven (I Love to Listen To)" (1987), Lennox makes high drama out of removing her wig, taking off the glam, ice-queen persona as easily as she had put it on. The Eurythmics' videos were clashes of ideas, positions, and personae, starring Lennox as the chameleon able to take on a multiplicity of roles and share the transformation with us. Unlike Madonna, who changed between one video and the next, Lennox made transformation an essential part of the videos themselves. By taking off her costumes, literally and metaphorically, Lennox ushered her fans behind the curtain of stardom's metamorphoses. Whether sexpot or dowdy housewife, feminine object of yuppie affection or butch male impersonator, Lennox turned the process of changing form into the mask she wore.

In "Beethoven (I Love to Listen To)" Lennox is an aggravated housewife who gives new meaning to the term "furious cleaning." Frantically scrubbing the counters and floors, straightening bedsheets, and inspecting toothbrushes, Lennox radiates with the insecurity and dissatisfaction of frustrated domesticity. The camera zooms in on Lennox, knitting agitatedly and muttering angrily about the "girl who thinks she should have everything." As we follow Lennox through her disquieting daily routine, we realize that the girl is Annie herself, haunted as she is by her impish childhood self. Wearing a platinum-blond wig and hot-pink lipstick, this mini-Annie follows her on her rounds, gleefully undoing her domestic work. When the adult Lennox takes a moment to reflect, sitting in front of her mirror, shadows playing over her face, she decides to pull the plug on her charade of housewifery. Yanking off her wig, she dresses herself as an adult version of the child Annie, in a platinum-blond wig, hot-pink makeup, and a silver cocktail dress. She gleefully shreds all the middle-class trappings of her apartment, attacking by inference the absent husband for whom all her previous ministerings had been intended and strides purposefully out of the dingy cinder-block building, away from her domestic prison. "Would I Lie to You?" (1985) featured the male significant other pointedly missing from "Beethoven," a sneering, insecure brat dedicated to making Lennox's life miserable. (A similar figure cropped up in Til Tuesday's "Voices Carry," where lead singer Aimee Mann announced her newfound independence from her constricting boyfriend-torturer by breaking into song from a seat in the audience during a Carnegie Hall performance.)

"Love Is a Stranger" approaches the same conclusion as "Beethoven" from the opposite direction, beginning with Lennox, looking glam in her fur coat, singing from the back seat of a luxury sedan. When the car comes to a halt, she pulls off her wig, looking into the camera and challenging her audience to find her less compelling, less attractive, without the luxurious accessories. These costume/persona changes were a coy reminder that everything here was performance—that any role taken on by Lennox was by necessity artificial and interchangeable. Nonetheless, Lennox accentuated the dichotomy between her two primary personae—that of the glamorous, sexy diva, and the frumpy, or masculine, odd woman out.

"Sweet Dreams" (1983) juxtaposes locales, not personae, switching Lennox and bandmate Dave Stewart at will between a corporate boardroom and a rural field. The two worlds increasingly intermingled over the course of the video, like an update of "Shock the Monkey," with a cow strolling around the conference room table and Stewart hunched over his computer, surrounded by snacking cattle. Lennox is an odd admixture of androgynous corporate cool and pixieish sexual heat, her masculine business suit and carrot-colored hair implying that no matter the context, Lennox would simultaneously fit in and stand out.

Regardless of what mask she wore, Lennox was, like Madonna, always herself, always finding room inside her capacious persona for one more role, one more costume, one more alias. By the time of "You Have Placed a Chill in My Heart," in 1988, the Eurythmics were hosting a convention of Lennox's past performances, where "Would I Lie to You's" spiky blond and "Beethoven's" housewife exchange phone numbers and recipes, and Lennox revels in her own mutability. Lennox's solo videos trawled similar territory, with "Why" (1992) a languorous look at her applying her performance game face, and "Walking on Broken Glass" (1992) a *Dangerous Liaisons* rip with Lennox stepping into the Glenn Close role opposite costar John Malkovich. "Little Bird" (1992) was "You Have Placed a Chill in My Heart" redux, with Lennox putting on a cabaret performance straight out of, well, *Cabaret*, and inviting all her past personae along to the party.

Where in Madonna's videos family was mostly absent, leaving her free to pursue whatever and whomever she pleased (with the obvious exception of "Papa Don't Preach," the single-mother melodrama with Danny Aiello playing her worried father), Cyndi Lauper's were dogged by parental and authority figures. They take place a step before Madonna's, detailing the process of breaking free, rather than its immanent actuality. "Girls Just Wanna Have Fun" (1983) features Lauper as the daughter of a traditional family whose stifling expectations shackle her. When she comes home for dinner, Cyndi gives her exasperated parents an impromptu lecture about the modern woman's wants and needs. Talking on the phone with her large array of rainbow-hued friends, she leads them on a trip to the big city, where they break into a kooky sidewalk conga line. Eventually, they all end up back at Cyndi's parents' house, where they pile into her tiny bedroom, *Night at the Opera* style. Lauper's energy overcomes the stultifying status quo in "She Bop" (1984) as well, where she takes on, for unclear reasons, the fast-food industry, emerging triumphant over Burger Klone and its brain-dead customers. "Time After Time" (1984) adopts a more elegiac tone, with Cyndi as a woman in a failing relationship who finds comfort in the solace of sad old movies. Sitting in her bedroom, crumpled and forlorn, her lover ignoring her for a few more minutes of sleep, she sings softly to herself. She remembers happier times, but when this proves to be not quite enough to sustain her, she packs her things and leaves, finding refuge in her mother's comforting arms.

If Madonna offered a fantasy of what it was to be an independent woman, Lauper's videos were a bit more down to earth. Independence was not just wild times and dazzling romance; it was also fighting with your parents and leaving your lover. There was a pleasing reality principle to Lauper and director Ed Griles' collaborations, one that served as a much-appreciated counterweight to Madonna and Lambert's fantasies of transformation. Where Madonna's videos held out the promise of ever-bigger, ever-better joys (and productions), Lauper's were far more mundane. In the consumption-happy world of MTV, that made Madonna the big winner, and Lauper something of a killjoy.

Other women turned to the theme of emerging female power for their videos, their narratives depicting woman triumphant, with none more notorious than Pat Benatar's "Love Is a Battlefield" (1983), directed by Bob Giraldi.

Benatar plays a teenage runaway, having run out on her parents to find herself in the big city. The video toggles between Benatar on a Greyhound bus, singing from the back row, and her misadventures in the metropolis. The city was big and dirty and loud and more than a little frightening, but Benatar survives the noise and the tough guy in a muscle-T who shoves her out of his way, and she makes her way to a local nightspot. There, she confronts a pimp who had been pushing women around, gathering her fellow females together to overwhelm him with their sexually aggressive dance. Suitably humiliated, he slinks away, and the new posse finish their dance down by the docks the next morning. Benatar and all her pals have found fashion by now, too, dressed in the tattered and shredded outfits de rigueur for the 80s urban-hobo look.

Like Madonna, and Olivia Newton-John, whose "Physical" (directed by Brian Grant) was a clever sublimation of lust into physical fitness, Benatar knew that sex sells, but the tale she tells is a fantasy whose uglier bits have not been excised. Life is tough, men are bastards, the big city is a rough place to be—but there are moments of grace. "Love Is a Battlefield" fits snugly into the cinematic tradition of the dance, where the very act of dancing can be powerful enough to move mountains. With its roots in the grace of Fred and Ginger, and Gene Kelly, the dance video placed its faith in the beauty of choreographed rhythmic motion. As with many of its antecedents, and descendants, "Love Is a Battle-field" used dance as a stand-in for the unmentionable, sex. In dancing so felici-tously, Benatar was asserting her newfound sexual prowess.

Embracing Simplicity

Even with the fashion-plate video ascendant, the notion of the video as short story survived, with two of its primary practitioners being the old-fashioned rock stars David Bowie and Bruce Springsteen. Their in-house directors, David Mallet and John Sayles, along with the DJ-turned-director Don Letts, whose videos for the Clash's "Rock the Casbah" (1982) (which featured an Arab and a Hasidic Jew cruising the Texas desert in a cushy Cadillac, looking for oil and set-tling for pogoing at a Clash concert) and the Pretenders' "Back on the Chain Gang" (1982) mingled narrative and punk-rock attitude, were crucial in crystal-lizing this more conservative take on the music video. Mallet, who directed so many of the abiding works of the early video era, collaborated with Bowie on his videos for "D.J.," "Ashes to Ashes," "Wild Is the Wind," "Let's Dance," "China Girl," and numerous others. In videos like the Boomtown Rats' "I Don't Like Mondays" and Def Leppard's "Photograph," Mallet had epitomized a brand of videomaking almost as polished as Russell Mulcahy's, but with an occasional, humanizing ragged edge. "Let's Dance" and "China Girl," from his 1983 comeback album *Let's Dance*, features Bowie as an ageless blond satyr with a tan suit and a million-watt smile. Much like "Girls on Film" and "Hungry Like the Wolf," "Let's Dance," "China Girl," and "Blue Jean" turn Bowie into a glamorous jet-setter—a music-video James Bond, suave and self-confident. "China Girl" and "Blue Jean" sustained the exotic, colonialist bent of "Let's Dance," set as it was in the Australian outback. "China Girl," marred by sophomoric orientalist touches like Bowie pulling his eyes into Asian-looking slits with his fingers, features Bowie making sweet love with his Red Chinese amour, and "Blue Jean" paints him silver and white, outfits him in Bedouin garb, and has him performing at a supper club with a backup band garbed like harem eunuchs.

"Blue Jean" also appeared in a twenty-minute incarnation, "Jazzin' for Blue Jean" (1984), that made a big splash in Britain. Director Julien Temple was among the first practitioners of the long-form music video, looking to expand the music video beyond the artificial boundaries of the song itself. "Jazzin' for Blue Jean," which (fleshing out the plot of the shorter version) starred Bowie as both a superstar singer and the working-class yob desperate to see him in concert, and ABC's "Mantrap" (1983) were Temple's contributions to the fledgling long-form aesthetic (which had begun with Michael Nesmith's long-form video album *Elephant Parts,* in 1981)—a form that never quite caught on, although Neil Young's *Greendale* (2003) was an intriguing late addition to the fold. Temple had a sly eye for debunking the mythology of celebrity (as with the stinging Hollywood parody of Neil Young's "This Note's for You" [1988] and Tom Petty's "Into the Great Wide Open" [1991], starring Johnny Depp as a clueless rock star), but was equally fond of videos with an air of romance and mystery, ranging from the reverse-motion fairy tale of Enigma's "Return to Innocence" (1993) to the malevolent female sexuality of the Rolling Stones' "She Was Hot" (1984) to the doppelgangers of "Jazzin' for Blue Jean" and the Stones' "Undercover of the Night" (1983). Temple's videos often romanticized performance, with videos like "Blue Jean," the Kinks' "Come Dancing" (1983), and Sade's "Smooth Operator" (1984) taking place in elegant nightclubs whose hushed lighting and alluring décor were miles away from the deafening roar and impersonal vibe of the average real-life rock show. The swooping crane shots and elegant time structure of "Come Dancing" imbued the Kinks' music with a romance and allure that his later video for "This Note's for You" would have mocked mercilessly.

Temple enjoyed the ambience of the spy thriller—a genre he returned to time and again, with "Undercover of the Night" the most prominent example. Like Bowie in "Jazzin' for Blue Jean," "Undercover" features twin versions of Stones lead singer Mick Jagger—one kidnapped by a shadowy gang of criminals led by guitarist Keith Richards, and one attempting to track the first Mick down. Jagger and Richards are at war here (with Richards apparently at the head of an army of police officers and soldiers), but Jagger is also at war with himself, one hand not knowing what the other was doing, and desperately seeking to find out. With its masked death's-head figures, mysteriously intertwined doppelgangers, and overhanging cloud of impending doom, "Undercover of the Night" was like *Black Orpheus* for the age of Reagan.

"Undercover" was not the only video to play spy versus spy—Golden Earring's riotously enjoyable "Twilight Zone" (1982), directed by Dick Maas, is every bit as claustrophobic, double-cross followed by double-cross, with no one to be trusted—even in bed. A mysterious man waits anxiously in a hotel room, fearing the dreaded knock on the door. Even when the unwanted guests finally arrive and shoot him, the video continued, as if unsatisfied with its own resolution. "Twilight Zone" enjoys a laugh at its own expense, its secret agents, interrogation rooms, and John le Carré-brand paranoia becoming nothing more than a theatrical performance, with East German secret agents in black leather and devilish interrogation specialists all part of the show. "Twilight Zone," in its own unsophisticated way, made like Brecht, reminding us that all we were watching (that all we would watch) was artifice, nothing more.

Where Bowie was a suave international lover, equally at home in London and Beijing, Bruce Springsteen's videos cast him as a good-hearted working-class soul, tradition-minded and unsophisticated. In "I'm on Fire" (1985), he plays a mechanic with a hankering for a high-class woman in a white dress and matching Cadillac (narrative ground previously covered, far less memorably, in Billy Joel's accidentally ridiculous video for "Uptown Girl" [1983]), and in "Glory Days" (1985), he is a crane operator with fond memories of his years as a high-school hurler. In each, Springsteen yearns for something just beyond his reach; but even in dreams, he remains firmly tethered to the ground. Fantasies of facing the San Diego Padres in a major-league game, or romancing the lady with the mansion on the hill, were of an entirely different bent than cavorting in Moroccan nightclubs.

John Sayles' film work found poetry in mundane American life, and his videos for Springsteen are similar in effect, investing auto-body shops and vacant sandlots with the hunger and romance of the Boss' songs. Similarly unadorned was "Brilliant Disguise" (1987), directed by Meiert Avis. In this one-take clip, Avis slowly zooms in on Springsteen, strumming his guitar at a plain-looking kitchen table and singing of his trail of broken promises. Springsteen looks directly at us, offering his unblinking gaze as his bond, but when the camera pulls into very tight focus, leaving us trapped between his forehead and his lower lip, we are suddenly not so sure we trust his artless visage. Is star power just a "brilliant disguise"? The video fades out before offering an answer.

"Atlantic City" (1982) had gone even further in eliding the star-making machine, removing Springsteen from the picture entirely. As befitted his anthem about the low-rent New Jersey gambling mecca, "Atlantic City" shows the ugly side of an already unattractive city. Images of neon lights and casino action were overwhelmed by shots of tacky billboards, wrecked neighborhoods, and bumper-to-bumper highway traffic. The gleaming glass casinos and office towers seem to be in danger of being swallowed whole by the encroaching darkness. Atlantic City, in the video's estimation, had become a raisin in the sun, shriveled and unwanted.

Dime-Store Surrealism

While Madonna, Bowie, and the like used their own glamorousness as selling points in their videos, musicians with less physical charm turned toward a workaday brand of surrealism in order to glam up their own drab surfaces. Influenced by Dali, Magritte, Cocteau, and above all Luis Buñuel, whose *Un Chien Andalou* (1929, codirected by Dali) became the touchstone of early music video, surrealism became the dominant mode of a certain adventurous brand of videomaking. For no one was this more true than the profoundly unphotogenic Ric Ocasek, and his band, the Cars. The band's 1981 "Shake It Up" frolics at the intersection of language and image, with Ric a mechanic (he works with Cars— get it?) out for a night on the town. The video shakes up everything from dice and drinks to viewer expectations, with wizened grannies turning into gorgeous young women, and other miracles of transformation.

"You Might Think" (1984), directed by Jeff Stein and Charlex, ventured deeper into the realm of dime-store surrealism. Ocasek showed up everywhere in "You Might Think," plaguing the existence of a flustered young woman—at the movies, he morphs into the monster onscreen; at the dentist's, he leaps onto her teeth, sporting a mini-drill; she unrolls a lipstick tube and finds him ensconced inside. He even weasels his way into the framed snapshot of the woman and her boyfriend, elbowing the frozen figures out of the way to make room for himself in the center. Mini-Ric's opposite, Mega-Ric, pulls a King Kong with his intended paramour in the Fay Wray role, hanging off the Empire State Building while grasping her in his palm. He drops her, and before impact she wakes in bed, her nightmare seemingly over. Glancing over at her alarm clock, she sees Ric inside it, his hands the hands of the clock and his head the head of a buzzing fly.

There was something to be said about the video's obsessive interest in the stalking and possession of women, with Ric and the boys hounding an unfortunate girl until she finds herself shrunken and acquiescent, but "You Might

Think" was less prurient than sublimely silly. "You Might Think" revels in the notion of omnipresence, imbuing a dull interior landscape with a touch of creaky magic. MTV crowned "You Might Think" its first Video of the Year (over "Thriller" and "Girls Just Wanna Have Fun"), but after a while, viewers must have started to sympathize with the feminine star of the video, also sensing that everywhere they turned, there were the Cars. The band's "Hello Again" (1984), codirected by Andy Warhol and Dan Munroe, was like a 1980s Factory party, with all the freaks coming out of the woodwork bearing the song's title imprinted on their earrings, tongues, and torsos. Warhol, nearing the end of his life, makes an appearance as a bartender, looking a bit confused, but "Hello Again" nonetheless retains some of his classic work's aura of straight-faced consumerist burlesque.

Possibly even more ubiquitous as MTV wallpaper was one-hit wonder a-Ha's epochal "Take on Me" (1985), directed by Steve Barron. Splitting the difference between art-school collage and straightforward narrative, "Take on Me" borrows heavily from the conventions of comic books, imagining free-floating transport between the real and fantasy worlds. The video's heroine has the best of everything: she gets to leap into her favorite story, fall in love with its hero, and bring him home. Its message of fantasy fulfillment was a thoroughly appropriate one for a medium whose intended purpose was to bring stars bodily into fans' homes.

The non-narrative clip took the turn to self-parody with Dire Straits' "Money for Nothing" (1985) (also directed by Barron, whose other most notable video was the Human League's *Day for Night*–inspired "Don't You Want Me"). In this gleeful biting of the channel that feeds, a cartoon character, hanging out in his living room with his dog, is sucked into the world of MTV, joining Mark Knopfler and the rest of the band onstage. "Money for Nothing" renders the band in hand-painted psychedelic colors, like a garish LeRoy Neiman painting come to life. The live footage had a certain propulsive magnetism, but the highlight of the video are the (now ancient-looking) computer graphics of two working-class slobs in overalls watching videos as they carry boxes to and fro. These proto-Beavis and Butt-heads critique the (fake) videos on their screens, which include a male singer-songwriter's sensitive ballad and a metal babe's strutting soft-core clip. The song's lyrics refer to the former as "the little faggot," and of the latter, they disdainfully note "that ain't workin." The only video the duo seems to enjoy, of course, is "Money for Nothing." Much like their disciples Beavis and Butt-head, "Money for Nothing" left its intentions blurry. What is being parodied here—the stupidity and narrow-mindedness of these MTV-watching lunks, or the dumb videos shown by the channel? The uncertainty allowed "Money for Nothing" to become one of the biggest successes in MTV's history, and an icon of the channel's willingness to poke fun at itself, down to the imitation channel bumpers that opened and closed the video. Other, later videos that took more explicit potshots at MTV icons, and iconography, like Neil Young's "This Note's for You," would have a harder time penetrating the channel's protective wall.

Comedy was a regular presence in the music video, ranging across video styles and musical genres. Paul Simon's "You Can Call Me Al" (1986), lacking the conceptual apparatus of "Money for Nothing," went for a simpler video premise: casting comedian Chevy Chase as Simon's comic sidekick. Simon twiddles his thumbs as Chase fills in for him in lip-syncing the song, comically overemoting to reach the high notes of "You Can Call Me Al." Chase is typically poker-faced and effervescently silly, but the real comedy of "You Can Call Me Al" stems from the disconnect between real musicmaking and video fakery; Chase takes over the entirety of Simon's role, with Simon only playing the musical parts in the video that others had played in the studio. Thomas Dolby's "She Blinded Me with Science" (1982) had looked all the way back to the silent film for comic inspiration, interspersing mock-serious intertitles ("Mr. Dolby Rejects Science and All Things Scientific") in its humorous takeoff on the mad-scientist flick.

The comedy of mutable identity was a constant in the music video, substituting the unfamiliar for the familiar. Talking Heads' "Wild Wild Life" (1986), directed by David Byrne, transformed the song into a karaoke-bar roundelay, with the joke being that the video's oddball singers (a librarian, a Rasta lover-man wearing a fedora, John Goodman) were no more unlikely stars than Byrne himself, whose rubbery facial expressions and flailing limbs rendered him a deeply implausible rock singer. Byrne's contortions were reminiscent of his hilarious starring turn in "Once in a Lifetime" (1981), which went beyond comedy and tapped into a wellspring of deeply American weirdness, with the Talking Heads lead singer part televangelist, part limbo dancer, and part children's-show host, all bathed in the flop sweat of nerdy exertion. The band's "Love for Sale" (1986) was a brilliant indictment of consumerism—a smiling dagger stuck in the heart of corporate America. A multitude of later videos would eventually borrow this fake-products motif, including George Michael's "Killer/Papa Was a Rolling Stone" and Jewel's "Intuition." While flipping channels, the band come upon a series of ornate images of conspicuous consumption. Byrne, on an assembly line of polo-shirted, well-appointed yuppies, is unceremoniously shoved out of line, as commercials for Isuzu, Pan Am, Colgate, Old Spice, Snuggle, and other products intimately familiar to any 80s consumer flashed across the screen.

"Love for Sale" makes use of an ingenious visual metaphor to link commercials and consumers. The band members' motions match the movement of the commercials they parody—wrenched apart like cookies being split in half, spun outward and upward like tubes of lipstick, and knocked down like mown grass. After a montage of the band being turned into a desirable consumer product themselves—dunked in chocolate, then wrapped in foil, like human Hershey's bars—"Love for Sale" ends with hands grabbing at displays of these delectable commodities, followed by couples embracing. Directed by Byrne and Melvin Sokolsky, "Love for Sale" renders explicit the band-as-commodity equation, wherein the hot new video on MTV is just another type of candy bar available to be purchased. Rather than swim against the tide, though, "Love for Sale" was arsenic wrapped to look like candy; its glossy visuals and ad quotations made it a perfect fit for music video's upwardly mobile aesthetic, its stinger only emerging on repeat viewings.

"Road to Nowhere" (1985), codirected by Byrne and Stephen R. Johnson, was its diametric opposite, stylistically speaking. Rough and casual where "Love for Sale" was diamond-sharp, "Road to Nowhere," like "Wild Wild Life," was a populist gesture, offering the song up to its distinctly unglamorous fans. The video stars a chorus of average-looking folk clad in shorts, T-shirts, and sundresses, singing the song's chorus in an impromptu performance at the local community center. "Road to Nowhere" features a quick-change montage of a married couple changing clothes and hairstyles, and adding children into the mix—an indicator of Johnson's emerging interest in the use of special effects. But it would be Johnson's next video that would set MTV afire and fully reflect the capabilities of the medium to dazzle.

Magical Montage

No other video symbolized the form's growth into maturity, and its concomitant embrace of seriousness, like Peter Gabriel's "Sledgehammer" (1986). "Sledgehammer" was as FX-intensive as its predecessors, if not more so, but it was less silly, less self-deprecating, than "Money for Nothing" or "You Might Think." With its surrealist swirl of imagery, time-lapse photography, and overarching sensation of operating according to a mysterious but coherent logic, "Sledgehammer" is like a modern update of the classic scene from Buster Keaton's *Sherlock Jr.* (1924), where Keaton finds himself, through the miracle of film montage, transmuted from one landscape to the next without warning. Using drawing, painting, claymation, Arcimboldo-like fruit collages, and postproduction effects, "Sledgehammer" is the history of art tossed into a shredder, with the resulting pieces reassembled into an ungainly but alluring new hybrid.

It was also the most dramatic extension of music video's capabilities to date—much more so than "Thriller," which was epic in length but deeply familiar in tone to any horror-film buff. "Sledgehammer" was an eruption of the avant-garde onto MTV screens, but an avant-garde more interested in the wonders of montage on a major-label video budget than *epater le bourgeoisie*.

Opening with bodily images of swimming sperm and streaming blood, pulsing in time with the song's rhythm, "Sledgehammer" cuts to a set of extreme close-up shots of Gabriel's face. The next series of shots pull back for a close-up of Gabriel's strangely palpitating face, looking as if he had lost control over his own facial gestures. His mouth flits open and closed, his eyebrows toggle up and down, and his eyes blink rapidly as he sings. A model train appears and circles his head, and a paper airplane floats past his ear. Gabriel's face turns blue, and painted clouds pass over his cheeks and forehead. He holds a striped bullhorn to shout, then uses it to listen, but it, too, disappears almost as fast as it has appeared. A white seatbelt holds him in place, and a chalkboard behind his head fills with drawings of a racing roller coaster. Gabriel's head disappears, replaced by a head-shaped block of ice, with his face dimly visible inside. A sledgehammer emerges from off-screen and smashes the ice, and fish swim out of his skull, along with a large pile of fruit, which gathers together, like the famous Renaissance paintings of Arcimboldo, to form an approximation of his face.

Continuing the transformation, slivers of wood fly together to form an imprisoning shackle over Gabriel's face, leaving only his mouth visible. Next, Gabriel is rendered in claymation, his hands miniature sledgehammers that knock a tiny clay creature out of its refuge inside his face. His face becomes a yin and yang, then two leaping fish, then a dancing headless chicken—then two dancing headless chickens. As the song repeats its mantra of "shed my skin," entire sets of Gabriel's clothing fly off, only to reveal yet more layers underneath. The room's furniture swirls around him, dancing, and the stars themselves, glimpsed in the sky, form themselves into a human figure that clambers out of the room, waving its arms from side to side.

"Sledgehammer" exists to celebrate its own magnificent powers of imagination and the varied palette it brings to the formerly limited expanse of the music video. "Sledgehammer" was the epitome of the non-narrative video in the era, expressing within its five minutes the visual jumble many thinkers saw in MTV: a pileup of discordant imagery, tied together only by its propulsion and voluptuous magnetism. Johnson's directorial taste ran toward images of ever-proliferating growth, a preference cemented by his other collaboration with Gabriel, "Big Time" (1986), in which a bubbling primordial ooze inexorably grows to become the universe as we know it. His raucous videos treat the screen as a canvas, against which an infinite variety of sketches, doodles, and jokes could be tossed. Like the later work of director Michel Gondry, "Sledge-hammer" establishes a quasi-magical premise, one that leaves viewers doubtful that its flights of whimsy can be maintained for the entire length of the clip. The final product is less a cohesive whole than a series of eye-catching images and clever jokes, but when they work, as they did in "Sledgehammer," the result is a spectacular mishmash.

"Sledgehammer" marked the triumph of FX as video vanguard. Like a low-budget version of Hollywood, the music video thrived on slack-jawed awe, constantly aiming for the next "wow." While their budgets could never compete with the *Aliens* of the world, FX-heavy music videos looked to special effects as an all-purpose salve, a relatively easy method of garnering airplay and buzz. The effects on display ranged from the animation-live action hybrids of a-Ha's "Take on Me" and "The Sun Always Shines on TV" (1985) and the Rolling Stones' minstrel-show "Harlem Shuffle" (1986) to the bodily mangling via FX of David Byrne's "She's Mad" (1992) (a direct descendant of "Sledgehammer") and the more sophisticated CGI of Godley & Creme's facial-morphing extravaganza "Cry" (1985). "Cry" features a passel of rapidly changing faces lip-synching the words to the song, white turning to black to brown, male becoming female, in a never-ending carousel of transformation (a trick later swiped by Michael Jackson and John Landis for "Black or White").

As directors, Godley and Creme were ceaselessly inventive, chameleons whose work was recognizable primarily for its elegance and spareness, not any particular formal properties. They were also the quintessential video directors of postpunk, which by the early 1980s had grown enamored of a certain chilliness, misanthropy, and taste for science-fiction roboticism perfectly encapsulated by Godley and Creme's stark, still work. The painted faces and abstract imagery of Visage's "Fade to Grey" (1980) and "Mind of a Toy" (1981) were the products of a deranged children's story, or a particularly unhinged cabaret performance. Godley and Creme's video for Herbie Hancock's "Rockit" (1983) resembled an abandoned mad scientist's lair, whose forsaken creations had been left to their own devices, with Hancock's music an instigator to go buck-wild. The manic robots pumped their legs to the music, dancing themselves into a frenzy that could only end in their own destruction. (Art of Noise's equally industrial "Close (to the Edit)" (1984) was a close relative of "Rockit." Excessively literal in its desire to take apart the music, it dispatches three men (and a little girl) with chainsaws, hatchets, and hammers to smash, saw, and clobber a wide assortment of musical instruments. Directed by Zbigniew Rybczynski, "Close" is the physical embodiment of its song's aural urge toward musical deconstruction.)

Like their work on "Cry" or "Girls on Film," "Rockit" triumphed due to Godley and Creme's combination of technical wizardry and playfulness. Their videos were dazzling, but warm, their skill and taste for formalist exercise leavened by a winning sense of humor. Godley and Creme could also, when circumstances demanded it, be as graceful and timeless as a well-designed wristwatch; witness their video for the Police's "Every Breath You Take" (1983), whose stately camera work and elegant lighting was the height of hushed 80s splendor. Duran Duran's "A View to a Kill," George Harrison's "When We Was Fab," Frankie Goes to Hollywood's "Two Tribes," Peter Gabriel's "Don't Give Up": the list of Godley and Creme smashes was lengthy, a product of the duo's remarkable innovativeness and sense of play. Until the mid-1990s, and the emergence of Spike Jonze, Michel Gondry, and Dayton and Faris, Godley and Creme would stand as the foremost masters of the music video.

Godley and Creme's influence, along with the looming brilliance of "Sledge-hammer," meant a new era of intellectual and technical playfulness for the music video. X's wonderful "Burning House of Love" (1985) messes with perspective, cutting between playful posings of dolls and human matches on action. With a frame like a crazy-quilted photo collage, "Burning House of Love" deliberately confuses spatial continuity, sticking the drummer into the same shot twice, or cutting just his feet out of an otherwise untouched shot and replacing them with empty space. Tom Petty and the Heartbreakers' "Don't Come Around Here No More" (1985), an homage to *Alice in Wonderland,* similarly took delight in deliberate visual confusions, rendering the small large, and the large small. Converting *Alice* into a drug-laced fairy tale (or was it that already?), "Don't Come Around Here No More" (directed by Jeff Stein) turns oversized cups of tea into miniscule dolls' furniture, infants into pigs, and Alice herself into a delectable cake, served by the slice. In these videos, special effects are themselves the centerpiece, intended to dazzle viewers with their ingenuity and bathe the music video in the aura of fashion-forward hip. Music videos became something of a catch-all experience, a television vaudeville—a little funny, a little scary, and a little sexy.

Not all the era's videos were possessed of so healthy a sense of humor. To many videomakers and artists, "good" meant "classy," and "classy" meant "strained seriousness." "Every Breath You Take's" deep-focus perspective, classical lighting, and lap dissolves skirted the boundary of self-parody, but its solid assembly, and close relation to its song's tone, kept it honest. Don Henley's "The Boys of Summer" (1984) on the other hand, while similarly well-built, strained credulity. Directed by Jean-Baptiste Mondino, "Boys" (also in black-and-white) projects a couple's remembered moment of bliss onto the walls and lives of yuppies, child drummers, and bored adolescents. The sun sinks lower in the sky as the video progresses, until, in the final shot, Henley drives through the city, the skyline awash with lights as nighttime settles in. Mondino was a skilled director, but the metaphor at work here was too simplistic for words (the setting sun equals the loss of 1960s idealism).

There is a reason why "Boys of Summer" makes the richest target for parody in Paula Abdul's video parody "Forever Your Girl" (directed by David Fincher), where a kid with slicked-back hair holds his head in his hands, a cigar gripped between his teeth. Mondino was usually in better form than "Boys of Summer"; videos like Me'Shell NdegéOcello's "If That's Your Boyfriend," Scritti Politti's "Wood Beez," and Madonna's "Justify My Love," "Human Nature," and "Open Your Heart" (as well as Mondino's video for his own "La danse des mots") evince a gift for alluring surfaces and polished visuals. "La danse des mots" (1984) attempts to translate the then-nascent five elements of hip-hop to a predominantly French audience, with Boy Scouts, boxers, and schoolteachers all popping, locking, and robotically gyrating to the beat. Mondino was a serial referencer, paying homage to hip-hop, Charlie Chaplin, and surrealism while never straying far from his fashion-inspired intention to inject unfailingly beautiful imagery into MTV's bloodstream.

Watching in the Dark

Still and all, in this era as in the ones to follow, the primary mode of videomaking was the concert or performance clip. Dominant in wallflower fashion, the performance video sought to blend into television rotation without attracting much attention to itself. Lacking ornamentation or distinction, the concert music video meant to give off the appearance of being organic to the medium, the baseline from which other videos digressed. Its conformism meant that the overwhelming bulk of performance videos were dull by nature, adhering closely to a pre-approved script of camera angles, cuts, and actions. Most offered a third-row center view of the band in concert, or chopped together a variety of onstage and offstage points of view without clear logic or intention. If music video was a miniaturized Hollywood, the performance clip was the equivalent of the straight-to-video film, catering to an undemanding audience and giving them the mediocre product they expected. The typical performance video was the concert experience rendered glittering and unblemished, with all of the live show's hassles and flaws removed. What these made clear, though, was how little the concert experience was transferable to television screens. Music videos could not serve, artistically speaking, as suitable stand-ins for the live show; with this in mind, they had to serve as something else. This was a message that many to most music videos ignored, which is, not coincidentally, why so many videos of the early MTV era have aged so poorly.

Some performance videos skirted the sea of MTV mediocrity. Like genre filmmakers investing a tired plotline with fresh technique, they did so by livening up the already-ancient clichés of the music video. Primarily, they drastically slowed down the live clip's hectic cutting, knowing that the presence of their stars would be spectacle enough. Two of the most notable performance videos of the era featured two of its biggest stars: Prince and Bruce Springsteen. The former, in his clip for "Purple Rain" (1984) (directed by A.I. Magnon), casts the R&B deity in heroic mode. Sticking primarily to close-ups of Prince singing, or shots of lone audience members, "Purple Rain" is individualist, where most other videos of its genre celebrated the overwhelming spectacle of the gathered masses. Most concert videos framed audiences in whirring overhead shots or wide-angle shots that took in as wide a swath of people at once as possible. The action onstage was usually handled similarly, with rapid cuts between band members emphasizing their interaction, as opposed to individual musicians' personae.

"Purple Rain" veers in the opposite direction, shooting Prince from a low angle, concentrating almost exclusively on him, and making the elfin singer appear larger than life. Similarly, shots of the audience are long, searching close-ups, highlighting Prince fans as set apart from the teeming mass. The earlier "Little Red Corvette" (1983) had also bathed Prince in a lone spotlight, his spangly blue suit painted red by their iridescent glow. Prince romances the camera by steadfastly avoiding its gaze, singing with his head down. Director Brian Greenberg's array of metallic red panels (positioned behind the singer) makes the video an inspiration of sorts for Mark Romanek's 2005 video for Coldplay's "Speed of Sound."

It was mostly the shock of the (somewhat) fresh, rather than any inherent superiority of technique, that set "Purple Rain" apart from the average concert video. Bruce Springsteen's "Dancing in the Dark" (1984) (directed by Brian De Palma) also invigorated the concert clip by offering a distilled essence of the Boss' appeal. The camera never leaves Springsteen for the first two-thirds of the video, loving his presence far too much to abandon him for glimpses of the E Street Band or his audience. Springsteen stares directly into the camera, demanding our attention, cajoling our collusion in the group experience happening somewhere on the periphery. If most concert clips offered the perspective of the fan, shifting between band and audience in imitation of the experience of being part of the crowd at a show, "Dancing in the Dark" provides the perspective of the obsessive: nothing, absolutely nothing exists other than

Bruce—not the other fans, not the band, nobody. There is merely Bruce—his stare, his rolling shoulders, his masculine swagger, his plain white T with the rolled-up sleeves, his Travolta-esque dance moves.

The camera loves Springsteen's star power, waiting until nearly two and a half minutes pass before providing its first shot of the audience. There we see an ecstatic young female fan with a pixieish haircut who cannot refrain from grinning at her nearness to the Boss. She is a collective stand-in, an Everyfan meant to represent the entire audience's mixed glee and thankfulness for the miracle occurring onstage. This is the occasion for a bit of ex post facto cognitive dissonance, as Everyfan is none other than the now-world-famous Courteney Cox of *Friends* renown. Springsteen pulls her up onstage, and the pair dance together, platonically and a bit awkwardly. Even this is part of the show; "Dancing in the Dark" gives the impression of Springsteen as a naturally gifted performer, enthralling but unpolished. The essence of his live performance, according to the video, lies less in technique than sheer will, and their awkward dance is crucial to this effect. "Dancing in the Dark" balances the view of Bruce as showman extraordinaire, too gifted to take your eyes off of, with Bruce as self-made star, too blue-collar and untutored to know how to dance with panache.

"Born in the U.S.A." (1984) similarly dramatizes the Boss-ness of Springsteen. Clad in a leather-sleeved jeans jacket and black headband, unshaven, Springsteen looks like a cross between Bob Dylan and a down-at-the-heels Vietnam vet. Eyes squeezed shut, his hand tightly gripping the microphone, the expression on Springsteen's face lay somewhere between a grimace and a sneer. "Born in the U.S.A." was an attempt on Springsteen's part to write the iconic song of post-Vietnam American life, its promise and its ugliness, and "Born in the U.S.A." the video likewise sought to summarize the experience of being American. Springsteen's clothing is only one part of the equation, which includes an array of familiarly "American" imagery—used-car lots, training soldiers, endless rows of identical white headstones in a cemetery, factory workers, a baseball game. "Born in the U.S.A." ends with an interpolation of the album's famous cover image—a shot of Springsteen in blue jeans, a red cap in his back pocket, and an American flag fluttering in the background. "I am America," "Born in the U.S.A." told us, and the video made good on depicting both sides of the American coin.

Always a music-video staple, the live video would undergo a reinvention in the late 1980s—at least in some precincts. Seeking to invest the most conservative, bland brand of video with some much-needed pizzazz, daring directors and performers sought to re-create the live clip. In fact, the late 1980s as a whole were marked by an effort to take the music video's incremental advances in the early years of MTV and crystallize them, making them permanent. This was partially a product of certain musical genres (including hip-hop, indie rock, and country) belatedly discovering the value of the music video, but it was also due to the wearing off of the shock of the new. With the music video no longer thrilling simply for existing, videomakers had to seek out new methods of captivating audiences, hoping to extend their stranglehold over the hearts and minds of youth culture.

CHAPTER 3

This Video's for You

The streaming fans. The screaming fans. The pumping fists. The swooping camera. The guitar solo. The bass solo. The drum solo. The keyboard solo. The backup singers. The horn section. The stage dive. The head bang. The sweat band. The fainting females. The screeching teens. The mosh pit. The closed eyes. The sweat-drenched faces. The sing-alongers. The ecstatic masses. Running up the stage. Running down the stage. Running along the stage. Leaping into the drum kit. Pounding the chest. Stripping off the shirt. Touching the fans' hands. Close-up on the guitar frets. Close-up on the microphone. Close-up on the bass drum. Close-up on the cymbal. Close-up on the impassioned fan, eyes closed. Close-up on the impassioned fan, mouthing the words. Close-up on the luscious female fan. The bow. The high-five. The fist in the air. The clap. The shout. The devil's horns. The index finger to the sky. The jog off stage. The crowd streaming out. The tour bus. The highway. The road.

Could the performance clip have been any more clichéd?

With the average video still a relatively dull affair, depicting the artists dutifully strumming their guitars, thwacking their drums, and pounding their pianos while lip-syncing to their latest single, it came as little surprise that as the music video entered a phase of increasing maturity, savvy videomakers sought to reinvent the live clip. Taking the essential working parts of the performance video, which consisted of a concert hall or rehearsal room setting, upfront presence of band members, and a focus on the performers as musicians, they sought to make this oft-staid brand of video funky, interesting, funny, or clever. The impetus stemmed from a wide range of performers; from metalheads to rock saviors, from jam bands to hip-hop groups. What united them all was a desire to find excitement in the most benighted aspects of the videomaking process.

With their roots in the counterculture scene of mid-1960s San Francisco, there was something profoundly strange about seeing the Grateful Dead on television screens in the late 1980s promoting their latest single "Touch of Grey" (1987). Knowing that to most MTV watchers they would have the approximate hipness quotient of their grandparents in Boca, the Dead, along with director Gary Gutierrez, had fun with their old-fogy reputation by depicting themselves as animated dancing skeletons. Ageless and jolly, the skeletons were dressed in the band's trademark clothes, down to drummer Mickey Hart's Hawaiian shirt. With shots of leg bones shoed in Converses thumping the kick drum, and arm bones pounding the snares, "Touch of Grey" bears a distinct resemblance to Tim Burton's mordantly funny cinematic necropolises. The fans at this arena show cheer on the musical skeletons, not noticing anything unusual onstage, even when, in the video's final shot, a skeleton-puppeteer's hands move the marionettes onstage. In this playful clip, even God was a skeletal old codger.

A younger, hipper band looked to the tradition of the live clip as a means, not of having a good laugh at their own expense, but of burnishing their reputation as rebels with a cause. The very act of performance here was an act of rebellion, an expression of individuality at odds with societal strictures. Irish rockers U2, on top of the musical world with the release of the instant classic *The Joshua Tree*, intended their video for "Where the Streets Have No Name" (1987) to pay tribute to the Beatles' legendary rooftop performance of "Get Back" from their farewell film *Let It Be* (1970). The video, directed by Meiert Avis, also takes viewers "behind the scenes" to show the band battling it out with the Man, played here by the officers of the Los Angeles Police Department, in an attempt to bring their music to the People, a role filled here by the lunchtime workers of L.A.'s downtown garment district. The cops who fitfully attempt to shut down the concert—and only succeed (at least in the video) after the band has concluded playing—bring a soupçon of drama to the proceedings and would become a staple of antiauthoritarian videos to come. In fact, the entire narrative and structure of "Where the Streets Have No Name," moved to Wall Street, would be ripped off by Michael Moore for his (admittedly excellent) video for Rage Against the Machine's "Sleep Now in the Fire," and parodied by Marc Klasfeld in his video for Alien Ant Farm's "These Days."

Aggressive without being violent, AC/DC's "Thunderstruck" (1990) turned rebellion into a group activity. Directed by David Mallet, "Thunderstruck" offers a first-person point of view on the performance video. The camera peers down at the drum kit as offscreen hands emerge to pound out a rhythm and at lightning-quick hands working the frets of the guitar. Unlike "Where the Streets Have No Name," the locus of rebellion was to be found in AC/DC's fans, not the band itself. Everyone, fans and band, thrash around inside an enormous cage-in-the-round, with headbangers hanging off the rafters. "Thunderstruck" conveys the sensation of live performance from the perspective of the performers themselves, providing an unusual take on the performance clip. Lead guitarist Angus Young executes his traditional hotfoot guitar solo, skipping across the stage, with the camera filming him from underneath the floorboards.

Less interested in the performers than the offstage action, Extreme's "More Than Words" (1991), directed by Jonathan Dayton and Valerie Faris, is an imitation "unplugged" video (soon to be an MTV icon via the enormously successful concert show), with warm lighting, tastefully arranged candles, and slow lap dissolves, but with a healthy dose of satirical irreverence. "More Than Words," an acoustic-guitar-heavy duet between singer Gary Cherone and guitarist Nuno Bettancourt, left the other two members of the band with little to do, and the video has a blast with their inactivity, showing them kicking up their feet, flipping through magazines, hanging out with their dog, and, during the power ballad's quiet moments, worshipfully holding up lighters in tribute.

All these videos, whether comic or serious, were careful not to stray all that far from the tradition of the well-lit, impeccably filmed, aesthetically unthreatening performance clip. The most impressive live video of this era, and the one that completely upended the already well-established standards of the genre, is the Pixies' "Head On" (1991). Beginning as an unadorned live clip, "Head On" transitions into art-world minimalism, exchanging the faux objectivity of its opening sequence for a delightfully subjective take on the live performance. The video's opening shots show the band performing in silhouette, with close-ups of tapping feet and fingers on instruments, but soon splits the screen into twelve equal-sized boxes: four heads, four torsos, and four sets of feet. The rapidly shifting lighting, visible in the background of each individual square, make it clear that this is a record of a live show, just a highly unusual one. "Head On" immerses us so deeply in the action as to render the familiar deeply foreign, turning a rock concert into an opportunity to study the human body in motion in scientifically precise detail.

The Minimalist Minority

Video minimalism, which reached its apex among the postpunk groups of the pre-Nirvana era, was grounded in a philosophy of respecting the integrity of performance. In place of the elaborate and, in its opinion, unnecessary gussying up of the music video with rapid-fire cutting, special effects, and the like, the minimalist video sought to strip video of its vanity, leaving it beautifully unadorned. "Head On," coming from one of the iconic artists of postpunk, embraces minimalism in surprising fashion, by taking the meat-and-potatoes live video and stripping it of any familiar markers. The Pixies' video was more at home in the art gallery than on a television screen, but was nothing if not respectful of the music. Splitting the band into its constituent parts onscreen, and then splitting each band member into pieces, we grow fully aware of the small tics, hand movements, and facial gestures that go into stage performance. "Head On" takes away the illusion of wholeness inherent to the performance video, the sensation of seeing all there is to see, and by so doing returns some of its intimacy.

The ground zero of the less-is-more philosophy, the ne plus ultra of video minimalism, was the Replacements' unforgettable "Bastards of Young" (1986). Like one of Andy Warhol's 1960s cinematic experiments, "Bastards of Young" was delightfully empty, sheared of all excess baggage. Looking like a drastically shorter version of *Empire* (1964) or *Sleep* (1963), Warhol's famously narrative-unfettered, multiple-hour films, "Bastards of Young" (along with its equally spartan compatriots "Left of the Dial" and "Hold My Life") is so content-deprived that each of its small shifts became freighted with enormous, outsized significance. Opening with a close-up shot of a speaker woofer pounding in and out, the camera very slowly and delicately pulls out to provide a slightly wider, more inclusive viewpoint. Joining the speaker in the frame are a pile of records haphazardly leaning against its base and a record player poised precariously on top of a milk crate. The human presence here is minimal, confined to the background of the video's action. A man's jeans-clad legs pass in front of the camera, then return to pick up a packet of cigarettes. The smoke from his lit cigarette swirls lazily across the screen. Adjusting position while recumbent on the couch, his slightly out-of-focus arm disappears, replaced by his left sneaker. Once the camera concludes its initial motion, it remains still, meaning that all the video's action can only be guessed at. We never see "Bastards of Young's" ostensible protagonist, and we don't much care. The drama of the video was found elsewhere, in the hypnotic motion of the woofer, in the slow drift of cigarette smoke, in the way his disembodied hand bounces ever so slightly to the song's rhythm. Even the peak of its narrative excitement, when the video's nonprotagonist leaps out of his seat, sweeps the top of the speaker clean, and kicks a hole in it, before storming out the door, was curiously unthrilling. Lulled by the careful attentiveness of the video, we remain at the micro level, more intrigued by the now-disabled speaker's anguished buzz than the human drama taking place outside the frame. Like Warhol's cinematic experiments, "Bastards of Young" embraces boredom, hugging it so closely it reveals unexpected nuances. "Bastards of Young" was a beautiful expression of an unabashed message from the notoriously conflicted indie heroes: "Just listen to the fucking song."

Minimalism in the music video was a credo that took many forms, not all as strict as "Bastards of Young." Others sought to use minimalism as a way of returning some of the self-respect to an art form sapped by the booze-and-babes ethos of metal bands. Looking to film history (always a potent source of material for the music video), videomakers embraced the long take as a mark of high seriousness and as a touchstone of realism. Realism, a principle heretofore mostly absent from the spectacle-craving music video, meant stripping away the unnecessary and returning dignity to the musician's labor.

New Order's "Perfect Kiss" might appear to have more in common, at first glance, with "Thriller" than "Bastards of Young." Directed by Jonathan Demme (*Melvin and Howard, The Silence of the Lambs*), "Perfect Kiss" (1985) was the music video as feature film, complete with Hollywood-style opening and closing credits and a big-name filmmaker at the helm. Beyond these surface similarities, though, "Perfect Kiss" existed in a realm worlds away from "Thriller." In long, unblinking takes, the band is recorded at their work, while keyboardist/guitarist Gillian Gilbert futzes with her lipstick and fiddles with studio equipment. The video as a whole is made up almost entirely of single-person shots, with nary a band shot to be seen until the eight-minute mark of this ten-plus-minute video. This may be a statement about New Order's alienation in the aftermath of the suicide of Ian Curtis, lead singer of their previous group Joy Division (present here in the hovering silhouette repeatedly glimpsed in the doorway), but it also invests their work with a certain grace and simplicity of purpose. They are musicians, and their work is making music, with no need to gussy things up with fancy sets or elaborate effects. "Perfect Kiss" is a film of people at work, doing what they do best. That the people happen to be the members of New Order, and the work the recording of their latest single, is beside the point. There is also a musical message to be gleaned here; New Order being a proudly synthetic band, integrating synthesizers and drum machines into the musical mix, "Perfect Kiss" is a forthright statement that this brand of music, too, requires the toil of performers to bring to fruition. Beautifully photographed by legendary cinematographer Henri Alekan (*Wings of Desire*), the video ends with the band exchanging contented looks, like a team of miners satisfied with their day's work.

The movement toward the unadorned took a slightly different tack with Sinead O'Connor's "Nothing Compares 2 U" (1990), directed by John Maybury. The video sought to cut away everything with the exception of her face, focusing almost exclusively on O'Connor's visage. "Nothing Compares" opens with brief glimpses of a rural road before a lap-dissolve reveals a close-up of O'Connor. With her striking, rough-hewn features, buzz-cut hair, and pale skin, O'Connor met no traditional standard of feminine beauty, but some combination of her skill as an actress and the sheer force of her personality, clear even here, made it difficult to look away. Maybury makes more of O'Connor's peculiar power by making less of the video's surroundings; and in fact, there is little grounding to "Nothing Compares 2 U." The world outside O'Connor's face is only a shadow here, with each of the shots of stone walks, statues, bridges, and lonely men gazing off into the distance clearly marked as products of her own memory. Small changes loom large in "Nothing Compares 2 U"; O'Connor begins the video in a close-up shot, avoiding the camera's searing gaze when singing, and only looking up when silent. As her singing grows more forceful, she grows more willing to look directly into the camera while singing, before returning to averting her gaze.

O'Connor's shaved head and intense manner cannot help but bring to mind one of the great icons of the silent cinema, Maria Falconetti in Carl Theodor Dreyer's *The Passion of Joan of Arc*. O'Connor was a singer-icon, like Falconetti an emblem of suffering and Christian forbearance. That Sinead is mourning the loss of romantic love, rather than matters spiritual, becomes irrelevant, lost in the passion of the sole tear that runs down her cheek. The statues that serve as a recurrent motif in "Nothing Compares 2 U" made much the same point, comparing O'Connor to icons of passion, sadness, and endurance, with the woman holding her brow in her hand being perhaps the most explicit. The tear, though, is essential to the nature of the minimalist ethos. In a less austere video, the single tear would be little more than a cliché, a sappy convention of deeply felt emotion. It is the long takes of "Nothing Compares 2 U" that render the emotion a matter of spiritual significance. The long take gives "Nothing Compares" a sense of duration, of one event organically following the next. As spectators, we see the song sung, and the emotion that wells up, and they emerge from the same shot, out of the same milieu. There is no cut-separation, nothing from the toolkit of the FX-savvy filmmaker to establish distance from the action. The minimalist video reaches for a truth it finds in the emotion of one song, one event, one face.

Few videos could compare to "Nothing Compares 2 U" in austerity, or emotional forthrightness, but many of postpunk's leading lights found a home in a looser version of minimalism that sought to embrace its simplicity of task. Much of this was due, of course, to the constricted budgets of college-rock bands in the 1980s, who simply could not afford to make videos like "Sledgehammer" or "Janie's Got a Gun." Groups like R.E.M., the Cure, Depeche Mode, Black Flag, Hüsker Dü, and Sonic Youth turned a constraint into an aesthetic, crafting clips that were small, clever, and cool.

The Cure's videos, many of them collaborations with director Tim Pope, emphasized their own lack of frills. "Primary" (1981) is like a low-rent "Perfect

Kiss," highlighting the musicians' work via carefully framed close-ups of Smith's mouth in midsong, drummer Lol Tolhurst's tensed shoulders, and the flexed fingers of the guitar and bass players posed against their instruments' strings. "Love Cats" (1983) confines lead singer Robert Smith's high-energy flailing to one sparsely decorated room. "In Between Days" (1985) attaches the camera to a zip line, with Smith rocking the camera back and forth as he sang. Similarly juxtaposing nearness and distance, "A Night Like This" (1986) is a series of close-ups of Smith's face, captured in concert, which slowly, smoothly backs farther and farther away. Pope's videos capture something of the Cure's inherent playfulness, filling their videos with German Expressionist sets, bunny costumes, and shadow play. They may have been inexpensive, but the Cure's 1980s videos are overstuffed with visual cleverness. New Order's videos were equally catch-as-catch-can, employing William Wegman dogs and dancing elves as brightly colored accompaniments to their dance-punk anthems. The Ramones' "Psycho Therapy" (1983) would eventually inspire Green Day's "Basket Case" and Eminem's "The Real Slim Shady"; in it, the Queens, New York, punks inspire a locked ward of shufflers and droolers to rebel against their *Cuckoo's Nest* incarceration.

Sonic Youth's "Dirty Boots" (1991) (directed by Tamra Davis) is a performance-clip-cum-indie romance, with a long-haired Thurston lookalike and a cutie in a Nirvana T-shirt finding love, or at least a long, passionate kiss, onstage during a Sonic Youth show. "Kool Thing" (1990) conflates the oppression of women and black men, pressing sensitive cultural buttons with its sexualized imagery. A blond woman, seen exclusively from behind, caresses the ankles and legs of a black man standing on a pedestal, untying his shoelaces with her teeth and pressing her finger into his ribs. Public Enemy's Chuck D appears on a TV screen egging lead singer Kim Gordon on, one oppressed group helping another—"tell it like it is." A black kitty makes circles around the band, and black dancers shake and shimmy off to one side, while the band grows increasingly raucous, and Gordon spins like a ballerina. "Kool Thing" aims to reconcile postpunk with hip-hop, but it serves more as a sexy provocation.

These videos appeared to have come together more by chance than rigorous editing, and they bore resemblance to minimalist efforts like "Nothing Compares 2 U" only inasmuch as they also avoided the pomp and circumstance of their mainstream compatriots. These videos make a studied effort to appear as natural, organic outgrowths of the music. The Smiths' catty, literate videos, and R.E.M.'s mysterious, gnomic clips, provide further examples of bands striving for a video aesthetic in lockstep with the music.

At the start of their career, the Smiths had been strongly opposed to the idea of shooting videos, having been burned by their American label, Sire, making their own unauthorized clip for "How Soon Is Now?" It was not until filmmaker Derek Jarman's work with the band (which includes the elegantly homoerotic "There Is a Light That Never Goes Out" [1986] and the manic "The Queen Is Dead" [1986]) that the Smiths came around to appreciating the music video. "Stop Me If You've Heard This One Before" (1987) features lead singer Morrissey riding a bicycle while pursued, at a suitably worshipful distance, by a passel of Moz imitators, all wearing the same trench coat, clunky plastic eyeglasses, and pompadour hairstyle. Whether these figures were intended as a swipe at his fans, or his musical imitators, is left up to the viewer.

In an introduction to a collection of their videos, R.E.M. jokingly referred to the music video as the contemporary equivalent of the hula hoop and the Edsel—"an outmoded art form." Nonetheless, their early videos (especially the enjoyably casual "Radio Free Europe" [1983]) offer a portrait of the band as Southern boys, version 2.0—wandering the back roads of Georgia, messing around with country folk, building homegrown artworks out of rusty bicycle parts and other detritus. The jittery camera work and blue and green tints of videos like "Feeling Gravity's Pull" (1985) and the long-form "Left of Reckoning" (1984) makes them, in many ways, just as mysterious as Michael Stipe's half-mumbled, cryptic lyrics. Even at this early stage of their career, R.E.M. were already thinking about breaking out of the indie straitjacket—both "Can't Get There From Here" (1985) and "Fall on Me" (1986) transcribe Stipe's lyrics onscreen for the benefit of puzzled listeners. "Orange Crush" (1988), directed by Matt Mahurin, engages with the song's anti-Vietnam War, Agent Orange imagery in gnarled, convoluted fashion, employing the band's familiar visual obscurantism amid half-buried homoeroticism. A man rubs his hands in dirt, erotically thrusting his pick, time and again, into the ground, and a soldier emerges from the water, smears himself with dirt, and opens his fist to reveal a bullet. "Orange Crush" conflates lead singer Michael Stipe's unclothed torso and a dog-tag-wearing soldier, jamming together two brands of male physical effort into one frame.

An artier, higher-gloss minimalism was on display in R.E.M.'s clip for "Losing My Religion" (1991). "Losing My Religion" is the epitome of postpunk's movement from poverty to aesthetic splendor, from crude low-budget efforts to polished, tasteful videos. R.E.M. themselves are representative of the shift, having gone from low-budget, rapidly assembled works to the MTV-friendlier "Losing My Religion." Lit and shot to resemble an Italian Renaissance painting, or some admixture of Andrei Tarkovsky and Michelangelo Antonioni, "Losing My Religion" (directed by Tarsem) wanders through time and space, watching angels and angel-manqués suffering under the gaze of the unbeliever. A teenage St. Sebastian poses, pierced by arrows in an erotically charged tableau;

a father mourns his dying son; Eastern Bloc workers pound at a piece of steel; and interrogators poke around an old man's chest, sticking their fingers under a winglike protrusion on his breast. The mournful tone of the stream of images, each as carefully composed and lit as a painting, was a reminder of Tony Kushner's famous statement, from his play *Angels in America*, that "there are no angels in America."

Meanwhile, the band wander across an empty room, a jug of milk smashes on the ground, and Stipe does a flailing solo dance. Everyone in the video, from Stipe on downward, poses with angels' wings, and the video's tableaux of beautiful freaks clothed in gloriously colorful costumes gathers force with each repetition, each intonation. Tarsem's skilled craftsmanship made him a new kind of minimalist director—one who did not believe in the catch-as-catch-can visual aesthetic of "Perfect Kiss" or "Kool Thing." "Losing My Religion" endorses the minimalist ethos in its all-in-oneness. The video was a unified object, leaving meaning to be sorted out by others. "Losing My Religion" is like an early-90s update of a certain brand of 1960s art-house film, meant to be seen repeatedly, and argued over. Its fundamental purpose is to be beautifully gnomic.

Anton Corbijn was better known for his photography than his video work, having served as house photographer for prominent bands ranging from U2 to Depeche Mode to the Red Hot Chili Peppers. Corbijn's partnership with Depeche Mode, especially, was a unique one, collaborating on twenty videos spanning the length of the band's career, from "Strangelove" (1987) to "Suffer Well" (2006). Corbijn favored stark, resonant imagery for his Depeche Mode work, often invoking deserts, empty rooms, Western-flavored setups, and other markers of classical, muscular individualism. "Personal Jesus" (1989) (later mocked/honored by the Killers' "All These Things That I've Done," also directed by Corbijn) features the band as lonesome cowpokes strolling into a dusty town, assessing (and being assessed in turn) by the lovely lasses at the local brothel. Corbijn turns the Wild West into a sexual wonderland, with the band members each caressed by their own set of frisky women. "I Feel You" (1993) is equally frolicsome, with the band adrift in the highlands, and a beautiful blond dancing for the camera in a rustic shack. Gahan does his own striptease for the camera, meeting its gaze head-on while removing his shirt and joining the woman in a lustful embrace as shadows fall over the frame.

Corbijn favors the texture and grain of black-and-white stock for most of his videos, and when shooting in color, often depends on an overprocessed, supersaturated stock that makes individual colors (like the red of Gahan's kingly robes in "Enjoy the Silence" [1990]) pop off the screen. His Depeche Mode videos often emphasize the archaic (kings, cowboys, shacks, lanterns, even old cars) out of a desire to frame the band's timeless qualities and the cinematic scope of their songs' landscapes. Corbijn is expert at emphasizing the mythic qualities of his clients, with videos like Red Hot Chili Peppers' "My Friends" (1995), U2's "Electrical Storm" (2002), and Echo & the Bunnymen's "Lips Like Sugar" (1987) accentuating the larger-than-life mystiques of his clients.

Corbijn's mystical side found a fitting client in the mournful posthumous video he shot for Joy Division's "Atmosphere" in 1988. In a landscape of dead trees and heavy shadows, the remaining members of the group watch as diminutive monks trudge through the desert, marching in packs while bearing their burdens through the still wilderness. The monks carry larger-than-life photographs of Joy Division lead singer Ian Curtis (who committed suicide in 1980). "Atmosphere" is a belated funeral procession, its medieval religious feeling a fitting tribute to the austerity and high moral purpose of postpunk heroes Joy Division. Curtis is designated a monk of pain himself here, trudging through the desert of his own aching psyche, and the relative disparity in size between Curtis and those who honor him is no accident; by "Atmosphere's" dint, Curtis was a giant among midgets.

The last great video of the postpunk minimalists leaned more toward the building-a-mystery strand of "Losing My Religion" and "Nothing Compares 2 U," and away from the here-I-am-I-can-do-no-other of "Bastards of Young." U2's "One" (1991) would ultimately require three separate videos from three different directors for its promotion, each with its own merits. But none would be quite as unforgettable as Mark Pellington's remarkable clip, which did not feature the band at all. In Pellington's video, a herd of buffalo surge in slow motion through an empty landscape. The buffalo dash across the screen in black and white, consistently off-center—now slightly to the left, now to the right. A field of sunflowers in full blooming color appear, only to fade away, replaced by the same buffalo. The word "one" flashes onscreen in a variety of languages, ranging from Spanish to Hebrew. The buffalo progress onward inexorably, with a brief interruption for "One" to run its footage backward, propelling the bison forward momentarily, until the final sequence of three freeze-frames of buffalo in different stages of plunging over a cliff—an image preserved onscreen for ten seconds. In highly mysterious, allegorical terms, Pellington's "One" contributes an indelible portrait of impending tragedy and death from the natural world—a supremely apposite framework for a song whose half-buried back story revolved around a disconsolate father comforting his AIDS-afflicted son. The senselessness of the suicidal beasts was a deeply compelling metaphor in the era of AIDS, a powerful illustration of the horror of the disease, and its seeming unstoppability. "One" was intended to be a meditation object, more inspired by the emotion conjured up by the song than directly stemming from it. As a result, it is perhaps the subtlest message video ever made, and the last gasp of video minimalism in its classic form.

The ability of the music video to take on serious political and social issues was another sign of the form's growing maturity. In fact, this era saw videos engage as never before with current events, parody, and pastiche, embracing the world beyond the music video in the hopes of staying cutting-edge. Even more appealing to bands and videomakers, though, considering the sudden ubiquity of music videos, was to engage with videos themselves, riffing on them as ripe subject matter for disgust, approbation, and good-hearted parody. These self-referential videos—some exercises in nostalgia, some vicious slaps at MTV icons—were self-congratulatory pats on the back for the television audience, congratulating them for their savviness in getting the joke.

The most outspoken of the bunch was Neil Young's "This Note's for You," directed by Julien Temple. "This Note's" was good enough to be named MTV's Video of the Year for 1988, but also suitably incendiary for the channel to ban its play during prime-time hours. Taking a sledgehammer to established superstars like Michael Jackson and Whitney Houston, Young's video bashes pop music's relentless commercialization, its transformation from rebel music into multinational ad jingle. Bathed in a golden glow meant to evoke the sheen of "classy" beer commercials, "This Note's for You" intentionally emphasizes the gap between Young's unfettered, rebellious image, and the premature nostalgia of the video's mise-en-scène. Young wanders into a club advertising his upcoming concert, a large sign reading "BEER ON TAP" casting a neon pall over the room. A saxophonist wails pleasantly as a couple huddle their heads together, a comely brunette leans in closer to catch her drinking partner's conversational patter, and amber liquid flows freely into glasses. Young straps on his guitar, hits the first raucous chord of his song, and the lighting instantaneously changes to something darker, more "rock." "Ain't singing for Pepsi," Young sings, and a Michael Jackson lookalike moonwalks across the screen; "ain't singing for Coke," and a diva with a marked resemblance to Whitney Houston smiles beatifically onstage. Beginning with those noted corporate shills, "This Note's for You" proceeds to lay into the faux good times of beer and soda commercials, wickedly parodying the look and feel of then-ubiquitous ads like the Bud Light Spuds MacKenzie campaign. The video has its comeuppance on these commercials, wreaking its havoc on their carefully manicured scenarios. A blond-mulleted wildman bursts into a Fellini-esque scene of unintelligible non sequiturs ("Give me back my shoes!," "Ah, if I could only pluck her brows"), grabs a hardhat's beer, and bites off its neck. The faux Michael, dancing and grabbing his crotch, watches helplessly as his hair bursts into flames, only to be rescued by Whitney, who dumps a beer on his head to put out the blaze. A gathering of blue-collar types swigging beers chime in for the chorus, "This note's for you" (itself a play off the memorable Budweiser motto, "This Bud's for you"). Young has cast himself here as the scruffy, decidedly noncorporate Real Thing, a real man standing in opposition to the froufy, effeminate nonsense of corporate America. His ax magic cuts through the bullshit of the Madison Avenue vision of alcohol-fueled good times so gleefully parodied here.

Paula Abdul also parodied her fellow musicians, albeit with a far less jaundiced eye, in "Forever Your Girl" (1989), directed by David Fincher. The video good-naturedly mocks the pretensions of some seminal late-80s music videos, releasing some of the hot air of clips like Don Henley's "The Boys of Summer." Pre-adolescent boys and girls, carefully made up to resemble their elders, imitate the singing models of Robert Palmer's "Addicted to Love," and the leather-jacketed machismo of George Michael. The kids-as-adults motif would later come to fruition with Spike Jonze's witty clip for the Notorious B.I.G.'s "Sky's the Limit" (1998). Abdul's later "Rush Rush" (1991), an interpolation of *Rebel Without a Cause*, costarring Keanu Reeves, and directed by none other than George Lucas, would have made a delicious subject for a parody video of its own.

Parody came naturally to the music video, already so self-aware, and self-referential, a medium. Videos like John Mellencamp's "Pop Singer," the Clash's "This Is Radio Clash," and (later) Bowling for Soup's "1985" got their jollies comedically tearing the music-video form to shreds. And for hip-hop, a musical genre that thrived on the sample, sampling the video work of others for parodic purposes was a natural, logical development. Public Enemy, the Roots, and De La Soul all poked playful holes in hip-hop videos' pretensions, gleefully shredding rap clichés by the dozens. Public Enemy's "Give It Up" (1994) bashes the rise of mock gangsterism, while the Roots' "What They Do" (1996) apes the tone of ghetto-fabulous hip-hop videos while pop-up titles ("the Goldstein estate (rented for the day)") relentlessly mock their pretensions to grandeur. Less mercenary in its intentions, Tone Loc's "Wild Thing" (1989) borrowed the severe beauties from "Addicted to Love," sampling the now-famous models for his own low-budget, black-and-white clip. Expanding the horizons of parody to include all of television, Redman's "I'll Bee Dat!" (1999) simulated the experience of flipping channels, with Redman himself on every station (like Eminem in his later television-parodying videos "My Name Is" and "Without Me")— stealing cars, hosting a morning workout show, sharing a cloud with Reggie's Secret models, and hawking Redman Cola, cereal, and long-distance plans. Hard-rock and metal bands also took to parody, but their efforts smacked more of desperation than inspiration; Bon Jovi's "Something for the Pain" (1995) took aim at the new stars (Eddie Vedder, Courtney Love, Dr. Dre) who had knocked them off their perch as MTV darlings, but the result was more sour grapes than comedic masterpiece. And some artists made entire careers out of parody, cherry-picking the latest hits and studiously mocking them. Weird Al Yankovic took on Michael Jackson's "Beat It" ("Eat It") and "Bad" ("Fat") and Nirvana's "Smells Like Teen Spirit" ("Smells Like Nirvana"), among others, each video so lovingly taking off from their objects of parody that they were practically shot-for-shot remakes.

Fresh from "Forever Your Girl," David Fincher directed two videos for Madonna that made hay of a different brand of borrowing, ransacking cultural resources past and present for the necessary inspiration for his icy-cool formalist aesthetic. Madonna had often turned to classic films for inspiration, with videos paying homage to *The Blue Angel* ("Open Your Heart"), *Citizen Kane* ("Oh Father," also directed by Fincher), and *Trash* ("Deeper and Deeper"). Shot in the midst of Madonna's glam phase, "Express Yourself" (1989) recast *Metropolis* as erotic thriller. Much like Fritz Lang's classic silent film, and Queen's video homage "Radio Ga Ga," "Express Yourself" depicts a world starkly divided between an upper world of privilege and pleasure, and a lower one of unceasing toil. Only here, the toilers were mostly shirtless hunks standing in rain-dripped bunkers, gazing up in awe at projected images of Madonna, playing a variation on the film's Teutonic industrialist. "Express Yourself" takes place in a brutal, violent world, where monocle-clad ogres delight in the performance of caged musicians, and boxers exhaustedly slug it out. This being a Madonna video, the proposed solution to these social and economic inequities is resolutely sexual. The boxing match is intercut with Madonna being taken by force by a sweaty working-class lug, the images clearly coded to indicate her enjoying every second of it. Echoing the famous final intertitle of the Lang film, the video ends with a quote: "Without the heart, there can be no understanding between body and mind." In *Metropolis*, this was a call for greater sensitivity on the part of the wealthy (mind) toward the working class (body). In "Express Yourself," it is a request for a few rushed endearments before another installment of the old in-out, in-out. "Vogue" (1990) makes the debt owed to gay culture yet more explicit. Shot to resemble a high-class perfume commercial, with every image buttery perfection, "Vogue" mixes stark close-ups of Madonna with shots of black and Hispanic men voguing. Voguing, a practice that emerged from New York City drag culture, was taken mainstream by Madonna and Fincher, dragging underground, vanguard culture onto television screens nationwide.

Fincher himself, as his later Hollywood work would make clear, was the master of a certain brand of perfectly coiffed formalism (perhaps epitomized by his video for Nine Inch Nails' "Only" [2005], which imprisons lead singer Trent

Reznor behind a scrim of impersonal, soulless electronic equipment). The video parodies of "Forever Your Girl" notwithstanding, Fincher was a dependable source of fashion-ad videos: lovely, immaculate, and more than a little humorless. Like his colleague Herb Ritts, Fincher was notable for the amped-up sexuality of his clips. From the posing, lip-syncing supermodels of George Michael's "Freedom 90" (1990) to the temptress-yuppie pas-de-deux of Billy Idol's "Cradle of Love" (1990) to the fifty-foot tall models of the Rolling Stones' "Love is Strong" (1994), Fincher's video work is liberally doused in sexuality, and yet its aesthetic neatness belies the ostensible message. For all their vigorous carnality, Fincher's videos were just a little too carefully put together to expel any real heat. "Freedom 90" quixotically attempted to reinvent Michael as a serious musician by bringing in a brigade of supermodels to sing in his stead. "Freedom 90" self-importantly casts off the shackles of Michael's past stardom, setting his leather jacket, guitar, and jukebox from past videos ablaze.

Michael had done better with the more explicitly lowbrow videos he had codirected with Andy Morahan, "I Want Your Sex" (1987) and "Father Figure" (1987). In the former, a scantily clad woman rolls around provocatively on an unmade bed, and water splashes on bare torsos and backs. Released, as it was, at the apex of the AIDS crisis, in 1987, its unbridled sexuality is tempered by Michael writing "EXPLORE MONOGAMY" in lipstick on a woman's nude body. Mixed message it may have been, but "I Want Your Sex" is clear about Michael's presentation, his dangling-cross earring and Don Johnson stubble conveying an image of sexually dominant alpha masculinity. Michael is a working-class tough with a taste for high-class women, a storyline made explicit by "Father Figure," where he is a cabdriver who seduces a model. Michael's cabbie finds love on the runway, but the romance fizzles almost as soon as it begins, with the woman reduced to just another of the beauties whose photographs decorate the wall of his dingy apartment. With the benefit of hindsight, and revelations about Michael's homosexuality, the overexaggerated (hetero)sexuality of his videos becomes clearer as a dodge, an inoculation against repressed truth, but regardless of Michael's sexual proclivities, these early videos possess a sexual charge that later, "classier" works like "Freedom 90" sorely lack.

Twee

Not all pastiche sought to make the underground mainstream, like "Vogue," or to mock the pretensions of Madison Avenue, like "This Note's for You"; many videos were perfectly content to borrow from sources already tiresomely familiar. Two of the worst offenders in this respect were Billy Joel's "We Didn't Start the Fire" (1989), a visual compendium of every hack cliché of the preceding forty years, and U2's "Angel of Harlem" (1988), a tribute of sorts to Billie Holiday. "We Didn't Start the Fire" finds Joel in a stereotypical suburban kitchen, watching the ups and downs of an average American family and post-World War II American history. Dinner burns in the oven, Mom starts popping pills, her daughter burns her bra, and a series of burning photographs appear onscreen: a 50s car, Jack Ruby shooting Lee Harvey Oswald, Eddie Adams' famous photo of a Vietcong execution. Appropriately enough for a song that is just a laundry list of TV-era names, the video is a flashy montage of iconic images stripped of any specificity or relevance—baby-boomer nostalgia of the shlockiest variety.

Where "We Didn't Start the Fire" looks to position Joel as onlooker-chronicler of the times, "Angel of Harlem" seeks to elevate U2 to the status of the icons the video celebrated. Archival footage of Billie Holiday (the angel of the song's title) and holy sites of musical pilgrimage like Birdland and the Apollo intermingle with the Irish rockers exiting a New York City cab, surrounded by awestruck fans, and playing a show at Manhattan's Beacon Theater. The presumptuousness of crowning themselves equals of the legendary jazz singer is presumably lost on the band, but the video was part of music video's regression into pale nostalgia and self-serving "historicism." Michael Jackson's "Man in the Mirror" (1988) is a similarly tired compilation of video footage already wearyingly familiar from countless news shows and CNN montages, conflating starving Africans, Adolf Hitler, John Lennon, Dr. Martin Luther King, and Ku Klux Klan members into a single watery stew of misplaced good intentions.

Where "We Didn't Start the Fire" had been content to entertain baby boomers with the iconic images of their childhood and adolescence, the nostalgia trip of "When We Was Fab" begins with the soundtrack itself: a virtual carbon copy of middle-period Beatles jangle. The video for George Harrison's hit 1988 single, directed by Godley and Creme, similarly quotes classic Beatles iconography, echoing the trippy, psychedelic feel of their film *Yellow Submarine* (1968), its effects grounded in a series of quicksilver changes to the surrounding landscape. Harrison sings and plays his guitar while standing against a faded brick wall. Obstructions and diversions repeatedly distract us from looking at Harrison—trucks and fruit carts blocking our view, the arrival of ex-bandmate Ringo Starr, a brief glimpse of Harrison in full-on *Sgt. Pepper's* costume. "When We Was Fab" is twee music video, intended as a kinder, gentler counterpoint to the roar and bash of youth-centric videos.

"When We Was Fab" would not be the only twee video that became an aesthetic embraced by performers with older fan bases less interested in flashy editing or sexual come-ons. In their place, the twee video borrowed the collage aesthetic of modern artists like Robert Rauschenberg and James Rosenquist and the formal daring of legendary performers like the Beatles and Bob Dylan, combining its influences into videos at once deeply familiar and avant-garde. INXS' "Need You Tonight/Mediate" (1987) channels Bob Dylan's "Subterranean Homesick Blues," and by extension the 1960s legacy of restless artistic experimentation. Lead singer Michael Hutchence casually tosses away a pile of cards like Dylan's famous video, each illustrating a word or phrase from the song's lyrics. The video's first half is a video collage set up like a stage, with one set of images sliding off the screen, only to be replaced by a newer, shinier set. Director Richard Lowenstein (who had also made "Angel of Harlem") fills the frame with action, expanding and shrinking different segments of the image at will, turning live-action footage into pencil drawings, and injecting the video with a fidgety energy. Los Lobos' "Kiko and the Lavender Moon" (1992) directed by Ondrej Radovsky, betrayed a similar restlessness, its imagery constantly on the ascent. Angels, demons, and religious symbols spiral around the frame, surrounding the band in a cocoon of spirituality.

Howard Jones' "The Prisoner" (1989), brilliantly directed by Danny Kleinman, played with photographic images, engaging, much like "When We Was Fab," in a series of variations on a theme. A scorned lover defaces a pile of photos of Jones, while his ripped visage sings from a series of contact sheets and developing photos. In the video's most impressive effect, the two halves of a chopped-up photo of the couple move together, dance, and embrace against a backdrop of photographic confetti. (Grace Jones' "Slave to the Rhythm" shows a similar propensity for messing around with snapshots, using photographic trickery to enlarge Jones' mouth to superhuman size, turn her neck into golden plates, and Jones herself into a beefy, brawny bodybuilder.) Kleinman was one of the most impressive artisans of the music video, his clips for Adam Ant, ZZ Top, the Pretenders, and others possessed of a similarly wry sense of humor and eye for distinctive, unusual imagery.

Looking like a Pop Art adventure ride through Richard Hamilton's landmark collage work *Just what is it that makes today's homes so different, so appealing?*, Michael Jackson's "Leave Me Alone" (1989), directed by Jim Blashfield, was a last-ditch attempt to prove that the King of Pop possessed a sense of humor. Poking fun at the wild rumors swirling around him (many of which later proved to be true), Jackson is a mere passenger on the carnival ride of his own life. Flying across the sky in a silver rocket, Jackson jets past tabloid headlines about cosmetic surgery and alien marriages, hyperbaric chambers and pet chimps. Like a guided tour through Jackson's skull, "Leave Me Alone's" landscape is dominated by images of imprisonment and intimidation—the popping flashbulbs of paparazzi, a car driving directly into a set of oversized, gaping choppers, Jackson dancing with a ball and chain around his feet. "Leave Me

Alone" is a blast directed at his critics, doubters, and tabloid scavengers, its vitriol leavened by its sense of humor and the cool pungency of its imagery.

Much of Jackson's success had stemmed from his ability to project a realistic aura of urban life, and "The Way You Make Me Feel" (1987) echoed the earlier "Billie Jean" in its depiction of the ugly-beautiful city: graffiti, heaps of trash, wrecked cars, and loitering teenagers. The other major videos from Jackson's *Bad* album were expressions of other, similarly familiar fantasies: squabbling gangs in "Bad" (1987) (directed by Martin Scorsese); Michael as a mobster straight out of *The Public Enemy* (1931) in "Smooth Criminal" (1988); and a strangely pitch-perfect imitation of a hair-metal video for the hard-rocking "Dirty Diana" (1988). "Bad," echoing the earlier "Beat It," is an epic-length tale of gang warfare, this time in the New York City subway system. Scorsese stirs together a dash of *West Side Story* and a pinch of *The Warriors* (1979), and makes use of some lovely crane shots, but the end result lacks the big-event feel of "Thriller" or the compulsive watchability of "Billie Jean." Instead, "Bad" felt surprisingly obligatory, a meshing together of Jackson's prior videos with Scorsese's cinematic favorites to no particular effect. The video was simply too familiar to impact audiences in the fashion it intended.

A Fistful of Dynamite

Madonna, the quintessential shape-shifter of the 1980s, was engaged in a one-upsmanship contest with herself, always on the lookout for a persona more scandalous or tantalizing than her prior incarnations. With "Like a Prayer" (1989), she hit the trifecta of flashpoint topics, mingling sexuality, religion, and race into a single white-hot cauldron of scandal; later, with "Justify My Love," directed by Jean-Baptiste Mondino, she would take a shot at softcore porn. Directed by Mary Lambert, "Like a Prayer" was an instant cause célèbre, its concomitant, abortive Pepsi campaign (designed around an adapted version of the video) raising an enormous ruckus among religious conservatives, and pulled after a single airing. Knowingly pushing the buttons of the easily offended, "Like a Prayer" stoked the flames of controversy to maintain Madonna's status as outlaw icon. In the video, Madonna plays a waifish runaway who takes refuge in a run-down church. Staring intently at a statue representing Jesus as a black man shedding a single tear, she grips the bars that cage Him in. After lying down on a pew, a sensual look on her face as if waiting to be ravished by God, she strokes the statue's face and he comes alive, kissing her on the cheek and forehead. Catholic imagery dominated "Like a Prayer," from the stigmata that appears on Madonna's hands to the crucifix that dangles between her breasts. The representations of Catholicism mingle everywhere with those of oppression, of a particularly African-American variety. Madonna/Mary sings in front of an array of burning crosses, and the modern-day Jesus is a railroaded black man. After an extensive makeout session between Jesus and Madonna, the performance ends with a visual match between the still statue of Christ in church and the black man locked in the jail cell. And performance it is, for "Like a Prayer" ends with an explicit reminder of its theatricality. A curtain comes down onscreen, and when it goes back up, the cast of the video come out and bow. "Like a Prayer" may have attempted to cram its narrative into the comforting realm of fiction, but its subject matter was simply too explosive, and the manner of its telling too explicit, to make this distanciation a feasible means of avoiding controversy. A sexualized, black Jesus, falsely imprisoned in an American jail, making out with Madonna? The effect of the falsely soothing ending was equivalent to lighting one hundred sticks of dynamite and attempting to put out the blaze with a leaky water balloon. "Like a Prayer" intended to start an inferno, and considering how many taboos it shattered, how could it fail?

"Justify" was the raw, unfettered side of "Like a Prayer," knowing, like all videos worth their weight in MTV airplay, that to capture viewers' attention, you must hint at more than you actually show. "Justify My Love" rewards multiple viewings, which are necessary merely to determine who was doing what to whom. Shot in silvery black and white, the video owes a significant debt to the work of Robert Mapplethorpe, whose photographs' aura of sexual licentiousness hangs over every frame here. Madonna touches on every possible kink, within cable-television limits, presenting an ambisexual gathering of sexually ambivalent types. "Justify My Love" is knowingly incoherent, aggressively confrontational in the hopes of stirring up the almost-inevitable controversy; it is no accident that Madonna leaves the room at video's end, clearly unable to stifle a smile and a laugh—presumably at her video's sheer silliness. But Mondino's eye for captivating imagery, and the Abercrombie & Fitch-quality air of sexual omnivorousness, makes for primo video fodder. "Erotica," from two years later, is a reprise of "Justify My Love," albeit stripped of that earlier video's groundbreaking daring. "Erotica" manifests a smorgasbord of sexual tastes, with Madonna at the center of the action. Consistently hinting at truly shocking activities taking place just beyond the camera's reach, "Erotica" presents Madonna as the MC and participant in a festival of diverse sexual proclivities. From the riding crop and whip she struts around with to her sapphic dance with Naomi Campbell to her inspection of a muscular man's unclothed torso, "Erotica's" eroticism was intended to shock an increasingly unshockable audience. "Erotica" was a superb example of why Madonna rarely went to the same well twice; by the time she dipped her bucket into the waters of sexual decadence a second time, the subject had become old hat, yesterday's excitement.

Aiming slightly higher on the high-art spectrum, Chris Isaak's "Wicked Game," directed by Herb Ritts, is similarly softcore, intended to keep a nation of horny teenage boys glued to their TV sets in the hopes of catching another near-glimpse of model Helena Christensen's bare breasts. Taking place on some celestial beach paradise, "Wicked Game" features Isaak and Christensen canoodling in a miasma of sexual bliss. Christensen gazes into the camera, her stare oozing sensuality, her eyes dissolving into a shot of moving clouds. The promise of heavenly sex is everywhere in "Wicked Game," from the couple's playful nuzzling to the tease of Christensen's almost-visible breasts. Heaven is short-lived, though; soon enough, even as her lover croons to her, Christensen begins to look bored with his caresses, chewing her fingernails and looking off into the distance. The duo gambol once more on the beach, but it is now clear, from the far-off look in Isaak's eyes as he sings, and the rapidly moving clouds that serve as counterpoint to the couple's romps, that these images are nothing more than memories of the now-irrevocably lost past. Christensen runs along the beach, away from the camera, receding into memory. "Wicked Game" is softcore with a soul, its effortless beauty rendering it a cut or two above its competition in the zipless-fuck category. "Wicked Game," along with other Ritts videos like Janet Jackson's "Love Will Never Do (Without You)" and Madonna's "Cherish," was an affordable luxury; it looks like a million bucks, but serves as a free tropical vacation for teenagers bathed in a cathode-ray glow.

"Wicked Game's" sensual longueurs make it a close relative of the era's yuppies-in-lust subgenre of videos. These clips, which mostly took place in a hi-fi world of lofts and horny professionals, were epitomized by two iconic late-80s clips with remarkably similar scenarios—Billy Idol's "Cradle of Love" and Aerosmith's "Sweet Emotion" (1991). Like Isaak's video, these clips also made lavish promises of impending sexual bliss; but unlike "Wicked Game," that pleasure was resolutely terrestrial, a far cry from the celestial sensuality of Isaak and Christensen. In the former, an uptight yuppie studying wedding invitations on his computer is interrupted by a knock on the door. His next-door neighbor, an innocent-looking lass, asks to use his stereo, as hers is broken. Putting on "Cradle of Love," she proceeds to get nasty, stripping off her clothes as her new friend cowers in his room. After spilling wine on her shirt, she pulls it off, and he dashes away to wash it in the sink. Meek and socially awkward, he appears physically afraid of her, trembling when she comes near him. He watches through the blinds as she writhes on his bed, playfully embracing his pillows, and lets out a gasp when she does a full split. Looking to get rid of her at any cost, he tries to pull the plug on the stereo, and the song that has so riled her up, but to no avail—the music still plays, and his gourmet dishware crashes to the ground from sheer decibel violence. His temptress-abuser crawls along the ground over to him, grabs him by the tie, and kisses him forcefully, then immediately marches out of the apartment, where her boyfriend waits outside the door. In "Cradle of Love," women are nightmarish sexual predators, beautiful, confusing, and frightening, but the weak performance of the video's protagonist allows for alternate interpretations on the part of viewers—namely, that they would not have been quite so meek. Idol himself, appearing in the background of "Cradle of Love," acts as a Greek chorus for the action, his trademark sneer and air of sexual menace popping up on the computer screen and in the Warhol-esque prints on the wall.

Taking place in the loft next door, "Sweet Emotion" is yuppie love of a more alienated, dysfunctional brand. A teenager crouching under the covers of his bedroom picks up the phone and dials a phone-sex line while pretending to be a Beverly Hills entertainment lawyer named Billy, sitting in his enormous, half-empty loft. His operator, also alone in her spacious loft, cools out in front of an open refrigerator as she coos into the phone. Most of the dialogue is pitched too low to make out, muted by the roar of Aerosmith's hoary rocker, but the little we can hear (and visual clues strewn around his apartment) indicates frank sex talk. We see Billy in his imaginary loft, but his adult impersonation remains far from perfect, his voice cracking at crucial moments. The pair end their call, and Billy's dream girl hangs up the phone, gazing wistfully at the ceiling. But director Marty Callner has one more trick up his sleeve. Echoing her last line before hanging up, we now see the cooing, sexy voice belongs to a harassed, overweight housewife balancing a baby on her arm in a cramped kitchen. Billy reclines in his bed, gleeful and satisfied, but the joke, as we now know, is on him. "Sweet Emotion" knows that while images of yuppie love sells, the gap between fantasy and reality is often gaping.

Making its way down the class ladder, the music video clasped blue-collar workers within its lustful embrace as well. The bearded weirdoes of ZZ Top, not normally known for their mathematical talents, came up with an unbeatable equation for video success: beautiful women + hot cars = smash hit. Both "Sharp Dressed Man" (1983) and "Legs" (1984) feature posses of models intervening to save the hides of regular folk in distress. "Legs" is a parable of feminist awakening whose primary purpose is to show off as many lovely sets of women's legs as it can. This odd dichotomy between message and style is the tension in both of these videos, which celebrate everyday people while worshipping glamorousness.

Similarly simple-minded in their quest for the next good time, Van Halen had always depended on the antics of their wild-man lead singer, David Lee Roth, for video gold. Making the disconnect between the band's no-frills chops and Diamond Dave's Vegas antics explicit, "Jump" (1983) shows the band efficiently performing on a stage while Roth appears in close-up against a black screen. Roth, primped and powdered within an inch of his life, twirls the mike stand in slow motion, executing a nifty backflip while the band chugs along. With Roth onboard, Van Halen didn't need any explosions or convoluted storylines; they had their own special effect, and he was a member of the band. "Panama" (1984) gives Diamond Dave a zip line to play with, and features Roth whooshing through the air, clad in Vegas-ready garb. Only "Hot for Teacher" (1984) (itself a variation on the classroom lust of the J. Geils Band's "Centerfold" [1981], and the private-school riot of the Stray Cats' "Sexy & 17" [1983]) was slightly higher-concept, and its concept was pretty simple: swimsuit models as teachers.

Much like "Jump" and "Panama," "Hot for Teacher" depends on Roth to provide his class-clown antics; the only difference is that here, he could do so in an actual classroom. We begin with Waldo, a prototypical grade-school nerd with a bowtie and a cowlick. As his mother tries in vain to fix his hair, Waldo (with a completely disjointed adult voice) expresses his concern that he can never live up to the effortless cool of his savvier classmates. Later events prove him prescient. The schoolbus arrives, with Roth as the driver, and Waldo stumbles into his own personal hell. To the sound of the song's opening guitar lick, the camera pans across an array of kid-sized rockers, pausing before arriving at the inevitable sore thumb. One student wonders what this year's teacher will look like, and "Hot for Teacher" shifts from black-and-white to color stock for her arrival. A catwalk appears in the middle of the room, and the new teacher, clad in a swimsuit, struts her way down the classroom runway.

There is something profoundly disquieting about the sight of these preadolescent scuzzballs checking out grown women with a seemingly discerning eye, but "Hot for Teacher" quickly papers over the discomfort with the arrival of Roth and the band, who proceed to dance on the school desks. The classroom becomes a jail cell, with the student-prisoners waiting for the bell's reprieve; when it finally does, they are greeted by Roth, now a limousine driver waiting to escort them wherever the day may take them. "Hot for Teacher" was as shameless as the later Alicia Silverstone-Aerosmith videos in its lowest-common-denominator appeals to the male psyche, but where the latter looked like trailers for the next Hollywood blockbuster, Van Halen depended on Roth's comic skill to sell its versions of the good life.

Like any 1980s rock video worth its salt, "Hot for Teacher" promises a life that is a constant party, even for those fans whose most fervent dreams did not extend further than the ringing of the school bell. It was only with the departure of Roth from the band that its videos matured, becoming serious in a way that would never have fit Van Halen in its heyday, while solo Roth expanded on "Hot for Teacher" with "Just a Gigolo" (1984) and "California Girls" (1985), videos consisting of a mugging Roth surrounded by a bevy of bikini-ed babes. Van Halen's "Right Now" (1992) is a string of bumper-sticker slogans, all centered around the phrase "right now," and while the video is clever in a public-service-announcement sort of way, it was also a clear sign of how far the band had strayed from its original aura. Directed by Mark Fenske, "Right Now" mingled the flippant and the socially conscious, the personal and the utterly irrelevant with enough wit to overcome the shopwornness of its sloganeering theme.

Eros and Thanatos

All of these videos, even "Cradle of Love" and "Sweet Emotion," aimed for a touch of good taste in their raunchiness. This was not the case for "Wild Thing" (1988), the surprise hit from shock comedian/wannabe metalhead Sam Kinison, or for any of the metal videos whose tone Kinison so assiduously copied. Recruiting famous pals like Rodney Dangerfield and Jon Bon Jovi for his video, Kinison cast notorious bimbo Jessica Hahn (famous for her role in televangelist Jim Bakker's downfall) as his object of affection/disdain. Hahn writhes in a pit surrounded by Sunset Strip metal boys dressed in black, with Steven Tyler and Billy Idol among the crowd of leering onlookers. Kinison plays his psychotically angry anthem of hatred for women surrounded by "Addicted to Love"–brand backup singers, and when he wrestles with Hahn, at the video's climax, his efforts are more retaliatory than amatory. "Wild Thing," both the song and the video, are more interested in the boys having a good time than in Hahn, or at least any part of Hahn other than her ample cleavage.

The metalhead comic/goon's hit was only one permutation of the truly ugly attitudes displayed toward women in the metal videos of the era. Bands like Whitesnake, Def Leppard, Warrant, Poison, and Mötley Crüe were dedicated to an adolescent agenda of babes, brews, and the white man's burden—to party. Benighted attitudes toward women were far from news in the music video, or in pop culture as a whole; a famous *Hustler* cover had shown women being ground into hamburger, and an early video like Joe Salvo's "I Don't Wanna Hear It" (1983) had rendered women as raw meat, but these metal videos took things a step further, articulating a chilling animosity, or indifference, toward the women they ogled. The videos' glamorizing a dead-end lifestyle of mindless hedonism and lustful abandon, in the darkest years of the AIDS epidemic, was indicative of a contemptible lack of conscience. Their women were less sex objects (like the women of "Wicked Game" and "Justify My Love") than lust objects, their bodies there primarily to be drooled over and ogled. In these videos, beautiful women were like Porsches: another rare commodity to be prized, meant to be jealously guarded, but never humanized. The hair-metal madness left women little role other than sex kitten, and no option other than submission. The videos were lowest common denominator, but influential as all hell; watch any hip-hop video from the mid-1990s forward, and you can see their mark, and their attitude, everywhere.

It may be an era everyone except the genre's most diehard partisans would like to forget, but the metal video was a crucial component of the music video's adolescence. And adolescent they were; to see them is to be reminded of the horror felt when gazing on a particularly dreadful high-school photo, or a previous era's unfortunate hairstyles. While the great majority of the videos from the metal era are hideous to behold, they do present something like the essence of the music video, at its most primal and unformed: ass-kicking and babes. Seen in the right light, though, the metal video was an expression of what Sigmund Freud deemed the two most powerful human impulses: Eros and Thanatos, sex and death. Owing to metal's less-than-adult character, these two drives were kept fiercely separate, as if one would taint the other, and no two videos better express metal's Eros and Thanatos than Warrant's "Cherry Pie" (1990) (directed by Jeff Stein) and Guns N' Roses' "Welcome to the Jungle" (1987) (directed by Nigel Dick).

"Cherry Pie," which brought sex kitten Bobbie Brown to momentary prominence, is a slab of babealicious cheese that unabashedly celebrates the nature of the deal being offered: watch the babe, support our band. Jani Lane and the rest of the boys in Warrant wear enormous smirks throughout the video, winking at their video's fans: "We know you love it," they seem to say. Like the beer and car commercials that have dominated the airwaves for the last twenty-plus years, "Cherry Pie" is an invitation to a leer, informing male viewers that this, too, can be theirs with the right hair, the right clothes, and, most important, the right music. Simultaneously embracing its pre-feminist aesthetic and winking at its own silliness, "Cherry Pie" is the epitome of adolescent sexuality: all wink and ogle, no genuine engagement with scary womanhood. At least the jokes were mildly funny, if dazzlingly unsubtle: Brown, as a waitress, drops a piece of cherry pie right into her lap; the band, dressed as firefighters, hose Brown down; at the line "bring a tear to your eye," Lane blubbers from all the T&A on display.

While the competition was fierce, the prize for ugliest video personae would have to go to Mötley Crüe, beloved hard-rockers of frat boys everywhere. Their "You're All I Need" is simultaneously incomprehensible and indefensible, an aggressively mounted defense of murder. "You're All I Need" (1987) depicts

American man as henpecked, belittled, and finally forced by woman to murder, in order to save the remaining shreds of his dignity. Directed by Wayne Isham, the video makes the astonishing request of its audience of sympathy for its resident devil. Although not quite as jaw-droppingly amoral as "You're All I Need," "Girls, Girls, Girls" (1987), also directed by Isham, is a re-creation of the band's boys' night out, in all its puerile, infantile glory. The Crüe ride their Harleys to a Sunset Strip strip club, toss a switchblade at a patron, and leer at the pole-dancers. Like fourteen-year-olds (to whom this fantasy is obviously directed) with unlimited funds, the boys' sexuality appeared to be stunted at the smirking phase. Cinderella's "Shake Me" (1986) attempts to dramatize the fantasy lives of adolescent girls, to similarly dubious effect. Two stereotypical video vixens taunt a teenage girl for not being able to attend that night's Cinderella concert, but when she picks up a guitar that has magically fallen out of the band's poster, she finds herself transported to the front row of the show, now clad in artfully ripped black spandex. After the concert, the girl sneers at her tormentors, locked out of the show, before hopping into the band's limousine. In Mark Rezyka's touching feminist parable, girls dreamed of the day when they, too, could service the band.

Oozing sexuality became the primary commodity offered by the Led Zeppelin imitators in Whitesnake, who featured metal vixen Tawny Kitaen (lead singer David Coverdale's then-wife) in their videos for "Still of the Night" (1987), "Here I Go Again" (1987), and "Is This Love" (1988). "Is This Love," presumably a bittersweet breakup story, is more intrigued by Kitaen's butt packed into a skintight white dress, and her striptease for her boyfriend, than its ostensible plotline. "Here I Go Again" was their biggest hit, featuring Kitaen doing cartwheels over the hoods of a pair of Jaguars, cuddling up to Coverdale as he drives, sticking her tongue in his ear, and languorously purring in the passenger seat before doing the splits on the car's hood. The video, directed by Marty Callner, makes Kitaen a close relative of the Jaguar Coverdale drives: a fantasy object, purchasable with enough cold hard cash, and fully available to meet all of its owner's needs.

If "Here I Go Again" maintains an iota of wit in its use of Kitaen, Def Leppard's "Women" (1988) cuts directly to the chase, casting the band in a comic-book adventure to track down the ideal woman, conceived of here as a well-trained robot. The band break into a robot factory in order to kidnap their fantasy femme, taught by her teachers such essential principles of femininity as "When you serve your master's cocktail, shake, don't stir." Needless to say, this speech bubble is accompanied by a drawing of a droid-girl shaking her hips while holding a martini. "Women" makes the objectification of women literal, with boxes in a warehouse marked "Lips," "Mouths," and "Miscellaneous Parts."

In metal's cosmogony, fun and games were for men; women, in these videos, are just attractive spare parts.

Even female musicians got into the act, simplifying the metal-video equation even further: make the performer and the hot chick the same person! Lita Ford's "Kiss Me Deadly" (1988) has her writhing on the floor of a sparsely furnished loft, her teased blond hair and studded black leather jacket illuminated by director Marty Callner's expressionist lighting. Alternating between rock-star poses and *Playboy* pinup material, "Kiss Me Deadly" schizophrenically clatters between its dual ways of embracing Ford. Casting herself as lust object, Ford manages the neat trick of objectifying herself, taking a page out of Madonna's book while playing a role the Immaculate One would never have deigned to accept—metal chick.

"Welcome to the Jungle" takes the Thanatos tack, enraptured by the violence of everyday life. Lead singer Axl Rose, in his midwestern rube mode, stands in front of a bank of television screens, taking in their dovetailing images of violence, destruction, and death. Guns N' Roses, here, are the soundtrack to the forthcoming apocalypse, singing their discofied dirge of doom. Unlike "Cherry Pie," though, the video's subject is taken in at a remove. Where "Cherry Pie" offered the tantalizing possibility of Bobbie Brown's dancing for you, breaking the wall of separation between performer and spectator (a promise implicit in every onscreen depiction of sex), in "Welcome to the Jungle," the depicted violence is only seen on a television screen, one step further removed from reality. "Welcome to the Jungle," thus, is not really the soundtrack to the apocalypse; it is the soundtrack to a really great movie about the apocalypse. "Sweet Child o' Mine" (1988) only further emphasizes the yawning gap between GN'R and the average metal band, with Axl and his bandmates committing the cardinal sin of wearing punk-rock T-shirts (CBGB's, T.S.O.L.), rockers acknowledging dweeby, L-for-loser punk rockers in embarrassingly public fashion.

Marty Callner's videos for Twisted Sister had already promised harassed teenagers sweet revenge on tyranny, demolishing the authority of father and teacher (conveniently embodied by the same actor, Mark Metcalf) in "We're Not Gonna Take It" (1984) and "I Wanna Rock" (1984). In both videos, lone teenage boys chafing under the whip summon the forces of metal madness ("I wanna rock!") and bring down the wrath of Twisted Sister on their tormentors. Metcalf is put through the wringer in these videos: crashing through windows, clobbered by swinging doors, knocked out by exploding dynamite and grenades. It is a testament to Metcalf's acting, and the dead-on precision of the videos' summation of childhood serfdom, that no one ever felt the least bit sorry for him. Quiet Riot's "Cum on Feel the Noize" (1984) took on the band's own fans, their song's throbbing decibel overload setting in motion a rock earthquake in one hapless metalhead's bedroom. Even the infamous flopping fish of Faith No More's "Epic" (1990) betrayed a certain joy in needless cruelty that expressed the metal video's spirit, if not its essence.

Joining GN'R on the Thanatos side of the ledger were Bay Area metal purists Metallica. Latecomers to the video, the band did not shoot a video until "One" (1989) (directed by Michael Salomon and Bill Pope), a track from their fourth album, ...And Justice for All. "One" is a deeply unusual clip, a soundtrack video for a twenty-year-old film hardly anyone had seen. Mingling performance footage with huge chunks from Dalton Trumbo's raging antiwar screed Johnny Got His Gun (1971), "One" is a despairing battle cry of high moral purpose. It is no accident that "One" bore little resemblance to any video made by their heavy-metal compatriots. "One" uses overlapping dissolves to cut back and forth between Johnny, trapped in his useless body after the war machine has chewed him up and spit him out, and the band's precise thrashing. Salomon and Pope laid Johnny's lengthy soliloquies over the song's instrumental sections, making "One" the rare video (later joined by Daft Punk's "Da Funk," directed by Spike Jonze) to give its visual track priority over its soundtrack. Swimming against the tide of happy-go-lucky hedonism that dominated most videos, "One" is a howl from the depths, adeptly using its source material to convey the song's mood of spiritual emptiness.

Road to the Riches

While metal ruled the video roost in the late 80s, its two eventual successors were grooming themselves just offstage, waiting impatiently to displace the king. Indie rock, until then an underground, college-town scene, had been gaining strength, with the success of bands like the Pixies, R.E.M., and Sonic Youth soon to open the door for Nirvana and the Alternative Nation 90s; and hip-hop, no longer a fad, a fluke, or a regional phenomenon, gathering forces for its own eventual storming of the video airwaves. The push had begun in 1988, when MTV had debuted Yo! MTV Raps, a daily broadsheet of the latest and greatest in the hip-hop world. Hip-hop also grew into a musical force on BET, the African-American niche channel that dedicated much of its broadcast time to music videos.

In its earliest years, the hip-hop video had borne a certain resemblance to the indie-rock video, both being the product of small budgets and minimal commercial expectations. Many established rap artists did not have the opportunity to shoot videos for their singles, victims of the major record labels' hesitancy about both the lasting power of the music video and of hip-hop as a commercial force. After the enormous success of Run-D.M.C.'s album Raising

Hell, and the Beastie Boys' *Licensed to Ill*, both pushed along by extensive video airplay, the floodgates cracked open. These clips tended to fall into one of two (often overlapping) categories: the comic and the ghetto-realistic video. Hip-hop oscillated between playing class clown and street thug, embracing opposites in its quest to be simultaneously hard and fun. Taking the reins from its songs, hip-hop videos grew sample-heavy, borrowing images and themes from the movies and pop culture. In videos like Eric B. and Rakim's "Paid in Full" (1988), they even attempted to physically duplicate the DJ's scratching, backing up and replaying the same good bits repeatedly onscreen.

More than plot, the crucial aspect of the hip-hop video was always location. As an urban art form, hip-hop demanded an urban stage for its videos. Its lyrical and cultural concern with "realness" meant that when it came to videos, hip-hop would always be promoted as a musical form associated with city life, even when some of its foremost practitioners (Public Enemy, De La Soul) were from the suburbs. The urban locales were also simply good business—at this point in hip-hop's evolution, at least, no one wanted to see a hip-hop video that took place at the local mall's food court. Hence, hip-hop videos almost always restricted themselves to a small circle of familiar locales: city streets, parks, project buildings, and bridge underpasses.

The ethos of "realness" demanded a musical and visual aesthetic that matched its starkness of purpose. This often meant a deliberate confusion of character, blurring the lines between personality and persona. The gangster became the alternate video incarnation of the rapper, his fearless exploits the visual equivalent of the MC's verbal dexterity. That so many hip-hop artists chose to rap about the seamier side of urban life in the heat of the crack epidemic, and that they often did so in the first person, made it difficult to separate the performer from the performance. Were artists like Ice-T and Kool G Rap playing a role? Were they oral storytellers? Or were they speaking the unvarnished truth about their own lives? The questions were deliberately left unanswered.

Kool G Rap and DJ Polo's "Road to the Riches" (1986) has it both ways, its tale of the good life, criminal style, bookended by an explicit characterization as nothing more than a gangster fairy tale. Kool G, with his nephew sitting on his lap, begins his story as a warning to the next generation, overly enamored of gangsterism. He tells his nephew, "You could be a rapper, but you don't want to be a gangster." And yet, "Road to the Riches" is a celebration of the thrill of criminality: expensive jewelry, gunplay, punchouts, and briefcases filled with cash. The *Scarface* poster visible on the wall makes clear where this video's cinematic allegiances lie. Kool G Rap may be warning the young'uns off from the mistakes he made, but "Road to the Riches" still cashes in on the cachet of unlawful glory.

Similarly blurring the lines between himself and his persona, Ice-T plays a tough-guy Big Willie in his videos, a violent outlaw MC. Sometimes the violence (and crime) was metaphorical, as in "I'm Your Pusher" (1988); at other times, disturbingly literal. "I'm Your Pusher" turns T into a prison escapee on the run, locked up for the crime of musicmaking. In a world where rap music was against the law, Ice-T pushes his music clandestinely, selling CDs like bags of heroin. Sampling its chorus from Curtis Mayfield's famed "Pusherman," "I'm Your Pusher" enjoys the illicit appeal of that song's dope-dealing protagonist while explicitly condemning the drug trade. Gang Starr's "Just to Get a Rep" (1991) (directed by Fab 5 Freddy) comes down more explicitly on the side of reportage than "I'm Your Pusher" or "Road to the Riches," its video a hard-eyed, unsentimental look at the urban cycle of violence. Lead MC Guru is no tough guy, merely a poet of street toughs—silently noting the tragic impact of their impulse to destruction.

"I'm Your Pusher" was a clever suggestion of rap's outlaw status, but its ruling metaphor became a standard one for later graduates of hip-hop finishing school, the evocation of a drug-dealing past becoming de rigueur for any wannabe MC. "Colors" (1988), from the film of the same name, intercuts a scene of a community meeting from the movie with Ice-T's rap, positing his plea for a return to sanity in the inner city as a response to the concerns of average taxpayers. Articulating the dichotomy at the heart of Ice-T's persona, and the personae of so many other hip-hop stars, "New Jack Hustler" (1990) presents two views of the MC: one, wearing a Los Angeles Kings hat (known gang insignia at the time) and an enormous pistol necklace; and the other, dressed in a tuxedo. Were MCs gangsters, or were they storytellers? Did they belong in Raiders caps, or tails? "New Jack Hustler" refuses to answer, implying that Ice-T was not reporting reality so much as refracting it through the mirror of his voice.

"High Rollers" (1989) shifts the implicit violence of "I'm Your Pusher" to the forefront. Like an advertisement for the LAPD's malevolent lethality, the bulk of "High Rollers" consists of police footage of pulling guns and knocking down doors. Rapping at a news conference like he was the mayor of Compton, Ice-T simultaneously decries the destructive lifestyles of the rich and infamous, and celebrates them. "High Rollers" may be critiquing the Daryl Gates-era LAPD for its embrace of excessive force, but it also gets its kicks from footage of same. The tone here is less mournful, or angry, than jazzed.

As with Ice-T, much of the message of N.W.A.'s videos is encoded within their clothing choices. Rocking Raiders and Kings caps, black jackets, and bandannas, the L.A. rap stars, much like Tupac Shakur to come, are dressed like Crips and Bloods. Dr. Dre, Ice Cube, Eazy-E, MC Ren, and Yella were engaged in video gang warfare, with their primary opponents the officers of the LAPD. In "Straight Outta Compton" (1988), the group strides confidently through Compton's streets while an array of white cops with thin mustaches and swinging batons follows in hot pursuit. "Express Yourself" (1989) opens with black slaves working under the jealous eye of a white taskmaster, whip in hand. N.W.A. burst through a white sheet emblazoned "I Have a Dream," raising the implied question: Were they the dream's embodiment, or its violent dissolution?

"100 Miles and Runnin'" (1990), sticking with the one-note theme, has the band on the run from the police yet again. The video, directed by Eric Meza, is a bigger-budget affair, with a full-on action-film chase bursting through homes and warehouses, over chain-link fences, and under freeway overpasses. This time, the boys foil the cops—the LAPD burst into their room at the end of the video only to discover some white guys in N.W.A. caps have taken the band's place. As cartoonish as the videos may have been, there was an element of prescience involved as well; the videos' police officers are reminiscent of nothing so much as Officers Stacey Koon, Theodore Briseno, and Mark Furman, LAPD uniformed racists and protagonists of two of the most famous racial dramas of the decade—the Rodney King beating and the O.J. Simpson murder trial.

Not all role-playing in the hip-hop video was oriented around the cops versus robbers dichotomy. Nonetheless, most role-playing videos chose showcases for their performers that emphasized their virility and machismo. The videos served as metaphors for the songs themselves, and the verbal jousting of the MC. In "Mama Said Knock You Out" (1990), LL Cool J plays a boxer, handily dispatching all challengers with a vicious verbal right hook. His car-themed clip for "Goin' Back to Cali" (1988) is more interested in drive-by ogling of the voluptuous female scenery than any discharge of weaponry. LL was often a hip-hop loverman romancing your girlfriend with an impish, shit-eating grin. In "Big Ole Butt" (1987), he hands out diplomas for particularly superb derrieres, getting caught time and again cheating on his latest girl without mustering up a great deal of regret. "Backseat," "Six Minutes of Pleasure," "Pink Cookies in a Plastic Bag"—LL was the Don Juan of the hip-hop video, loving 'em and leaving 'em with impunity.

Big Daddy Kane was also a ring champ, in "Ain't No Half Steppin'" (1990), a rhyming pugilist whose facility on the microphone allowed him to snatch his opponent's gold chain. Eric B. and Rakim are 1940s-style gangsters in "Follow the Leader" (1988), dressed in tuxedos and matching gold chains and let loose in a world of swirling smoke, tommy guns, and drive-by machine-gunnings. KRS-One is a college professor in Boogie Down Productions' "My Philosophy" (1990), rapping onstage at a crowded lecture hall, a giant photograph of Malcolm X in the background to keep him company, and a renegade schoolteacher in "You Must

Learn" (1989), preaching the gospel of African-American history to a crowd of high-school students clamoring for knowledge. For the superstar collective assembled by producer Marley Marl for "The Symphony" (1991), the group plays a posse straight out of a spaghetti Western, complete with the Sergio Leone–biting opening title card, "Once Upon a Time . . . in Brooklyn." Also riffing off a film classic, "The Formula" casts Dr. Dre and disciple The D.O.C. as mad scientists à la Dr. Frankenstein, the duo at work in their laboratory on the formula for the perfect beat. In all these videos, the MCs took on roles that best suited their portrayal as men's men, less musical sissies than verbally agile bruisers.

"The Formula," before settling into its take-off on *Frankenstein*, dismisses a variety of wack pretenders to the hip-hop throne, including an R&B group comically kitted out in Raiders caps and hardcore gear, New Kids knockoffs, and MC Mallet, a dead-on parody of then-current pop-rap superstar MC Hammer. The comic video, in opposition to ghetto realism, opted for light-hearted good times. Slick Rick's "Children's Story" (1989), on the surface a ghetto-realist video, with its outlaw-on-the-run motif, overwhelms its ostensible plot with its Keystone Kops aesthetic. Rick, looking entirely out of place in his hip-hop threads, finds himself chased by police officers clad like turn-of-the-century coppers. Rick jettisons the bumbling cops with Chaplinesque insouciance and, after he is arrested, breaks out of jail with impunity. As suited his appeal to preadolescents, the Fresh Prince's "Parents Just Don't Understand" (1988) features him at the center of a similarly madcap adventure, where Will, under assault from an outbreak of hideously tacky plaid shirts, is ridiculed by his classmates, and his mother chases after him with a rolling pin. Taking place a million miles away from the cracked-out ghettos of "Express Yourself" or "Road to the Riches," "Parents Just Don't Understand" is set in a middle-class adolescent's wonderland of well-appointed homes and brand-new Porsches.

To Public Enemy, the ethos of realness meant something different altogether. Their videos sought to galvanize the politically moribund music video with the moral righteousness of the civil rights movement and the outspoken black nationalism of Louis Farrakhan. Anger and entertainment, political frankness and hip-hop posturing—Public Enemy's videos, much like their album, were a veritable hodgepodge of clashing styles, modes, and moods. Nonetheless, at their best, PE's videos preserved, if only momentarily, the flickering flame of a vanishing era in African-American politics.

"Night of the Living Baseheads" (1988) features Flavor Flav as an unorthodox newscaster uncovering the truth about the drug epidemic then ravaging the African-American community. Chuck D poses at a crime scene, a chalk outline prominently displayed behind him, and guest MC Lyte is an undercover investigator looking for addicts in the heart of that bastion of white privilege—Wall

Street. Even in this early video, Public Enemy are torn between tackling the issues and tickling fans' funny bones, with Flav and Chuck appearing to be coming from entirely different worlds, often working at cross-purposes.

"Fight the Power" (1989), directed by Spike Lee as an analogue to his film *Do the Right Thing*, is a combination live performance, movie-soundtrack video, and protest march, with Lee and PE organizing a "Young People's March to End Racial Violence" that took to the streets of Brooklyn, ending on the Bedford-Stuyvesant block where the film had been shot. The marchers hold up images of legendary African-American figures like Muhammad Ali, Jesse Jackson, Paul Robeson, Marcus Garvey, and Frederick Douglass, along with PE-specific signs that paid homage to band sidekicks Terminator X and the S1W's. Public Enemy's Chuck D and Flavor Flav perform on the float that leads the marchers, its backdrop a giant photograph of Malcolm X. Lee intercuts scenes from the film into the video, its tragic cocktail of police brutality and racially motivated violence providing the ostensible purpose for the march. Jokes about the commodification of dissent were almost too obvious to make, and "Fight the Power" acknowledges the contradiction at its heart, being a real-fake march in protest of a fictional event inspired by all-too-real tragedies. More troubling is the martial vibe lurking at the video's edges, with Fruit of Islam types in almost every shot, and the warrior posing of the backup dancers. For a video that began with footage of Martin Luther King's 1963 March on Washington, its understanding of Dr. King's ethos of nonviolence was imperfect at best.

PE's next major video, "Welcome to the Terrordome" (1990), is an odd combination of black-nationalist militarism and imprecations to party hearty. After portentously announcing that "FREEDOM IS A ROAD SELDOM TRAVELED BY THE MULTITUDE," Public Enemy proceed to seek freedom by the way of the gun, with men in black bum-rushing the show at a corporate office tower, and Uzi-toting PE soldiers appearing onstage at an outdoor demonstration. "Welcome to the Terrordome" is unclear about just whom, precisely, the enemy Public Enemy was gearing up for was, but "By the Time I Get to Arizona" (1992) is far more explicit. The song had been written as a protest against the lone state to reject the proposed Martin Luther King's birthday holiday, and the video imagines a detailed revenge against the racist politicians denying Dr. King his proper tribute. "By the Time I Get to Arizona" opens with a press conference, where a slick-looking white senator (meant to evoke David Duke and a standard-issue capitalist fat cat in equal parts) states his continued opposition to honoring Dr. King. The video proposes two responses to this deplorable state of affairs, one historical and one imaginary. In the former, stark black-and-white footage of African-American protesters show impossibly brave men and women being sprayed by fire hoses, attacked by police officers, and heckled by jeering whites, but standing firm in their commitment to asserting their dignity, and to demand equality under the law. In the latter, Public Enemy and their associates meet in a dimly lit lair to stock up on the latest weaponry. Present actions answer past misdeeds, as the violence grows uglier and uglier, leading up to a re-creation of King's assassination. In retaliation, Public Enemy place a bomb underneath the car of the racist senator, blowing him and his entourage to smithereens. Once again, as in "Fight the Power," the images are undeniably stirring, and the political awareness impressive, but—targeted assassinations in the name of Dr. King? Somewhere along the way, the message had gotten garbled.

By the time Public Enemy got to "Give It Up," in 1994, they had become the grizzled elder statesmen of hip-hop, which made their comic rants about the gangsta-fication of the genre both compelling and predictably whiny. Chuck and Flavor Flav flip channels, their eyes bugging out in shock at the latest group to jump on the bandwagon—little kids, women, and suburban whiteboys (their album released on Plain White Rapper Records). Each of these upstarts get their comeuppance, cut down to size by Public Enemy's dis song. It is hard not to take away the impression, though, that by the logic of "Give It Up," the only true practitioners of pure hip-hop are adult black men. Everyone else, it seemed, was little more than an interloper.

One of the many contradictions at the heart of Public Enemy's videos was the strange relationship between the intellectual vigor of leadman Chuck D and sidekick Flavor Flav's clownish antics (best seen in the humorous video for "911 Is a Joke"). Hip-hop embraced clownishness as a prized character trait, with Flav, Digital Underground's Humpty, and the outlandish Biz Markie among its foremost practitioners. His "Just a Friend" (1989) begins with Biz and friends exchanging mom jokes on a park bench, before outfitting him in white wig and tails, rocking out like a hip-hop Amadeus. Biz also sports preppy garb and a clunky pair of glasses for his trip to the local college, where he bursts in on his girlfriend and catches her in flagrante delicto with a campus stud. Knowing Markie's comic potential, Masta Ace's "Me and the Biz" (1991) turns him into an actual caricature, with a marionette filling in for the real-life Biz. "Biz" hangs out on the stoop, drinks coffee with Masta Ace, lounges in bed, and sits on the windowsill as Ace snuggles with his girlfriend.

Humpty, of Digital Underground, made a career out of blurring the boundary between hip-hop and comedy. In the video for his signature hit "The Humpty Dance" (1989), Humpty was dressed like an accountant, in a drab suit and matching patterned tie; but a CPA at his company's raucous holiday party, performing onstage at a club with his giant fake schnoz and white fur cap. Beyond the inherent humor of Humpty's ridiculous getup, "Humpty Dance" is funny in corny, wink-wink fashion. Humpty describes his nose as "big like a pickle," and measures the pickle in his hand against a ruler. Any double entendres about his big pickle were, of course, strictly intentional.

Introducing a more cerebral form of humor, A Tribe Called Quest hit the desert for "I Left My Wallet in El Segundo" (1990), got overly literal with "Can I Kick It?" (1990), and explored the dizzying possibilities of the computer revolution in "Scenario" (1992). Tribe were intellectual jokesters, their videos willfully silly but never as broad as "Just a Friend" or "Me and the Biz." "El Segundo" deposits the group in the middle of a desert stocked with white-trash cops and Mexican dwarves in ponchos. "Can I Kick It?" takes the titular question at face value, with Tribe and their friends taking turns knocking over a giant-sized I and T. "Scenario," their best video, offers viewers an opportunity to direct their own adventure, its dense frame resembling a PC screen with multiple open windows, outfitted with whimsical knobs and buttons that controlled camera angles, Tribe's hairstyles, and their backup dancers' swimsuit fashions. Above and beyond all the joking, Tribe were dead serious about their music and their videos. "Award Tour" (1993), directed by Josh Taft, was a challenge to the hiphop naysayers who doubted its enduring relevance. "Award Tour" bounds its loose, jocular rapping-in-the-park narrative in an elaborate gold picture frame. This, too, the video tells us, is art.

After "Bastards of Young," "Perfect Kiss," and "One," "Award Tour" was making explicit the argument that many music videos had been implicitly making for years: that music videos could and should be taken seriously as art. In the music video's next phase, which spanned the period from 1992 to 1997, when MTV began to pull videos from their central place in the channel's programming, the form embraced both the bigger-is-better philosophy espoused by superstars like Michael Jackson and Madonna—a way of thinking that would find its apotheosis in the remarkable trilogy of epic videos by Guns N' Roses—and an embrace of the artistry to be found in the disposable. In its maturity, the music video would become what it had long intended to be—brilliant, trashy, enjoyable, and entirely ephemeral.

CHAPTER 4

Video Follies

Around the time that Nirvana and Dr. Dre simultaneously revolutionized music with the release of their albums *Nevermind* and *The Chronic*, respectively, the music video seemed safe, assured of its central role in the promulgation of music and its place at the epicenter of youth culture. Even as "Smells Like Teen Spirit" and "Ain't Nuthin but a G Thang" were dominating MTV, and ushering in a new cohort of alternative-rock and gangsta-rap performers, the music video's position was silently, steadily eroding. In the meantime, though, the music video appeared as stable as ever, crucial in overseeing the cultural shift from the heavy-metal videos that dominated the late 1980s to the hip-hop and grunge-heavy early 90s. MTV, along with BET, was especially crucial in bringing hip-hop to suburban America, making figures like Dre and Tupac Shakur mainstream heroes to an increasingly rap-besotted culture.

G Thing to She Thing

After the menacing, antiauthoritarian hostility of N.W.A.'s videos made MTV blanch, hip-hop videos returned to being mostly unseen. *Yo! MTV Raps* still showed the latest and greatest in hip-hop, and regional services like Video Jukebox (The Box) were dedicated to playing rap videos, but MTV, and its compatriot BET, mostly kept away from rap, fearful of the consequences an overload of hip-hop videos might bring. The morality of hip-hop was a subject much in the news in the early 1990s, with Ice-T's "Cop Killer" debated in the halls of Congress, Time Warner heavily lobbied to divest itself of its rap holdings, and social conservatives like William Bennett and C. Delores Tucker portraying hip-hop as the death knell of the civil rights movement and a harbinger of crime waves to come. Second Lady Tipper Gore called for a renewed censorship effort, in the form of parental-advisory stickers, to keep harmful music away from minors. In this environment, it was almost understandable, although cowardly, that major purveyors of music videos would shy away from hip-hop. It would take a video drought, and the creation of a new brand of hip-hop fantasy life, to spark a resurgence of hip-hop videos and bring about the genre's domination of MTV and BET.

N.W.A. had been doomed to minimal MTV airplay from the start, their videos rife with imagery redolent of gang life, their songs given titles like "Fuck tha Police," and their visual concepts more police chase than fashion shoot. But when ex-N.W.A. member Dr. Dre came back in 1992 with his album *The Chronic*, the formula had been tweaked, and his videos were a different, substantially more TV-friendly affair. N.W.A.'s videos had pegged the group as police-hating outlaws on the run, but the videos from *The Chronic* ("Ain't Nuthin' but a G Thang," "Dre Day," and "Let Me Ride") were more ghetto daydream than urban reality. Eschewing the paranoid realism of N.W.A.'s "Express Yourself" and the Geto Boys' "Mind Playing Tricks on Me," and his own previously stated lack of interest in drug culture ("Yo, I don't smoke weed or cess/cause it's known to give a brother brain damage"), Dre's solo videos were jovial, depicting a fantasy existence of parties, backyard barbecues, and tricked-out cars. Choosing to turn away from its role as "the black CNN" (as Chuck D had pegged it), hip-hop, and its music videos, chose to become the black MTV instead, embracing a (white) teen-friendly vision of the good life. Hip-hop videos grew glossier and more audacious, emerging out of their initial confines to become something stranger, stronger, and more wide-ranging than anyone might have expected.

A 24/7 party, jam-packed with easy sex, pot smoking, binge drinking, vomiting, and barbecues, if not in that order, "Ain't Nuthin but a G Thang" is a light-hearted fantasy tailor-made for wannabe hip-hop fans scared off by the political agenda of "Fight the Power" or the violent propulsiveness of "Straight Outta Compton." Hip-hop video as endless party was a mantle taken up by many early- and mid-90s clips: Naughty by Nature's "O.P.P." (1991) and "Hip Hop Hooray" (1993), Coolio's "1,2,3,4" (1996), and Wyclef Jean's *Saturday Night Fever*–quoting "We Trying to Stay Alive" (1997), to name just a few. "Ain't Nuthin' but a G Thang," directed by Dre, is a day in the life of an imaginary Compton, one that obviously bears little relationship to any real locale of the same name. The fantasizing was of an altogether more prosaic type than, say, "Wicked Game"; and the hidden political and social content of videos like "G Thang" and its successors lay in the relative paucity of its idealized worlds. Dre's fantasy extended as far as an entire day free of violence, free of strife, altogether lacking in the free-floating paranoia of "Straight Outta Compton" or "Express Yourself."

Pulling up in his powder-blue 1964 Chevy, Dre heads into his protégé Snoop Doggy Dogg's house, passing Snoop's deadbeat father and layabout siblings before finding him in his bedroom, pulling his shoes on. The pair head out of the house and roll down the street in Dre's coupe, the car's pounding hydraulics causing the twin marijuana-leaf baseball caps atop their heads to bounce rhythmically. They arrive at a barbecue and hit the stage to perform, the camera getting right up into their faces, bobbing and weaving along with the beat. "G Thang" takes in the day's humorous events with an amused eye: the chef throws burgers onto the fire, a pistol tucked into his waistband; a tot dances with his father in the parking lot during the concert; a woman in a bikini top gets it stripped off during a volleyball game.

Day turns into night and cars roll up to a party in a warehouse space, its refrigerator jammed full of ice-cold forty-ounce malt liquor bottles. Dre and Snoop hit the stage to perform again, and the video alternates between them and the inevitable comeuppance dealt to an unpleasant woman. She enters during their performance, grasping the railing to walk down the stairs into the party, and almost instantly pulling her arm back, recoiling as if she had already contracted a deadly disease from its touch. Pretty, but snobbish, she is irritated by the pushes and shoves of the overflow crowd and the advances of pushy men. Soon enough, two men emerge from the crowd with bottles of malt liquor, shake them up, and spray her.

In this fantasy, there was little room for women except as sexual objects and subjects of derision. "G Thang" and its successors take place in a hip-hop star's imaginary playground of all-night parties, loose women, and endless, lush expanses of marijuana, but the entirety of the fantasy is confined to a working-class world easily identifiable as Compton, South Central Los Angeles, and its urban equivalents across the United States. Setting the table for a seemingly infinite parade of clips with twentysomething men posing meaningfully around restored 70s muscle cars, cavorting with surgically enhanced beauties, and throwing back a few at their local club, Dre and Snoop's videos established an infinitely appealing world of masculine fantasy; a space where boys could be boys, uncensored by the demands of pushy feminism or the necessities of the working world.

"G Thang's" successor, "Dre Day," is an ugly slap at former bandmate Eazy-E, depicting him as an indentured servant of Ruthless Records boss Jerry Heller, possessed of a pitiful stable of midgets, half-wits, old fogies, and other never-gonna-be rappers, and ending with him standing at the onramp to the Pasadena Freeway, holding up a sign labeled "WILL RAP FOR FOOD." Dre has his symbolic revenge on Eazy, following up his lyrical assassination with the implication of impending violence. The guns that made a brief appearance in "G

Thang" are out in full force here, but the effect is still comic, not dramatic; no one is in serious fear of being shot here. The guns are merely extensions of the bullets being spit by the song's MCs, a further threat of emasculation at the hands of their rapier tongues.

"Let Me Ride" is an expansion of "Ain't Nuthin' but a G Thang's" laid-back sensibility, zooming in on that video's car-culture motif. A video inordinately fond of overhead crane shots, "Let Me Ride" follows Dre as he cruised around town in his '64, popping two-wheel turns and attracting the attention of all the neighborhood ladies and their gearhead boyfriends. Dre raps from amidst the crowd at a gathering of souped-up automobiles, each bouncing up and down on its hydraulics. He picks up a woman sucking lasciviously on a popsicle on a street corner, then ejects her from his car when he spots another more to his liking at the car wash. "Let Me Ride" is as vivid a fantasy of Southern California car culture as the Beach Boys' odes to their little deuce coupes, a raunchy car commercial the likes of which would never make network TV.

Dre's sidekick Snoop Doggy Dogg devoted his videos to a similarly laid-back aesthetic, pegging him somewhere between teenage miscreant and post-juvenile delinquent. In the cartoonish "What's My Name?" (1993), Snoop possesses the ability to morph into a canine at will, simultaneously literalizing his name and providing himself with an easy escape route from angry fathers. Dogs are everywhere in this video—digging up holes in front yards, being chased by dog-catchers, interrupting barbecues, rolling dice, drinking, and smoking cigars. "Gin and Juice" (1994) has Snoop graduated to more adolescent affairs, throwing a bash at his parents' house after they head out for the evening. The video was not all that different from "G Thang" or "Let Me Ride," but if you look hard enough, especially at the scenes of an impromptu dance and car show, you might be able to spot, in the mingling blue and red bandannas, evidence of the post-L.A. riot gang truce that kept the City of Angels' streets quiet for nearly a year in the early 1990s. Even in Snoop's *Home Alone*–biting comedy, a touch of reality manages to creep in. "Doggy Dogg World" (1994) is a nostalgia party that invites all the half-forgotten African-American stars of film and television of the 1970s to join in the fun, with Snoop himself a hustler in a fur-lined coat, oversized glasses, and fedora, leading the band in a finger-snapping rendition of his G-funk slow jam.

Dre and Snoop's future labelmate 2Pac (Tupac Shakur)'s videos took place in another realm entirely, a no-future zone of hopelessness and despair worlds away from the ghetto-fabulousness of "G Thang." Videos like "Trapped" (1991) and "Papa'z Song" (1993) revolve around a tightly constricted set of locales—prison cells, dingy homes, and street corners. Tupac often raps from behind bars—harassed by guards in "Cradle to the Grave," singing through a prison phone in "Trapped," and watching his son playing forlornly with a ball as he is locked up in "Papa'z Song." Tupac was a poet of the streets and prisons, rocking a baby in his arms as he tells the story of its mother in "Brenda's Got a Baby" (1992) and in a bulletproof vest, lit by flame-like strobes, in the crime tale "Holler If Ya Hear Me" (1994). In these videos, and "Keep Ya Head Up" (1993) (directed by Dave Dobkin), Pac is the strong, sensitive type, his soulful eyes, brimming with emotion, rage, and calculation, the constant visual focal point. Shakur was unfailingly political in these videos, opening "Keep Ya Head Up" with the inscription "Dedicated to the Memory of Latasha Harlins . . . It's Still On," evoking the tragic death of a South Central Los Angeles teenager killed by a Korean shopkeeper, and implying that the L.A. riots, which had rocked the city only the year before, would be but the first skirmish in an ongoing war. Shakur was simultaneously warrior and elegist, mourning the tragic waste of African-American life, experiencing it personally, and demanding vengeance— a strange cocktail of responses that would only grow in flammability as his commercial star brightened.

2Pac's next videos were made under an unusual constraint, with Shakur incarcerated on a sex-abuse charge. Unable to be physically present in his videos, both "Dear Mama" (1995) and "So Many Tears" (1995) depend on archival footage and visual trickery to keep Shakur in the frame. In "Dear Mama," Tupac's mother Afeni Shakur looks at old photographs of her son, punctuated by dimly lit scenes that dramatized moments from their shared past—Afeni smoking crack during her period as an addict, Tupac languishing in jail. Afeni watches Tupac's "I Get Around" video on television, and in considering his legacy, finds herself considering her own as a former member of the Black Panthers, with one yellowed newspaper clipping reading "Black Panthers vs. Police." "So Many Tears" mixes old footage, outtakes from previous videos, and darkly lit scenes of Pac lookalikes hooded in shadow or with their backs turned to the camera. A New Orleans–style second line group, complete with dark suits and fedoras, appeared onscreen, with a widow in black crying over her loss and a drummer tapping a snare drenched in a waterfall of tears. The mournful tone, the crafty use of recycled imagery, the visual sleight of hand—in a tragic irony, the techniques necessary to keep Shakur's career going while he was imprisoned became de rigueur once he was murdered in 1996. 2Pac's strange video afterlife made his image a slave to these postmortem tricks of the trade, and Tupac Shakur, dead, became a bigger video celebrity than he had been alive.

Before his death, though, Shakur switched record labels to Suge Knight's Death Row, and transitioned into a series of flamboyant big-budget videos that stood in diametric opposition to his earlier work. "California Love," directed by

Hype Williams, is the splashiest of all, a *Mad Max* rip-off with a raft of guest stars (including Chris Tucker and George Clinton) that dominated MTV for all of 1996. Shakur disavows his earlier incarnations here; the sensitive soul of "Keep Ya Head Up" is overwhelmed by the cartoonish testosterone overload of "California Love," all thumping chests and deep, booming voices. Inoculating himself against past sins of weakness, Shakur was the star of his own post-apocalyptic action flick, looking immensely at home amidst the play-acting carnage. "California Love" is incoherent, its narrative muddled to the point of unintelligibility, and saddled with a sophomoric "it was all a dream" ending, but it captured viewers' attention nonetheless with its epic scope and Shakur's dangerous magnetism. An experienced actor, Shakur comfortably expands his persona to fill the wide spaces of Williams' phenomenally expensive video. Shakur had entered the second phase of his career, with videos portraying him as a mercenary, avenger, or violent outlaw. In "2 of Amerika'z Most Wanted" (1996), Shakur appears in bloody white garb, his arm in a sling, marching into a Notorious B.I.G. stand-in's office as faux Big and Puffy discuss their failed hit on their rival Shakur. For an artist whose early videos had been dedicated to mourning the vicious cycle of violence and incarceration endemic to African-American life, it was a gruesome irony that Shakur would turn so quickly to celebrating that same violence and thuggishness. In September 1996, less than a year after the triumph of "California Love," Shakur was gunned down by unknown assailants in Las Vegas. His mortal career had come to an end, although in a yet-more-unlikely turn of events, his video career would possess one more act.

Posthumous Pac became something of a cottage industry, beginning before his death with "I Ain't Mad at Cha" (1996) (codirected by Shakur and Kevin Swain), which plays with the notion of a dead Tupac hanging out with peers like Miles Davis and Billie Holiday. Its death-scarred imagery and heaven motif became unexpectedly poignant, and a little creepy, after Shakur was shot to death. Later, legitimately posthumous videos picked up on these themes, with "I Wonder if Heaven's Got a Ghetto" (1997), directed by Lionel Martin, flipping the script. If the former imagined him dead while still actually alive, the latter imagines him still alive when actually dead, only further inflaming the conspiracy theories that swirled around his (still unsolved) murder. Skirting the issue of Pac's absence by employing a first-person point of view, "I Wonder" has the rapper, now only injured after being shot, airlifted to a Catholic nunnery in New Mexico (don't ask), nursed back to health by black nuns (really, don't ask), and eventually picked up by a busload of African-American musical legends, including Jimi Hendrix. The video is structured like a puzzle for Pac's faithful, with little hints meant to be worried over, including the restaurant called the

Amaru Diner (Tupac's middle name) and the final dissolve from a nun holding beads to Tupac's logo. The figure of Tupac Shakur is invested with an aura of holiness in "I Wonder," capped by the scene where his hand reaches out from offscreen, offering his blue (Crip) bandanna to a suffering little boy. Tupac as miracle worker, and gangs as protectors of the forsaken? Only Tupac Shakur had the accumulated cultural capital to get away with so shameless a posthumous transformation.

"Changes" (1998) employs Ken Burns–style camera trickery, using zooms to juice up stills, and mixes in footage from Pac's films (*Juice*) and other videos ("Papa'z Song," "California Love") to create the impression of activity. The whitewashing of Tupac crystallized with the video for "Do for Love" (1998) (directed by Bill Parker), which turns Shakur into an animated figure straight out of Saturday-morning cartoons. Cartoon Pac romanced, gambled, fucked, and hung out with his pals at his mansion. Rendered entirely two-dimensional, and lacking any of the complexities that made him so alluring a cultural figure during his life, Tupac Shakur became a fun-loving gangsta with rippling muscles and bandanna. Needless to say, "I Wonder if Heaven's Got a Ghetto" and "Do for Love" were far cries from the prisons, ghettoes, and abandoned women of his despairing early videos.

Shakur's late-career move toward big-budget extravaganzas was echoed by contemporaries like Ice Cube and Bone Thugs-N-Harmony, whose videos were markers of hip-hop's move toward the video mainstream and its embrace of glitz over grit. "Natural Born Killaz" (1995), directed by F. Gary Gray, stars Cube and Dr. Dre as a team of psychopathic killers on the run from the police. Dre, never the most convincing tough guy, made for a weak serial killer, looking better as a tango-dancing, tuxedo-clad entrepreneur in his premature kiss-off to the gangsta game, "Been There Done That" (1996).

The extent to which hip-hop had gone Hollywood was made crystal clear by Puff Daddy's 1997 tribute-cum-cash-in, "I'll Be Missing You," directed by Hype Williams. Ostensibly an ode to Puffy's lost comrade-in-arms, the Notorious B.I.G., "I'll Be Missing You" embraced Hollywood cliché, with Diddy dancing in the rain like a rap Gene Kelly, crashing his motorcycle on the open highway, and surrounded everywhere by lit candles and children in snow-white uniforms. Even in a video for his dead friend, Puff Daddy could not resist showboating, hogging the spotlight with his painfully sophomoric antics. Williams' video, while slick, is utterly devoid of any understanding of the complex figure it purports to celebrate, embracing eye-catching imagery in lieu of genuine grief or sentiment.

A better class of hip-hop video aimed to create visual analogues to the realistic reportage of their songs. The Fugees made literal their rejection of the grandiose in their video for "Killing Me Softly" (1996), sitting in a movie theater and throwing popcorn jeeringly at the screen, where a reel of a rejected, glossier video treatment unspools. Likewise Coolio's "Fantastic Voyage" (1994), whose beachfront fantasy was explicitly labeled an escape from the stultifying inner city, miles away (both geographically and mentally) from the water. The Pharcyde imagine a topsy-turvy world of black plantation owners and white slaves in "Runnin'" (1996), enjoying, if only momentarily, the delicious irony of turning the tables on four hundred years of oppression. Ice Cube's "It Was a Good Day" (1993), directed by F. Gary Gray, understood what a superb screenplay it had in the song itself, laying out the ingredients for a top-notch day in South-Central Los Angeles, and following its blueprints exactly. Geto Boys' "Mind Playing Tricks on Me" (1991) was similarly faithful to its song, illustrating its three brief, haunting stories of inner-city pressures. If "Mind Playing Tricks" suggested a malevolent force lurking behind the scrim of ghetto struggle, Bone Thugs-N-Harmony's "Tha Crossroads" (1996), directed by Michael Martin, looked at the same dismal picture and saw the hand of God protecting His children, even in death. While God was only implied, the Angel of Death is an explicit presence in "Tha Crossroads," pimped out in a full-length leather coat and sunglasses. His role, beyond looking faintly reminiscent of Isaac Hayes circa 1968, is to usher the recently and tragically deceased toward the light, leading a caravan ascending to Heaven. His reasons may be inscrutable, taking children along with the elderly, but "Tha Crossroads" is a video of beleaguered acceptance, encompassing the real-life death of band mentor Eazy-E into its framework.

The hip-hop videos of the late 1980s were notable for their relative lack of interest in sex. Big Daddy Kane may have played pool with a beauty in a leopard-print dress in "Smooth Operator," and LL rapped about a "Big Ole Butt," but most hip-hop videos elided the topic of sex entirely. In a surprisingly large percentage of the rap videos of the late 1980s, the performers are surrounded by male backup dancers. Women are often nowhere to be seen, barred from the boys' club of hip-hop. It was not until the early 1990s, the era of "O.P.P." and "Baby Got Back," that women as lust objects, intended to be ogled, made their first steady inroads into the music video. Taking a page out of heavy metal's playbook, hip-hop would increasingly depend on the bodaciousness of the female bodies on display to sell their videos, with male performers routinely paired with stunningly beautiful women as proof of their virility. No longer dressing their performers up as boxers or Wild West cowboys, later hip-hop videos would come to feature luscious arm candy almost exclusively as its primary visual accoutrement.

This trend began in earnest with 2 Live Crew and Sir Mix-A-Lot, and the respective videos for the Miami bass group's "Me So Horny" (1989) and the portly Seattle MC's unlikely hits "Baby Got Back" (1992) and "Put 'Em on the Glass" (1993). Crew honcho Luther Campbell wields a little black book the size of a Yellow Pages, playing the telephone like a musical instrument in the hopes of attracting some female companionship for the evening. The "Baby Got Back" video, directed by Adam Bernstein, underlines the humor inherent to its ode to ample asses. Putting womankind on a pedestal in order to get a better look at her butt, "Baby Got Back" pokes fun at the stick-figure ideal celebrated by publications like *Cosmopolitan*. Phrases like "REAR" and "MUCH BACK" appear in the frame in giant letters, twin lemons pop up to illustrate the ideal behind, and Mix himself declaims his verses while standing on a giant ass. Even the DJ's turntables had a little butt figurine over the needle. "Baby Got Back" was clever and articulate, but "Put 'Em on the Glass" steps over the line into borderline tawdriness. Taking the logical next step from butt-worship to mammarian devotion, "Put 'Em" equates beautiful cars with beautiful women, posing a slew of dancing girls in front of Mix's array of luxury cars. As he drives around town in his Lamborghini, women doff their tops for his visual delectation, and back at the ranch, Mix's breast brigade soap up while washing his cars, the video providing the requisite close-ups of well-scrubbed boobs. Mix was still funny (bowing to the camera at the song's close, as if in expectation of our huzzahs), but "Put 'Em on the Glass" is more Playboy Channel fantasy than music video. Music videos had always been about spectacle, and the promise of the unclothed female body had always been the spectacle of spectacles; but with "Put 'Em on the Glass," and its countless followers, sex and comedy divorced, and sexiness, in the hip-hop video, grew into a grim, joyless affair. With no Sir Mix-A-Lot to serve as master of ceremonies, his wink was steadily replaced by the leer of the metalheads.

The women of hip-hop and R&B chose to fight fire with fire—some of them, at least. En Vogue's "Giving Him Something He Can Feel" (1992) showed just how aware the trio was of their disarming effect on men. Singing at a swanky nightclub, decked out in slinky 40s-style gowns and elbow-length gloves, the women enjoy putting the hurt on their masculine audience. The men loosen their collars, pat their sweaty brows, fan themselves with their hats, and discreetly slip their wedding rings into their pockets; in short, they are rendered helpless in their desire for the women of En Vogue. The men also exchange glances over the course of the performance, as if silently asking each other, "Have you ever seen anything like this?" Enjoying their now-familiar power over men, the women bask in their well-deserved adulation, not even minding the ejaculatory fizz of overflowing champagne that stands in for their fans' amorous fantasies run amok.

The equally spunky, sex-positive feminists of Salt-N-Pepa turned the tables on their masculine counterparts in similarly knowing fashion. Their video

"Whatta Man" (1994) borrows liberally from the conventions of the hip-hop video, flipping the script by reversing the gender roles—women looking at, and evaluating, a series of men reduced to playthings, and little more. "Shoop" (1993) has the trio hanging out on the beach, good-naturedly assessing the physical attributes of the men doing jumping jacks, playing touch football, and stripping for an afternoon swim. In "Whatta Man," the women do the ogling, cat-calling, and fondling, and men pose in various states of undress, little more than video eye candy. Knowing its own audaciousness, "Whatta Man" (which featured guest singers En Vogue) refuses to take itself seriously, viewing its inside-out imagery as a strategic jab in the direction of the dominant video narrative. The absurdist heartthrobs of one-hit wonders Right Said Fred remove the female middlemen entirely, putting their pectorals on display in "I'm Too Sexy" (1991) for a putative audience of male modelizers with hardly a speck of self-consciousness.

Tainted Love

Homosexuality had always been a shadow presence in the music video, from David Bowie's videos of the 1970s onward. It had also been present through its absence, as in the aggressively heterosexual videos made in the late 1980s by George Michael, which hoped that a constant barrage of supermodels would distract his fans from any unsightly rumors about the heartthrob's personal sexual preferences. The explicit portrayal of homosexual desire onscreen, however, has a much shorter, more scattered video history.

The ur-text of gay-themed video was Frankie Goes to Hollywood's clip for "Relax" (1983), which imparted an air of Roman imperial decadence to the goings-on at a gay bar. Lead singer Holly Johnson arrives at a nightclub in a rickshaw (an odd touch that fits snugly with "Relax's" era-inappropriate vibe) and finds himself at the center of a wild bacchanal that mingles erotic passion and ancient-world debauchery. The gay bar, in this video's estimation, is the contemporary equivalent of the gladiatorial arena, with bloodthirsty mobs, sexual frenzy, and hedonistic abandon. Johnson is roughed up by the bar's mustachioed he-man patrons and tossed onstage, where he must quickly make his peace with a tiger. In the meantime, transvestites fondle their breasts, men pump their fists in ecstasy, and the obese man who runs the show pulls off his toga entirely. "Relax" ends with Johnson getting pasted in the face by a gusher of fluid, as he intoned "when you wanna come?" on the soundtrack—a surefire method of getting your video banned from MTV, as "Relax" was.

The mindless hedonism of "Relax" was nowhere to be found in the Coil's "Tainted Love" (1985), haunted as it was by the specter of AIDS. Its deceptively placid surface covered a narrative marked by disease and impending death—one whose depredations were explicitly compared to the video's buzzing fly, trapped in a ring of honey and unable to escape. "Tainted Love" intimates a dysfunctional relationship between the bed-ridden protagonist and his smirky, leather-jacketed lothario boyfriend (whose revelation was itself treated as a plot twist by the video), but the video is primarily concerned with presenting a small glimpse into the mundane reality of the AIDS-afflicted, ending with a note about its proceeds going to AIDS research.

It would not be until the mid-1990s that explicitly gay themes would return to videos with the unabashed intensity of "Relax." In contrast to "Relax," though, these videos would walk the darker side of gay life, exchanging hedonism for despair and disillusionment. Me'Shell NdegéOcello's "Leviticus: Faggot" (1996) (directed by Kevin Bray) begins with a cruel, bigoted father booting his gay son out of the house. Cast out to wander the streets with the hustlers and the addicts, the son is watched over by Me'Shell, his ministering angel. "Leviticus: Faggot" turns the tables on the gay-bashers, casting an accusatory finger at all the prim faces and righteous churchgoing sneers of the haters. Lit differently from the rest of her surroundings, to emphasize her outsiderdom, NdegéOcello is a fierce guardian, her unblinking stare a silent accusation.

Also taking place among the down-and-outs of the urban gay underworld, Extra Fancy's "Sinnerman" (1996) concerns a Bible-thumping, fire-and-brimstone preacher, who lectures passersby (presumably on the evils of homosexuality) while his head is turned by the men who come his way. After his day's work is finished, the preacher presses his face to the glass of the window of a gay laundromat, checking out the men inside, before biting the bullet and picking up a male streetwalker. Simultaneously relieved and horrified at giving in to his urges, the preacher eventually flees from his desires, running in slow motion away from his pick-up, and toward the light.

Taking place far closer to the mainstream than NdegéOcello or Extra Fancy could ever get, George Michael's "Outside" (1998) was the British singer's first video after his arrest for soliciting a male undercover police officer for sex. Meeting his shame head-on with a good-natured sense of humor, "Outside" looks around and sees a world of furtive sexual encounters, taking place in bathroom stalls, hotel pools, and parked dumptrucks. Surveillance cameras capture all these clandestine hookups, gay and straight, and it is never long before the police come swooping in, handcuffs and batons at the ready. "Outside" is less neurotic than parodic; its point is not so much to decry police invasion of privacy as to have a good laugh at Michael's public embarrassment. Michael is the definition of a good sport here, dressing up as a cop (albeit one more indebted to the Village People than the LAPD) and partying in a mirror-balled urinal-cum-dancehall.

Turning gossip-page infamy into comedic video gold, "Outside" also demands equality of craving; gay or straight, the video tells us, we are all, at times, slaves of our desire.

Heh Heh, Beavis—You Said "Incisive Social Critique"

No one would have been more pleased by hip-hop's new state of affairs than MTV's resident early-90s dumb-asses Beavis and Butt-head, who became famous for their animated acts of violence, buffoonishness, and general stupidity. Mike Judge's teenage metalheads, clad in Metallica and AC/DC T-shirts, soon became lightning rods for the misguided and ill-informed censure of politicians after an incident in which a teenage arsonist blamed Beavis and Butt-head's antics for inspiring his incendiary acts. Lost in the shuffle of hack politicians lining up to excoriate what they little understood (elderly Senator Ernest "Fritz" Hollings of South Carolina referred to the duo as "Buffcoat and Beaver") was the fact that Beavis and Butt-head were the sharpest, pithiest, flat-out best music-video critics—ever. Beavis and Butt-head had not been the first meta-stars of music video (*Max Headroom*, that momentary fad of mid-80s cyberpunk chic, had interspersed music videos among its celebrity interviews and monologues, and Rick Moranis' *SCTV* character Gerry Todd had been a biting parody of video-show hosts), nor would they be the last (VH1's *Pop-Up Video* would have its brief moment at the epicenter of the video-satirical cultural zeitgeist after the boys' star had dimmed), but they were undoubtedly the best.

Sitting in their dismal living room, with little to do other than watch television, Beavis and Butt-head invariably spend the interludes between their adventures watching a hilarious array of half-forgotten, bizarre, fiendishly bad, and/or rocking music videos, culled from the capacious archives of MTV itself. The duo have a simple, easy to understand critical framework for apprehending any given music video: fire, cars, tattoos, hot chicks, explosions—good; college music, stories, messages—bad. *Beavis & Butt-head* borrowed extensively from *Mystery Science Theater 3000* for its snarky, talk-back-to-the-screen aesthetic, but Judge's show hones in with laser intensity on the specific weaknesses of the music video itself. Picking off the weaklings from the herd, Beavis and Butt-head are at their best when taking on the ridiculous, the puffed-up, or the sentimental, deftly deflating the pretensions of the music video at its worst. Using five words where other, more intellectually gifted critics would require a thousand, Beavis and Butt-head delight us with the efficiency of their skewerings; once heard, they are not easily forgotten. Even the bands they loved were often pierced by the nature of their enthusiasm, serving as a back-handed compliment to the metal groups (and occasional others) they worshipped. Just a few examples will suffice; of a video by Kiss, Butt-head remarks "These guys are pretty cool for a bunch of mimes"; watching a Violent Femmes video, Beavis derisively notes, "I bet these guys went to college and stuff," and Butt-head, agreeing, adds, "Yeah, and I bet they paid attention"; and best of all, after observing Amy Grant's "Baby Baby" for a number of seconds in silent, slack-jawed shock, Butt-head befuddledly asks, "Is this a Clearasil commercial?"

Beavis and Butt-head direct their ire at the act of watching videos, but the show is never threatening to its viewers for a number of reasons. First, the duo usually let us in on the joke, allowing us to also feel superior to the shlocky videos on display; and second, they are so clearly pegged as Middle American doofus metalheads, idiot savants of video, that it would be hard to be insulted, even by their scorn. Beavis and Butt-head are numbskulls, their critiques indicative of a dead-end anti-intellectual mindset that deemed anything challenging off-limits. (Butt-head on subtitles: "If I wanted to read, I'd go to school.") Judge leaves open the question of whether the show's viewers are supposed to agree with Beavis and Butt-head's critiques. Teenagers mostly said yes, cultural conservatives, horrified by their immoral antics, said no, and academics told us we were supposed to laugh at their blatant stupidity. But from the mouths of babes emerge pearls of wisdom, and Beavis and Butt-head's amused asides were often the best things anyone ever said on the subjects in question.

Lifestyles of the Rich and Rapping

As hip-hop grew wealthier, taking in an ever-increasing share of music consumers' entertainment dollars, the videos began to reflect this change of fortune, with two directors in particular emerging at the forefront of the trend. Hype Williams and Paul Hunter perfectly exemplified hip-hop's increasing embrace of the intersection of thug life and conspicuous consumption, crafting a glossy aesthetic that became a necessary accessory for the properly attired hip-hop star. Hip-hop's house directors for the 1990s, Williams and Hunter were stylistic brothers, their visual signatures similar enough to be at times interchangeable. Williams, the more celebrated of the pair, was the more polished, with nary a hair out of place in his videos. Hype was like hip-hop finishing school, his videos providing the last primp and buff to stars on the rise. Hunter's work was often a mite darker than Williams', his videos borrowing almost as much from rock-influenced directors like Mark Romanek as they did from Hype.

Williams and Hunter were the smoothest, most polished directors the genre had ever seen. Their rise coincided with, and was made possible by, hip-hop's newfound interest in living large. Spinning as smoothly as a brand-new set of twenty-two-inch chrome rims, their videos were like hip-hop episodes of *Lifestyles of the Rich and Famous*, three-minute commercials for a fantasy world of effortless pleasure and bottomless luxury. The glamour extended to the texture of the videos themselves; using glossier, richer film stock, and carefully textured lighting, each video gleamed like a freshly waxed BMW. Williams and Hunter offered hip-hop's royalty the use of their personal film studios, crowning them American culture's new icons of free-wheeling consumption. In an era when movie stars professed their preference for hybrids over Bentleys, and McDonald's over Wolfgang Puck, hip-hop's players aimed to look like money, and Williams and Hunter were their go-to directors. In its early years, the hip-hop video had been concerned with replicating the grit and authenticity of the music, but now, following the lead of MCs who rhymed "tall" with "Cristal," the equation had changed. Their videos were less about narrative, or "realness," than the baubles of success, each luxury item highlighted and fetishized.

Williams' videos in particular were odes to the trappings of wealth, a celebration of the pleasures of limousines, Cuban cigars, endless cascades of bubbly, and well-appointed mansions. In his video for LL Cool J's "Doin' It" (1996), LL bites, in tantalizingly slow motion, into a perfectly rounded, cherry-red, juicy, flawless-looking apple—Original Sin in vibrant color. Williams' camera caresses the apple's unblemished texture, its well-appointed shapeliness, giving us both its untouched splendor and the allure of the first bite. There were no mere apples in Williams' videos; even in this throwaway shot, the apple had to look like the tastiest, most beautiful apple you'd ever seen. Williams extended this aesthetic to every frame of his work, with the result that all his videos, even those with ostensibly different motivations, became propaganda films for the upwardly mobile lifestyle. In Mase's "Feel So Good" (1997), the Bad Boy scion cruises the Las Vegas Strip, where every surface gleams with an immaculate, otherworldly perfection. "Down Low" (1996), casts R. Kelly in the John Travolta role from *Pulp Fiction*, asked by his boss Mr. Big (Ronald Isley) to squire his mistress around, but "never, never to touch her." Inevitably, love blooms in secret, and R. and his girl have a steamy erotic encounter, interrupted by the arrival of Mr. Big's henchmen, who beat them without mercy. "Down Low" is a tragedy, its romance ending in separation and death, but Williams is too material a director to fully embrace tragedy. "Down Low" loves the trimmings of success, from the beautiful cars to the classy mansions, too absorbed in its contemplation of the good life to truly accept its own unhappy ending. Even the grittier videos, like Nas' "If I Ruled the World" (1996) or DMX's "Get at Me Dog" (1998), feature Grit™, a glossy simulacrum of the realistic texture hip-hop videos had once specialized in. Each Hype video was like a James Bond movie, its intended plot of less interest to moviegoers than the shiny toys used along the way. Williams' particular genius was his ability to see the world as brighter, glitzier, and lovelier than it actually was. This was also his limitation; there was something profoundly odd about Nas, crucified like Jesus in his video "Hate Me Now" (1999), looking quite so radiantly pristine.

Williams also made a career out of his embrace of the fish-eye, a wide-angle lens that foreshortens the center of the frame and distorts its edges. Videos like Busta Rhymes' "Woo-Hah! Got You All in Check" (1996) and "Put Your Hands Where My Eyes Could See" (1997) make liberal use of the fish-eye, turning the already-energetic Busta into a walking special effect. The fish-eye was a captivating effect, but it also marked Williams' interest in artfully manipulating reality toward a desired end, a goal that his repeated use of slow-motion, lap dissolves, and crisp, supersaturated color only serve to underscore. In "Woo-Hah!" Rhymes is ringmaster of a one-man carnival, dressed in outlandish costumes and mugging shamelessly for the camera. Williams uses the fish-eye to accentuate Rhymes' hyperactivity, each limb and digit of his body bounding off in a different direction like a live-action cartoon. "Put Your Hands Where My Eyes Could See" further accentuates Busta's taste for absurdity, casting him as African royalty enjoying the fruits of privilege on an average day in the palace. The entire video lopes to the staggered beat of the song's drums, Williams picking up and dropping the African theme as it pleases him. Cannibals dance around a campfire, King Busta's mistresses compete for the honor of sharing his bed, and a team of servants are dispatched to brush His Royal Highness' teeth.

Working with a wider range of clients, it was no surprise that Paul Hunter's work was stylistically more adventurous than that of his brother-in-arms. Hunter was a cinematic chameleon, able to adapt rock video's aggro sensibility for a new generation of upwardly mobile hip-hop performers. His clip for Mack 10 and Ice Cube's "Only in California" (1997) looks like an interpolation of Mark Romanek's video for Nine Inch Nails' "Closer," crammed full of female storm troopers on the march, Teutonic scientists witnessing a series of gruesome medical experiments, and Ice Cube trapped inside a spinning steel cage. The unsettling, Victorian-themed tableaux (Snoop Dogg dressed as a top-hatted English gentleman, an ostrich running loose in an elegant living room, Mack 10 suspended in midair by a knot of tangled black cables) make clear just how closely Hunter had studied Romanek's work, especially his video for NIN's "The Perfect Drug." Hunter was one of the first major video directors to form a visual aesthetic out of imperfection, flawlessly rendered; his videos are dotted with scratched frames, out-of-place leaders, warped colors, and herky-jerky images. "Only in California" and Puff Daddy and the Family's "It's All About the Benjamins" (1997) are both speckled with stray leaders, as if we were unexpectedly trapped in a movie theater run by an amateurish projectionist; and "Benjamins" is shot on a grainy, greenish stock that brought to mind the likely view from behind a pair of night-vision goggles. Hunter's work artfully sold its own (extremely purposeful) imperfections as beautiful, and the director made a fetish out of damaging his footage—witness his video for Lenny Kravitz's "Fly Away" (1998), whose shaky frames and distorted colors resemble a mangled VHS cassette.

When appropriate, though, Hunter could be just as sumptuous as Williams. His video for Lil' Kim, Christina Aguilera, Mya, and Pink's "Lady Marmalade" (winner of the MTV Video Music Award for Video of the Year in 2001) pours on the *Moulin Rouge* frills, possibly even outdoing Baz Luhrmann's musical spectacle in its crushed-velvet lavishness. Missy Elliott is the hawker/MC at a Victorian-era theatrical performance, introducing each member of "Lady Marmalade's" impromptu quartet. Dressed in fin-de-siècle nightwalker fashion, each of the women cavorts in her own personal boudoir, stalking the boards and stretching their vocal cords. Hunter enjoyed borrowing from Hollywood history for his videos, making reference to *The Wild Bunch* (Enrique Iglesias' "Bailamos"), *The Hudsucker Proxy* (Eminem's "The Way I Am"), *Singles* (TLC's "Unpretty"), and the James Bond oeuvre (Britney Spears and Madonna's "Me Against the Music"). Hunter also went to the adventure-flick well repeatedly, with the Notorious B.I.G.'s "Hypnotize" (1997) joined by Busta Rhymes' "Turn It Up/Fire It Up" (1998) and Mariah Carey's "Honey" (1997) as Michael Bay–damaged blockbuster clips. Hunter's abiding fascination with scientific experimentation and technology were regular motifs in his work as well, turning up everywhere from "Only in California" to Marilyn Manson's "Dope Show" (1998) to Jennifer Lopez's "If You Had My Love" (1999).

Perhaps the most famous of Hunter's videos is the now-iconic clip for "Hypnotize." Biggie and his sidekick Puff Daddy gallivant around the world in a series of fast cars and motorboats, outgunning the police while maintaining the presence of mind to look fabulous every step of the way. "Hypnotize" borrows liberally from the conventions and aesthetic sensibilities of the Hollywood action-adventure film, filling the screen with surveillance-camera snapshots, green columns of streaming data, and speeding motorcycles, SUVs, and motorboats. Biggie and Puffy are lovable Scarfaces for the late 90s, effortlessly avoiding the long arm of the law and making their escape to the tropical-island happy ending familiar from countless jewel-heist flicks. This style of video became such a cliché that Spike Jonze directed a hilarious parody of it, with remarkably similar-looking pre-adolescent stand-ins for Biggie and Puffy sipping champagne in a Jacuzzi in the Notorious B.I.G.'s "Sky's the Limit."

It should come as no surprise, then, that even when Hunter chose to make a minimalist video for D'Angelo, the product that emerged, while lovely and arresting, was like "Nothing Compares 2 U" arriving at the far end of a game of Telephone, slightly garbled in the transmission. "Untitled (How Does It Feel)" (2000) is a lush slice of man-porn, one where a rigorous aesthetic is linked to an understanding that the number of square inches of nudity revealed in a video bore a direct correlation to the number of units sold.

The video begins with an exceptionally tight close-up of an ear, slowly panning down that appendage to a pair of eyes, and then further to a goatee-surrounded mouth. Hunter's camera was tightly reined in, only revealing a small portion of D'Angelo's body at any given time, creating a pent-up demand for a fuller view. Hunter, normally a proponent of rapid-fire cuts, here restricts himself to a single shot, and one with minimal, slow-motion camera movement. It takes nearly a minute for Hunter's camera to begin zooming out, pulling out to a full close-up of the singer's face, then farther out to a medium close-up of face and chest, ending with a shot whose bottom is tethered to the farthest nether reaches of D'Angelo's torso.

"Untitled (How Does It Feel)" is nudity of two kinds; that of the nudity of the singer singing his song unfettered and unencumbered, and the nudity of the unclothed body, now subject to the prurient gaze of the spectator. The former attests to the video's genuineness, providing filmed proof of the singer's physical effort in singing. D'Angelo being naked, we can watch the play of his stomach muscles, heaving inward to take in breath, and pushing outward to expel air in the effort of singing. The latter is a product of Hunter's roots in glossiness, where even the minimalist aesthetic becomes an opportunity to provide elegant lighting to D'Angelo's torso, taking in the crucifix pinned between his pectorals as he simulates being on the receiving end of a blowjob. The camera repeatedly teases with the singer's body, juking in the direction of his most private parts without actually revealing anything onscreen that would be inappropriate for MTV. Updating "Nothing Compares 2 U," Hunter chooses to provide O'Connor's unfiltered expression of romantic ennui with a little of that Hollywood razzle-dazzle, and a dollop of populist beefcake.

Magnificent Megalomania

Legal and commercial problems notwithstanding, Michael Jackson spent the first half of the 1990s acting as if he was still the world's biggest pop star, and when it came to music videos, the claim remained legitimate. It was only Jackson who could turn the premiere of each of his videos into a major event, debuting them on network television in prime time. The songs may not have been hits at the rarefied level of "Thriller" or "Billie Jean," but videos like "Black or White," "In the Closet," "Jam," and "Earth Song" were nonetheless epic in scope and ambition. Switching between his three well-defined video modes (carnal loverman, globe-healing diplomat, and action star), Jackson maintained his position as the world's foremost pop icon, in part through a savvy mobilization of video as a counteroffensive to bad publicity. That that effort ultimately crashed and burned, and Jackson's fame turned to notoriety of the worst sort, owed less to the videos, which are dazzling in their own right, than the effect of the King of Pop's bizarre, possibly criminal, behavior.

Reuniting Jackson with John Landis, director of "Thriller," "Black or White" (1991) pegs Michael as the world's pop star, stripped of all specificity in his quest to represent the citizens of the globe entire. "Black or White" drops Jackson in among the tribal warriors of the African bush as they stalk their animal prey. Jackson plays air guitar in the tall grass as the painted warriors serve as backup dancers, then the entire group makes their way across the screen and onto a waiting sound stage. The Africans disappear, replaced in short order by Indian women with metallic headdresses, Native Americans shooting guns and parading around Jackson's raised platform, and balalaika dancers performing in the shadow of the Kremlin. Jackson is the world's chosen performer, a fact crystallized by the video's final two sequences. In the first, Jackson sings on a platform with an ornamental torch, and a slow zoom out reveals him standing on the Statue of Liberty, in the harbor of an imaginary global city that includes the Acropolis, Taj Mahal, Eiffel Tower, and Big Ben within its confines. Once it has been established that Michael Jackson is the people's pop star, "Black or White" takes an extra step and proclaims that everyone, in some way, is themselves Michael Jackson. Using digital morphing technology, then the height of FX trickery, a series of faces metamorphose into each other, a black woman becoming a white woman with flaming red hair, an Asian woman becoming a blond-haired surfer dude, with Jackson himself an integral component in the tableau of quicksilver metamorphoses.

The other videos from Jackson's *Dangerous* album sought to dazzle the old-fashioned way—with celebrity. "Remember the Time" (1992) features an Egyptian motif and an array of famous faces, including Eddie Murphy, Iman, Magic Johnson, and the members of the Pharcyde. Murphy is a bored pharaoh desperate for entertainment, and Jackson the magician-performer who captivates his wife Iman, sending the pharaoh into paroxysms of jealousy. "Jam" (1992) is a meeting of the two most famous African-American men in the world—Jackson and Michael Jordan—with each teaching the other something of their carefully honed wizardry. "In the Closet" (1992) turned to the old master of video sensuality, Herb Ritts, and model Naomi Campbell for a dash of the sensual heat so rarely found in Jackson's videos. Campbell's phenomenally luscious body is accentuated here by her skimpy white underthings and by Ritts' use of canted frames, which encased off-kilter close-ups of Campbell's chest, her bare stomach, and her crotch. "In the Closet" exists primarily to express its slack-jawed admiration for Campbell's physical charms, and by extension beef up Jackson's shaky heterosexual bona fides. Jackson and Campbell may slither around each other, and their hands may grope each other's silhouetted forms, but any heat in the video came from Ritts' expert craftsmanship and Campbell's voluptuousness, with little added by Jackson's wooden impression of sexual desire.

After the sci-fi gloss of "Scream" (1995), his duet with sister Janet, directed by Mark Romanek (see below), and the icky sensuality of "You Are Not Alone" (1995), in which Michael canoodled with then-wife Lisa Marie Presley, Jackson returned to the messianic fervor of "Man in the Mirror" with the environmentalist message of "Earth Song" (1995), directed by Nicholas Brandt. "Earth Song" is almost childishly simple, both in technique and implication, but it is surprisingly moving nonetheless. Beginning with harrowing imagery of environmental degradation—its shots of dead, de-tusked elephants, bare forests, and wrecked cities painted a gloomy metallic grey—"Earth Song" replenishes the exhausted earth by that oldest of cinematic tricks—running its footage backward. As Jackson falls to the ground, imploring us to realize that "this crying earth is weeping," the rest of the world joins him on their knees, from African farmers to Australian aborigines to suffering Yugoslavs, their hands picking up clumps of earth and letting it seep through their fingers. These tactile shots are soon followed by an almost-imperceptible backward motion, in which the earth itself rises back up into its supplicants' hands, and those on their knees rise once again. His arms spread as if to summon all the cosseted forces of history, grabbing onto two trees to hold strong in the face of the impending cleansing wind, Jackson stomps his foot on the ground, the camera registering the motion as the stride of a colossus. With everyone across the globe looking up, as if to register what God hath wrought, the earth magnificently rights itself, felled trees returning to their stumps, dead elephants regenerating their tusks and returning to life, the rumble of tanks receding, replaced by a glorious stillness. Dolphins swim freely, animals roam the land in splendid profusion, and the forest returns to its primeval fullness, with one last tree returning into place before a final shot of mist settling over an untouched world.

"Earth Song" is a fantasy of environmentalist regression, of erasing humanity's ugly footprint and restoring the earth to its prior perfection. It is also a fantasy of Michael Jackson's omnipotence, capable with a song and a stomp of waking a sleeping citizenry from their environmentally destructive nightmare. "Earth Song" is cheesy, hokey, absurd, and simplistic; it is also phenomenally effective propaganda. It would effectively be Jackson's last video hurrah.

Of all of music video's epic productions, of all its pretensions to glamour and glitz, none are quite so gloriously overblown as Guns N' Roses' magnificently melodramatic trilogy of videos from their 1991 double album *Use Your Illusion*. Even "Thriller" paled in comparison with Axl Rose and Co.'s megalomaniac trio of clips, which tell a discombobulated, symbolically fraught tale of lost love and shattered dreams. Having risen to take hold of the mythical "Biggest Band in the World" title after the enormous success of their debut album, *Appetite for Destruction*, Guns N' Roses attempted to make a series of videos that would match the band's outsized ambitions in their gigantitude. Film critic Stuart Klawans coined the term "film folly" to refer to hugely ambitious films like D.W. Griffith's *Intolerance* and Mikhail Kalatozov's *I Am Cuba*— epic productions stemming from vast budgets and gargantuan egos. Film follies, by their very nature, are always doomed to fail at some level, but their ambitiousness also renders them uniquely fascinating, and anomalous, the white elephants of film history. Guns N' Roses' videos "Don't Cry," "November Rain," and "Estranged" meet the definition of film folly beyond a shadow of a doubt. Where the average video confined itself to a narrow band of locations, and a modest budget, the Guns N' Roses trilogy ballooned to epic size, with all the trappings of a Hollywood blockbuster: multiple locations, fancy helicopter and crane shots, oversized length, and outsized emotion. Their enormousness made them ripe for parody (a 1994 *Spin* article poked fun at their tangled, near-incoherent symbolism), but they remain marvels of the video's ambitions to cultural significance and emotional heft. And with the ever-shrinking promotional budgets for videos in the new century, it is unlikely that their equal will ever be seen again. If the early era of music video was a gathering of strength, moving toward ever-bigger, ever-grander productions, these Guns N' Roses videos were the form's apex, the high point in a curve that swung downward in their aftermath toward the smaller, more economical, less heroically ambitious videos of today.

Assisting the band in bringing their vision onto the screen was director Andy Morahan, formerly best known for helming those celebrations of artful stubble, George Michael's "Father Figure" and "Faith." First to emerge was "Don't Cry" (1991), an enigmatic tale of love's dying fall. "Don't Cry" stars Rose and then-girlfriend Stephanie Seymour as a bickering couple whose squabbles echo with the sounds of impending madness and death. Present trauma is haunted by past joys; after Rose and Seymour drunkenly fight, the camera pans left to take in a picture of the formerly happy couple, picnicking in a cemetery. In the next scene, a somber Rose drives by the cemetery in his limousine, touring the far reaches of his own memory. Rose finds himself thrashing in the water, tugged down into the depths, toward death, by Seymour. He survives, but not without sustaining serious damage to his psyche; when we see him next, Axl is in a bare white room in patients' garb, distractedly mumbling to himself. In the meantime, guitarist Slash has his own female problems. Driving the coastline with his lady friend, she yells and curses at him, and he calmly veers his car over the cliff.

Death is always followed by rebirth in "Don't Cry"; after presumptively dying in a car crash, Slash magically reappears at the top of the mountain to play his solo, and Axl returns to the cemetery later in the video to visit his own grave. Tainted love is a form of death here, wrecking egos and poisoning even the charmed existences of big-time rock stars. "Don't Cry" dramatizes the multiplication of the psyche, with several Axls on the loose, talking to each other and suffering different fates. Where one Axl lives, bruised and battered, another is trapped under his own gravestone, literally buried alive. Like the bird that is his companion underground, this Axl is desperate to get out, and unable to find a way. "Don't Cry" provides a solitary ray of hope at its conclusion, the rebirth implied in the shots of a baby undergoing baptism which bookend the video promising escape from the seemingly eternal cycle of psychic pain and degradation.

As "Don't Cry" wryly notes in a final intertitle, "There's a lot goin' on." The next video, "November Rain" (1992), is equally dense, continuing backward and forward with the same plot, returning to Axl and Stephanie's wedding, and finding the roots of later tragedy in that moment of happiness. Death once again lurks around the corner, with a small crisis (rain interrupting the wedding) connecting inexorably to a larger one (Stephanie's death). "November Rain" is surreal in its illogic, with love and death like two links in a tautly formed chain. It is also melodrama in high dudgeon, simultaneously moving and supremely silly. The video opens with Rose in bed, shakily popping pills. Sitting at a piano in a spartan-looking rural church, Rose settles in to play before his surroundings disappear and he is left at his piano in the desert. Back in church, Seymour walks down the aisle, resplendent in her wedding-day finery, as Axl, dressed in a bolero jacket and skintight pants, nervously waits at the altar. As the happy couple exits the church, Slash, distressed, walks down the aisle and plays his wailing guitar solo in the church's dooryard while the camera swoops around and above him. Melodrama always teeters on the edge of inanity, and "November Rain" is no exception. Snickers often break out at the vision of Slash's seething (possibly homoerotic) jealousy, as expressed in his keening guitar solo, but "November Rain" does not mind. It is too much in love with its own swooning grandiosity, its opulence rendering all questions of taste entirely moot.

The wedding party moves on to a reception at a handsome home. Axl and Stephanie cut their cake, and he gives her the knife to lick. Rose's bandmates click glasses, and an older couple take a turn around the dance floor. The gentle moment is interrupted, though, by a sudden rain shower. Flowers fall into a puddle, a drunken man in a tuxedo slips and falls, and band members dive under a table for protection. In time with the song's final orchestral swoop, a partygoer dives through the cake, destroying it, and a glass of red wine spills like blood on the white tablecloth.

Much like in "Don't Cry," small-fry problems grow into tragedies, for reasons beyond reason. The cake, symbol of their love, is crushed, and the virginal purity of the tablecloth has been stained a bloody red. The fragile, unblemished order of the wedding has been disrupted, and in its place, death arrives with inexorable promptness. Rose appears next in a disheveled state, staring up at the sky as a priest eulogizes his wife, who lies in an open casket at his side. Her casket is brought to the gravesite, and mourners open umbrellas to shield themselves from the rain. In a flashback, Seymour is seen at the wedding, tossing her bouquet into a crowd of anxious women. Coursing through the air, the white flowers turn blood-red and land with a thud on her own casket. Axl wakes up sweating, back in his bedroom, and is seen in the last shot back at his wife's grave, crying as the flowers change colors again, fading from red to pink. Weddings become funerals, and the epic love story becomes a tragedy.

"Estranged," the last and best entry in the trilogy, returns to the theme of rebirth, emphasizing water's qualities of rejuvenation and tying the strands of all three videos together for a cautiously optimistic coda. In "November Rain," water, in the form of rain, was a harbinger of tragedy and death, but here, water reprises its role in "Don't Cry," as a life-giving element. GN'R's drive to monomania takes on enormous proportions here, with "Estranged" (1993) running close to ten minutes in length. Opening with the dictionary definition of the word "illusion" posted onscreen, "Estranged" finds the police breaking into Axl's house, guns drawn, stretchers at the ready, as he cowers in a corner. A toy dinosaur catches his eye, and he flashes back to an image of his son playing in the grass. Meanwhile, fans stream into a stadium in time-lapse photographic shots. Axl lays recumbent on a couch, and his double sits up, holding his head in his hands. He takes a shower while fully clothed, and he sits on the floor as the water runs. "Estranged" contrasts the glory of the stage, where we see the band perform, with the gloom of real life. Axl is forced by the police to leave his family's home, and the camera takes a long look at the giant crucifix hanging on the wall. Axl, too, presumably, feels crucified by his existence, and by the ignominious end of his relationship with Stephanie. The trilogy returns time and again to the notion of illusions, with the joys of love and companionship repeatedly revealed for the mirages they are.

Water is a comfort and a danger here, and with the element present in nearly every frame, "Estranged" proposes a means of survival within harsh, unforgiving nature via the symbol of the dolphin. The dolphin, swimming with effortless grace through the ocean, represents a resolution to the traumas of "Don't Cry," "November Rain," and the first half of "Estranged." The video's imagery turns liquid, and we suddenly notice dolphins everywhere: on the trunk of a car, on television screens, in the middle of the Sunset Strip, which has turned into a river. In a smooth pan, "Estranged" moves from the darkness of the Strip to an ocean scene, where an aerial shot takes in a giant tanker scuttling through the water. Axl, prowling the ship's deck, leaps into the water. Echoing the famous joke about the believer in God who turns down human assistance in the midst of a catastrophe, Axl stubbornly refuses help. Thrown a life preserver, he tosses it back; offered a helping hand by a man in a nearby boat, he ignores it. Waves buffet his head, and he sinks down into the depths, but unlike in "Don't Cry," the ocean is no longer the preserve of death, but rather of renewed life. During the dolphin-call guitar solo of the song's interlude, Rose swims with the cetaceans, riding one up to the surface. Slash also ascends, walking on water for his solo. A rescue helicopter flies over the water, and finding Axl thrashing about, pulls him out. In the video's last shot, Axl wears a bathrobe with a dolphin emblazoned on the lapel, and his band's trilogy fades to black with one final message: "Lose Your Illusions."

Axl emerges from the trilogy of videos older, sadder—and wiser. Having had and lost his love, he saves himself, and although no longer in possession of his illusions, he lives to see another day. Loss is the through-line of the trilogy—the loss of separation, of death, of illusions. For all their bombast, "Don't Cry," "November Rain," and "Estranged" are deeply adult in their evocation of wounded spirits, their summoning of the bittersweet and the tragic a far cry from the fantasy wish-fulfillment of the average music video. Guns N' Roses' grandiose ambitions, which led them to release two overstuffed albums on the same day, and Rose's tendency toward outsized displays of emotion, culminated in this trio of clips, the biggest and brightest follies in music-video history. Easy to disdain, but hard to hate, "Don't Cry," "November Rain," and "Estranged" are the epitome of the music video's crass magnificence.

Along with Guns N' Roses, the rock band most responsible for the epic-ification of the music video was Aerosmith. Their move toward jumbo-sized, Hollywood-style clips began with 1987's "Janie's Got a Gun," directed by David Fincher, but reached its apotheosis in the trio of videos from the band's 1993 album *Get a Grip*: "Cryin'," "Amazing," and "Crazy." "Janie's" melded some good ol' sex-and-violence with a quasi-empathetic message about domestic violence. Fincher's video cuts backward and forward in time, combining suburban ennui with the tang of looming violence. "Janie's Got a Gun" is not a bad video, although a bit naïve in its depiction of sexual abuse. More troubling, though, was the video's inability to serve its clients' interests. Aerosmith, the formerly party-hearty Boston rockers, may have written the song, but Fincher's video left them without much role to play, and the socially conscious elements of the clip feel grafted on. "Janie's Got a Gun" is a decent video, but the wrong choice for Aerosmith.

A far better fit for the band was their work with director Marty Callner, who gave the aging rockers a youthful glow with an injection of jailbait sex appeal. "Livin' on the Edge" (1993) makes a half-hearted stab at social significance, with Edward Furlong as a teenager wrestling with his conscience over an illicit gun. In what is intended as the video's climactic scene, he reaches into his backpack after being pushed around by a bully, and pulls out—a sandwich, to placate his hostile classmate. In actuality, the rest of the video is far more memorable, consisting primarily of Steven Tyler and his bandmates playing dress-up. Tyler sings with half his face painted black with gold accents (a lighting trick done with makeup), stands nude while cupping his manhood in his hands, wears a live peacock on his head, and outfits himself in a Weimar-era *Cabaret* top hat and cigarette holder. The video documents a world in crisis, with school violence, teenage hooliganism, and even sexual impropriety making appearances, but "Livin' on the Edge" is a video far better at partying than pondering.

Knowing where their strengths lay, Callner's next video for Aerosmith concentrated on oozing sex appeal, seasoning it with a hefty dose of teenage angst and dysfunctional relationships. Teen video vixen Alicia Silverstone made her MTV debut in "Cryin'" (1993) as a headstrong beauty who refuses to be tamed by her asshole boyfriend (the suitably slimy Stephen Dorff). Opening with Alicia poised over a freeway overpass, ready to jump, "Cryin'" flashes back to the early days of her relationship with Dorff. Their idyll is short-lived; Silverstone grows annoyed with Dorff at the movies, and when he smirkingly pushes her off him as she straddles him in their car, she punches him, kicks him out of the car, and drives off. Alicia leaves the car by the side of the road, dropping the keys on the ground, and in the image that sold the video to countless sexually deprived teenagers worldwide, took a pair of jeans out of the car's trunk, pulled them on, and stripped off her sundress.

Silverstone walking the highway in a tight white tank top and jeans was an indelible, iconic image of ripe teenage sexuality that intentionally overwhelmed the video's ostensible narrative. Back to the video's start, where Dorff arrives in the hopes of talking her down from her perch. Exhibiting the same weasely mien as before, he holds his hands up, palms out, at his shoulders, in a "what's the deal?" fashion, and gestures at her to come down. Alicia rocks on her heels, as if testing out the idea of actually going through with it, and then jumps, falling in slow motion. It is only at this point that we see the bungee cord she is attached to, and realize this mock-suicide has been an elaborate prank, played on her uncaring boyfriend and a hostile world. She hangs from the bungee cord, giving him the finger (blurred out for MTV) and looking triumphant, and even Dorff shakes his head in amusement. "Cryin'" was a video about women (and teenagers) ascendant, triumphing over adversity and looking sexy while doing it.

Their next video dropped even the pretense of social significance, keeping the sex and grafting it onto a techno-futurist narrative. In addition, "Amazing" (1993) reflects on its predecessor, turning the narrative of "Cryin'" explicitly into fantasy wish-fulfillment for pasty-faced computer geeks. A long-haired teenager with a monitor tan pulls up the "Cryin'" video on his computer and sets up a camera to record himself. Before inserting himself into the narrative via virtual reality, though, a few tweaks are in order; he makes sure to tighten his digital stand-in's chin, and he places a pair of sunglasses over his eyes for the appropriate veneer of cool. Slipping on a virtual-reality helmet and glove, he enters the fray, riding his chopper into the desert and picking up Alicia Silverstone. Sneering at his offer of a helmet, she hops on the back of her motorcycle, but as they progress through the desert, she makes her way up front, slithering her way onto his lap, her legs wrapped around his torso as they make out. While vigorously exerting his glove-sheathed arm, he knocks over his soda, with the liquid spurting out onto the keyboard. Needless to say, Alicia is disgusted by his virtual premature ejaculation and pulls away. Luckily for our geek, this isn't live, it's Memorex; he hits the "Replay" button and starts again. Having survived the makeout session without any unseemly spills, he smokes a virtual post-coital cigarette, and the duo hitch a ride on a Great War–era plane, then air-surf off its wing. At the close of their adventure, he prints out a photo of Alicia as a memento. In the video's final scene, and surprise ending, we see his face on the computer screen, and Silverstone printing out his picture, with a satisfied, half-guilty smile. "Amazing" posits male fantasy as female fantasy, asking us to believe that this video dream girl spent her nights in front of her computer, dreaming of adventure with the president of the AV club. As Silverstone famously said elsewhere: "As if!" The closing twist of "Amazing" may lack a shred of believability, but its tech-savvy, some ten years later, glows with the light of inadvertent nostalgia.

"Amazing" gussies up teen sexuality with computers, but its clever application of the technological motif, and its sly sense of humor, save it from softcore hell. The last member of the Aerosmith-Alicia trilogy reaches for no such hybrid, presenting its sex straight up. There was something more than a little icky about Tyler offering his teenage daughter Liv as fodder for the video's barely-legal sex appeal, but "Crazy" (1994) is effective entertainment, if not quite as much fun as its two predecessors. The video opens with a Catholic schoolgirl heading to the bathroom and climbing out the window. During her escape, her skirt gets caught on the window's handle, giving us a long look at her black panties. Unsurprisingly, it is Silverstone once again, but this time she is joined by Liv Tyler, who jumps into her convertible as she is pulling out from the school's parking lot. Having stripped off their button-down shirts, the duo pull into a gas station, where an old man leers at them, watching Liv's wiggling behind as she pumps gas, and a *Reality Bites*–style slacker behind the cash register watches impassively as they steal everything in sight. He only perks up when he receives their gift—a roll of photos shot in the store's booth that presumably, based on his double-take and their readjusting of their clothes as they leave, are of them in various states of undress.

Their next adventure takes them to a talent show, where Liv does a pole dance as Alicia, dressed in male drag, watches. Onstage, Liv does a fairly accurate imitation of her father's moves, spitting, kicking her leg out, and fluffing her hair in a manner impressively similar to the Aerosmith lead singer. In their final adventure, the girls pick up a hunky farmer as he works the fields, convincing him to go skinny-dipping with them, and then stealing his clothes. He chases after them and catches up to their car, leaping nude into their laps. "Crazy" lacks its predecessors' sense of future-forward modernity, appearing to take place in a nostalgic corn-fed wonderland. Aerosmith was undoubtedly guilty of selling their videos on Silverstone's back, pimping out her nascent sexuality as their prime selling point, but they possess enough wit, vigor, and feminist energy to justify their lubriciousness. These videos work because of their old-fashioned narrative drive more than anything else; they are stories that hold viewers' attention in fairly uncomplicated fashion. Unlike the Guns N' Roses trilogy, too, they did not require a Ph.D for exegesis.

Going Small(er)

For Michael Jackson, and other 90s video stars, nothing succeeded like excess. Believing that bigger was indeed better, megastars like Jackson, Madonna, Guns N' Roses, and Dr. Dre made the early and mid-1990s the golden age of the epic video. The scope and expense of videos like "November Rain," "Earth Song," and "California Love" was large enough to make merely large clips like TLC's "Waterfalls" (1995) seem positively diminutive. "Waterfalls," directed by F. Gary Gray, illustrated the song's bittersweet morality tale with two stories of urban tragedy, all buffed to a futuristic, silvery glow. In the first, a delinquent son abandons his mother for a life hustling on the streets; in the second, a lothario is charmed out of using a condom during a sexual encounter. Both end in disaster, with the wayward son followed to a crack spot and a run-in with gang-bangers by the shade of his mourning mother, and the foolish lover haunted by the rapid-fire post-coital display of his lover's past lovers in her picture frame. Even after realizing the error of their ways, it is simply too late to undo the past; attempting to hug his mother as she passes on the street, he passes right through her, a living corpse haunting the city. Meanwhile, the misguided woman of the latter tale sits at her bedside as her lover's picture fades to white-ness, soon to be joined by the woman herself, leaving only a condom. The women of TLC hover over the video as ministering angels, liquid beings levitat-ing on water and watching over the lives of its characters.

Across the Atlantic, the superstar girl group the Spice Girls had begun with a cheap, entertaining video for their smash hit "Wannabe" (1996), with the five women dashing into a posh restaurant and wreaking havoc with the stuffy clientele before escaping via public bus. But by the time of their second video, "Say You'll Be There" (1996), the group were superstars-in-training, complete with stage names ("Trixie Firecracker," "Midnight Miss Suki") for the faux widescreen kung-fu epic they appeared to be starring in. The Spice Girls' male counterparts in Take That made a similar rapid-fire transition, from the dingy boxing-gym homoeroticism of "It Only Takes a Minute" (1992) to the cine-matographic sumptuousness of "Back for Good" (1995).

On the whole, though, big-name British acts, especially those emerging from the 1990s Britpop movement, favored small-scale videos. Oasis mostly eschewed fancy scenarios for live clips and clunky, deliberately amateurish videos like "Live Forever" (1994), in which drummer Tony McCarroll is given a premature burial, and "Cigarettes & Alcohol" (1994), a concert video enamored with the band's groupies, who gather backstage to vegetate and booze. Cutting corners even fur-ther, all of Pulp's mid-90s videos (mostly directed by Pedro Rohanyi) seemed to take place in the very same disco. "Common People" (1995), "Disco 2000" (1995), and "Mis-Shapes" (1995) were tributes to the have-nots anchored by preening lead singer Jarvis Cocker, often rendered as a black-and-white cutout. In "Common People," Cocker engaged in a standoff with the slumming wealthy girl who wants to borrow his lower-class cred for an evening, talking intimately to the camera like a trusted confidante. "Disco 2000" was even more arch—a gar-ish-looking tribute to the hideous styles of the 1970s, and a pocket portrait of life at a third-rate British disco, with all of its suppressed emotion conveyed by the subtitles running at the bottom of the screen.

Jabbing in similar fashion at the hollowness of English conventionality, the satirical pop group Blur also favored cheesy, deliberately unimpressive-looking backdrops for its comic videos. Like Pulp's Cocker, Blur's lead singer Damon Albarn served as court jester and chief instigator for his band's videos, riling up the clueless and privileged with his schoolboy charm and occasionally demonic grin. Even when, for a brief moment, Blur rivaled Oasis for the title of biggest band in Britain, their videos remained enjoyably flimsy. This was not necessarily for the worst; what videos like "Country House" (1995) (directed by Damien Hirst), "Parklife" (1994), and "Charmless Man" (1996) (directed by Jamie Thraves) lacked in pictorial splendor, they made up for in wit. "Charmless Man" in particular was another example of Thraves' specialty—the mystery video (seen to best effect in Radiohead's "Just," of the same year). A polished, supremely confident master of the universe type is stalked by Damon and the band, his veneer of assurance steadily cracking under the weight of their relentless reappearance. The video begins with a panicked man running through a desolate urban alley, but it is not until the video's end that we realize the runner and our protagonist are one and the same. "Charmless Man" ends with Albarn smiling into the camera, his off-kilter grin proof of his, and the band's, dedication to chasing down the sacred cows all around them and reducing them to metaphoric tatters.

With a similar storyteller's feel for narrative to "Waterfalls," and concomitant fascination with death, Tom Petty and the Heartbreakers' "Mary Jane's Last Dance" (1993), directed by Keir McFarlane, stars Kim Basinger as a fetching dead woman and Petty as a morgue attendant bewitched into kidnapping her corpse and bringing her home. Eschewing the usual leading-man heroics, Petty is a creepy, disturbing figure in "Mary Jane's," a sexual deviant and fetishist of the kind you wouldn't invite home to Mama. Having stolen her out of the morgue from under a suspicious security guard's watchful gaze, Petty dresses her in an old-fashioned lacy dress (has he been saving the dress for just such an occasion?), seats her at a long table festooned with red candles, and drag-dances her across the candle-strewn floor, careful to hold her lifeless body up as they swivel around. Even fetishists must ultimately admit the impossibility of their desires, and once Petty despairs of keeping her head from flopping over when propped up on the couch, he takes her out to the lake, and with a heavy heart, drops her body into the water. Basinger's face, immobile as ever (has there ever been a better match of actress and role in music video history?), achieves a certain placidity as she sinks momentarily under the waves, before popping back up, her eyes wide open in death.

"Mary Jane's Last Dance" zeroes in on a single troubled figure with verve and a certain dark charm, while another literate video, R.E.M.'s "Everybody Hurts" (1993), directed by Jake Scott, extends its gaze to the trapped figures of an urban traffic jam. Returning to the long-familiar notion of the music video as silent film, the subtitles of "Everybody Hurts" illuminate the wayward thoughts and deeply held secrets coursing around its characters' minds. The interior monologues of "Everybody Hurts" are bittersweet, with intimations of heartbreak, loss, and death echoing from person to person. These stray senti-ments, grabbed from unseen, presumably longer interior monologues, conjure up myriad distinct thought processes, making "Everybody Hurts" an extraordi-narily dense, rich music video. The bumper-to-bumper gridlock both sum-mons up these thoughts, offering its drivers and passengers a moment of reflection, and symbolizes their situations, caught as they are in the grip of uncontrollable larger forces. These forces are primarily personal, not political. A teenager gripping a rosary thinks, "They're going to miss me"; a man standing on an overpass tears pages out of a Bible, accompanied by the thought "They that sow in tears shall reap in joy"; a mustachioed trucker keeps his thoughts to a pithy "17 years"; and, most touchingly, an old codger with piercing blue eyes accepts the fact that "She's gone," blinking before saying, "Goodbye."

The thought-subtitles are replaced by the song's lyrics for the chorus, when lead singer Michael Stipe gets out of his car and, looking forward mournfully, sings while distractedly hugging himself. Eventually, all the motorists exit their cars, and in a mixture of crane and ground-level shots, "Everybody Hurts" shows them escaping, if only momentarily, their prisons. A blurry television report describes how "they just, they just got out and walked . . . police cannot find anyone!" over an aerial shot of abandoned cars. Scott's video works as a tale of secular grace, achieved via the mercy of R.E.M.'s magisterial song, and as an allegory of the Rapture. The breathless reportage about the vanished motorists, combined with the subtly religious tone of many of the characters' silent appeals, posits a God offering respite from pain to some of His suffering souls. Playing a role similar to TLC in "Waterfalls," R.E.M., and especially Stipe, are intermediary figures here, leading the exodus from automotive prisons, and as the authors and performers of this prayer for relief.

Jake Scott's work was often surprisingly spiritual, from the hovering angels and mystical cycle of birth and death dramatized in Live's "Lightning Crashes" (1994) to the levitating bodies of Smashing Pumpkins' "Disarm" (1994). His videos were receptacles for pop religion: comforting, safe, and harmless. Son of noted filmmaker Ridley, Jake Scott's videos betrayed a technical agility reminis-cent of his father's feature-length work. His recurrent concerns were primarily visual—the fish-eye lenses of Oasis' "Morning Glory" (1995) and Bush's "Comedown" (1995); the harsh fluorescent lighting of the supermarket in Radiohead's "Fake Plastic Trees" (1995) and the apartment hallway in "Morning Glory"; the earth tones of the sick room in "Lightning Crashes" and the band hideout in "Morning Glory"; the omnipresent televisions of "Everybody Hurts" and Tracy Bonham's "Mother Mother" (1995). Scott was an impressive techni-cian, but "Everybody Hurts" is far and away his best video, invested as it was with an emotional charge mostly lacking from the bulk of his work.

Less explicitly spiritual than "Everybody Hurts," but still possessed of a collective grace, R.E.M.'s "Man on the Moon" (1992) (directed by Peter Care) had dropped Stipe into the modern-day American desert. The screen divides into an ever-changing pattern of boxes, its images repeatedly distorted by crackles, pops, and light effects. Looking like a latter-day Montgomery Clift (a lyrical touchstone here), Stipe makes his way through a desert of slithering snakes, Darwinian-evolution flipbooks, and eighteen-wheelers bustling through the emptiness, before arriving at a watering hole where guitarist Peter Buck doles out the drinks and bass player Mike Mills is a customer. The bar's patrons, ranging from the oldsters gathered at one table to the young waitress, all join together in singing along to "Man on the Moon," a touching and unexpected display of unity that markedly contrasts with the bulk of the video's air of glorious solitude. Both R.E.M. videos sought to imagine ways that the lonely souls of America could be brought back together—music proving the healing balm for bruised souls.

Stipe was a master of camera flirtation, engaging its attention while coyly looking away, romancing the camera, and by extension the audience, while never fully committing to its embrace. A neophyte to the game, Lisa Loeb proved equally capable of playing, with her debut video "Stay" (1994) (directed by Ethan Hawke) a masterpiece of the music video's capacity for small dramas. Beginning with a fixed shot of Loeb standing against a wall, the camera slowly zooms in on her face, then idiosyncratically follows her through a loft apartment as she sings. Loeb bounces around the apartment's confines, a mixture of close-ups and tracking shots following the arc of her pinball motion. Over the course of the video, Loeb appears to relive the events that inspired the song, her restless motion a symbol of "Stay's" confused emotional state.

Loeb alternately makes love to the camera with her eyes, milking the emotion out of each line of her song, and carefully avoids its gaze. "Stay" proves just how much drama there can be in one singer, one space, and one song, not requiring any special effects other than Loeb's own mesmerizing everygirl-ness (best symbolized by her nerd-chic tortoiseshell glasses) to keep audiences spellbound.

Even U2, those masters of well-heeled emotional bombast, went small with their 1993 videos "Numb" and "Lemon." "Numb" dares to pull focus away from lead singer Bono, putting guitarist The Edge front and center, and pelting him with a staggering variety of distractions and petty annoyances. Bandmates whisper in his ear, beautiful women caress his shoulders and nibble at his ears, little girls slap his face, and string is wrapped around his head. Most daringly, after he is pushed offscreen by unseen hands, the screen stays black for twenty seconds—an astoundingly extended period of time for as compact a form as the music video.

"Numb's" minimalist charms were matched by its companion "Lemon," which suggested a scientific study of motion as funneled through rock-star excess. The group poses against a graph-paper background, their images framed with captions like "Man with electric guitar swinging through 360°." "Lemon" possesses an arch, tongue-in-cheek sense of humor, as if all of human behavior were a mystifying matter, worthy of further scientific investigation.

The Poetry of Light

To his detractors, Mark Romanek was a serial borrower, at best. Lifting images, ideas, and entire scenarios from films, photographs, art installations, and the like, Romanek has a reputation as a music-video director with butterfingers, prone to aesthetic thievery. By picking out Romanek for abuse, the naysayers conveniently choose to ignore the degree to which those tendencies have become codified within the traditions of music-videomaking as a whole. Music videos have made a fetish of borrowing, and pop-savvy artists and videomakers made "Name that Influence" a favorite video parlor game. Romanek was only slightly more obvious about it than his peers, in part due to the voraciousness of his wide-ranging aesthetic curiosity. His archive-raiding videos, and his masterful eye for arresting compositions, made Romanek one of the most captivating music video directors around from the early-1990s onward.

Lost in the discussions of Romanek's guilt or innocence as a pilferer was a full understanding of the director's technique, which extends far beyond his borrowings. Treating the screen as a canvas, Romanek exhibits a painter's eye for filling the frame, and for the headrush of vivid color. Romanek's work aims for a pure videomaking that celebrates its own intermediate status, neither film nor television, providing unblemished spectacle for a form that craved it.

Romanek's work, from its earliest stages, exhibited two opposing, painting-inspired tendencies: the artfully arranged tableau and the whoosh of color in motion. As early as The The's "Sweet Bird of Truth," in 1986, Romanek aimed for the iconic, memorable image over narrative sensibility, with that video notable for its fish flopping in an urban puddle and the cracked painting of Jesus abandoned alongside a burning pile of garbage. With the exception of his color-field work, the bulk of Romanek's work had embraced narrative, but of a particular sort; one less interested in straightforward exposition than a series of arresting images. His videos for Madonna's "Rain" (1993) and "Bedtime Story" (1995) are less about their ostensible plots (a factory for dreams and Madonna shooting a Japanese commercial, respectively) than the imagery they produced: Madonna nude in front of a giant sunflower, a foot crushing grapes artfully draped atop Arabic calligraphy, doves flying out from a woman's belly, the twin walls of rainfall that tumbled on either side of Madonna in "Rain." The icy, bluish sheen of "Rain" echoed its contemporary, Lenny Kravitz's "Are You

Gonna Go My Way" (1993), the glow of lights at its end, bathing its cast and crew in a warm smolder, reminiscent of the descending chandelier in Kravitz's clip. En Vogue's "Free Your Mind" (1992) put the sultry trio onstage at a German Expressionist fashion show, strutting down the catwalk in black leather getups while Otto Dix–like portraits of grotesque faces bedecked the walls. "Free Your Mind" is a celebration of light, with strobes, paparazzi flashbulbs, and white flashes of light decorating nearly every frame of the video. Romanek's fantasy shamelessly mixes and matches, R&B singers in fetish gear joined by generic hard-rockers onstage, playing for a crowd of uber-hipsters wearing futuristic telephone headsets in a Weimar cabaret-cum-concert hall.

The scope of Romanek's borrowings was vast: Joel-Peter Witkin's avant-garde photography for Nine Inch Nails' "Closer" (1994), Chris Marker's classic short film *La Jetée* (1962) for David Bowie's "Jump They Say" (1993), Jean-Luc Godard's *Alphaville* (1965) for Sonic Youth's "Little Trouble Girl" (1996), the One-Minute Sculptures of Erwin Wurm for the Red Hot Chili Peppers' "Can't Stop" (2003). Selecting unique source material, Romanek's videos expected to stand out in the MTV crowd, their unusual tableaux designed to arrest viewers' attention. These works blur the line between homage and rip-off, taking their inspiration from other media and re-creating them wholesale on the video screen. Romanek transcends simplistic pastiche through his consistent aesthetic, which, regardless of the source, emphasized the sorts of moving still lifes that caught his eye: the exceptionally crisp shots of deserted corporate offices in "Little Trouble Girl," the Victorian Gothic landscapes of Nine Inch Nails' "The Perfect Drug" (1997), the distressed, washed-out close-ups of African men in Janet Jackson's "Got Til It's Gone" (1997), and the urban-paranoiac freeze-frames of Beck's "Devil's Haircut" (1996).

Romanek's career shuttled between funkier low-budget productions and video blockbusters. Both "Bedtime Story" and his video for Michael Jackson and Janet Jackson's "Scream" (cost: $7 million) were the most expensive music videos ever made at the time of their releases. "Scream" (1995) looks like money, the video equivalent of a summer blockbuster. Set on a floating space station, Romanek's black-and-white clip has a 1960s futurist feel, all clever gizmos and space-travel funk. "Scream's" primary purpose was to erase memories of Michael's child-molestation troubles by emphasizing Jackson family harmony (an effort duplicated by Jackson's unbearably mawkish "Childhood" [1995]), but Romanek is more interested in the toys than the actors: a remote control that zaps art-historical holograms onto the wall, the siblings playing Pong on a wall-size television, Michael smashing vases while playing a solo game of racquetball. "Scream" was intended to feature Michael and Janet as angry, paranoid victims of an intrusive media, but Romanek's polish swamps the pretend grit.

"99 Problems" (2004), the farewell video from Jay-Z's final album, also reveals a gap between intention and function in Romanek's work. Meant to effectively end Jay-Z's career as a performer, the video's most talked-about sequence features him assaulted by a slow-motion fusillade of bullets on a Brooklyn street. This symbolic death is overwhelmed by the video itself, which refuses to commit itself to Jay-Z's death, or even to its primary storyline. Following Jay and sidekick Rick Rubin on a borough-wide Brooklyn odyssey, "99 Problems" is captivated by the sights and sounds of its intended backdrop. Romanek's jittery camera work and canted frames lend the video a certain urgent intimacy, and its tableau of Brooklynites, from Hasidim to hood-rats, motorcyclists to airborne acrobats, renders the video a sideways city symphony. Romanek takes a page out of *The Godfather* for the final sequences, cutting between Jay-Z's assassination and Rubin in church in an echo of the famous Francis Ford Coppola montage of baptism and violent death, but even this plot movement was too drastic for "99 Problems." Jay-Z may be gunned down in the video, but "99 Problems" ends with the rapper triumphant, strutting down the street clad in a "Brooklyn" hoodie, throwing punches at the air, ready to take on all comers. For Jay-Z, death didn't take, because life in his home borough was simply too compelling to pass up.

Romanek's everything-and-the-kitchen-sink aesthetic was evident in his clip for Nine Inch Nails' "The Perfect Drug" as well, which crammed all manner of images Gothic into its frame. Romanek, a director whose work betrays a studied acquaintance with art history, borrows liberally from the work of Caspar David Friedrich and Giorgio De Chirico for the blue-tinted menace of "The Perfect Drug." Once again, Romanek moves the periphery front and center, elevating his foreboding landscape imagery to a prominent place in the video: fallen obelisks, hooded figures, bare trees, black-clad widows, and a De Chirico-esque giant hand. Reznor completes the compendium of Victorian bad-boy clichés, slashing his way through a maze, drinking absinthe, and suffering the green-tint nightmares that coincide with the song's drum-n-bass breakdown. Romanek enjoyed the game of picking a motif and running with it, pasting together a set of images on space travel, or Brooklyn, or dreaming, and working within those loose parameters.

Romanek's masterpiece, though, was the astonishing, utterly unique clip he put together for Johnny Cash's final video, a cover of Nine Inch Nails' "Hurt." Shot in the House of Cash museum in Hendersonville, Tennessee, "Hurt" (2002) blends a rapid-fire sketch of Cash's legendary career with an overhanging sense of impending mortality. Above all, "Hurt" is about the contours of Cash's visage. "Hurt's" grandeur stems from Cash's face—weather-beaten, flabby, lined, and scarred. Romanek gives Cash's unyouthful, craggy face the same respect, and the same attention, the music video normally lends only to twentysomething heartthrobs. Unsurprisingly, considering Cash's own illness, "Hurt" is consumed with the sensation of impending death. Death in "Hurt" is no mere thought experiment; it is a heavy, corporeal, ever-expanding presence. And when else in music video history has a face that old appeared onscreen for as long, without being ridiculed or intended as a counterpoint to glorious, effervescent youth?

"Hurt" opens with twin intimations of looming death: a golden statue of an elderly bearded figure astride a horse, and a bowl of ripe, luscious fruit. Romanek cuts from these traditional art-historical *mementos mori* to an image of Cash's hands playing the guitar. Cash's face is a punctuation mark to this series of images, its time-ravaged quality a synecdoche for the pocket career summary that follows. Looking away from the camera to his left, as if gazing out into the distance, or at something just out of our line of sight, Cash's performance is interspersed with images selected from his past: Cash driving a train, walking on the beach, strutting onstage.

It is this footage, above all, that gives "Hurt" its philosophical quality, as if weighing a man's entire life in the balance. The passage of time fades even these triumphs, and Romanek's imagery reflects its autumnal quality. Cash sits at a closed piano, bathed in a dim yellowish light; a gold record from *Johnny Cash at San Quentin* sits in a dusty corner, its glass cracked and broken; the still life of fruit reappears, now speckled by the black rot of death. Cash sits at a formal dining-room table, at which a meal has already been eaten, and the images of his past continue to rush past him like the flood that sweeps through the streets in one old clip. Cash pours his glass of wine out on the table, offering the blood of Christ up as absolution to the array of past incarnations that flash across the screen (echoing the import of this action, Jesus appears onscreen, nailed to the cross). "Hurt" ends with Cash at his piano again, the yellow light on his face like the last moments of daylight, closing the cover and running his hands over its wood. "Hurt" rings with the tones of death, looming as a shadow presence, but its tone is less tragic than somber. Romanek's video is a scrapbook for a dying man, weighted with the knowledge of death so studiously denied by the overwhelming bulk of its music-video colleagues. The great majority of videos were about the rejection of death, and the celebration of youthfulness and glamour; in contrast, "Hurt" is about nothing other than death, and taking place in the few minutes before the sun finally sank below the horizon, is about its acceptance. In "Hurt," memory and death become the two most trusted companions of old age.

Romanek had enshrined another brand of rock iconography as well, stamping rockers with the pure visual poetry of light. Lenny Kravitz's "Are You Gonna

Go My Way" cast the retro rocker in the 70s fantasy of his choice, a dream of Me Decade stardom complete with platform shoes, red wide-leg trousers, a backing band of hippie misfits, and a multicultural stew of joyous fans partying on terraces above the band. "Are You Gonna" fetishizes the tools of rock stardom, lavishing Kravitz's squat, classic-looking microphone and his flying V guitar with loving attention. Romanek frames Kravitz in a series of low-angle shots, for the appropriate guitar-hero dynamic, but also to honor the video's true star: the pulsating chandelier and overhead lights that drop from the ceiling at its outset. The lights pulse outward like a wave, propeller around, then finally darken for the guitar solo. "Are You Gonna Go My Way" is pure video, an unabashed celebration of rock's propulsive dynamism. Painting the screen with light, Romanek escapes the performance-versus-narrative dichotomy by creating a third way. His painterly dynamic treated the screen like a canvas, not a window—to be filled with light and color. "Are You Gonna Go My Way," and its successors, find a way to escape the crippling sameness of rock iconography while simultaneously carrying its banner. Its putative stars do not vanish from the screen; they are merely shunted to the side, not remotely as beautiful, or as fascinating, as the interplay of light and color taking place behind and around them.

Audioslave's "Cochise" (2002) is the most remarkable of Romanek's light paintings, its explosion of color so lushly beautiful it appears to have been designed for a screen larger than television. A pickup truck rolls into a construction site, its path lit by banks of lights flanking it on either side. Looking like a posse of tough guys from some grade-Z action flick, the three backing musicians of Audioslave head up in the manual elevator, emerging onto an open platform, where they are joined by lead singer Chris Cornell. The introductory guitar line activates the first burst of fireworks, an enormous array of reds, greens, and yellows that splatter across the screen. The rockets explode in every region of the frame, reflected on the bodies of the members of the band when shown in close-up. "Cochise" is simply the best fireworks show of all time, one pounding burst of light after another with no letup whatsoever. Romanek makes the music-as-sex equation literal here without resorting to the tired formulae of booze and babes; "Cochise's" explosions of light are one long onscreen orgasm.

Coldplay's "Speed of Sound" (2005) is a little brother to "Cochise," not quite as effervescent, but nearly as lovely. Here, instead of fireworks, the band plays in front of a light board whose colors surge upward and outward. Romanek's jagged camera work accentuates the vividness of the charge of colors. The purples, reds, blues, and yellows surge and fall like stereo volume meters, the colors reflecting in close-ups of lead singer Chris Martin's face. If "Cochise" is Abstract Expressionist in its unleashed bursts of color, "Speed of Sound" is cooler, more diffident and restrained. Like its predecessor, though, it flattens the video frame, interested less in three-dimensional motion than the motion of light and color across its canvas.

Romanek, along with Spike Jonze and Michel Gondry, would be one of the essential directors of the alt-rock ascendance. These directors, along with a host of others, defined the alternative-rock revolution to nearly as large an extent as the musicians, jointly crafting an aesthetic that matched the sometimes-anguished, sometimes-comic aura of performers like Nirvana, Beck, and Nine Inch Nails. Alternative rock, and its surrounding culture, came to dominate the music video in the 1990s, and its staggering array of permutations will be the story of our next chapter.

CHAPTER 5

Visions of a Youth Culture

Smells Like Youth Culture

Reports from two ends of the 90s alternative rock revolution: two youthscapes familiar to any middle-class suburban adolescent: the school pep rally and the house party. Two gatherings of teen pettiness, hormones, and angst, but where the first is a reclamation of disputed territory, a surge of adolescent power announcing the triumph of the downtrodden outsider, the second is a rueful acknowledgment that while the alternative revolution may have occurred, the bad guys emerged as the winners, leaving the sensitive adolescent, tormented soul that he is, no better off than he would have been in the era of Whitesnake and Warrant.

But first, the revolution. In a high-school auditorium so devoid of color or decoration it could be located anywhere, the students are seated for a pep rally. Quickly, though, it becomes evident that this is no run-of-the-mill gathering. The rally's musical accompaniment is, of course, Nirvana, and their song "Smells Like Teen Spirit" (1991) is the anthem of the outcast, a call to arms under the freak flag. The video, directed by Samuel Bayer, is a vision of the nascent post-postpunk movement ascendant. Sons of the Pixies, Jane's Addiction, and the other quasistars of the late-80s underground, Nirvana was a group whose moment had come, and "Smells Like Teen Spirit" reveals an innate understanding of their musical dynamic.

Singer Kurt Cobain, a pale wraith with shoulder-length blond hair, was the picture of the teenage loser ten years down the road, and yet here he was, in the epicenter of the pull to adolescent conformity, the pep rally, a star. Where the pep rally traditionally asked its celebrants to dampen their individuality in the name of a group ideal, part of the teenager's acclimation to the inevitable compromises and conformity of adulthood, "Smells Like Teen Spirit" presents an alternative. Rather than direct its anger to a simplistic desire for destruction, "Smells Like Teen Spirit" maintains the structure of existing institutions in order to twist them, pretzel-like, into a new, more accommodating shape.

The band thrashes through their song, the pom-pomed cheerleaders shimmy and strut, looking a bit too world-weary (and tattooed) to be teenagers, but nonetheless.

Here, then, was a high school where the loser was ascendant, but his reign did not result in burning the schoolhouse down, or beating up the jocks; Bayer's video makes a statement for inclusiveness, for a velvet revolution of manners. Even the awkward, somewhat frightening figure of the school janitor is compelled to join in, dancing while wielding his mop. Any relationship between the school metaphor and Nirvana's desire to maintain their identity while serving as employees of a major record label, Geffen Records, was, of course, purely coincidental.

Eleven years later, the revolution has become a fading memory. Nirvana may have triumphed, but their victory was distinctly Pyrrhic in nature; Kurt Cobain died for our sins, leaving us with the diminishing returns of Sugar Ray, Creed, and Limp Bizkit, the dying embers of the alt-rock conflagration. One video succinctly summarizes the failure of "Smells Like Teen Spirit's" dream to come to fruition, while simultaneously serving as a pungent metaphor of the "alternative" scene circa 2002.

In a quiet suburban neighborhood, a teenage boy and girl, seen from behind, walk up to the front door of a comfortably upper-middle-class home. A few steps before reaching the door, the girl removes her shirt and strips down to her bra and panties. The boy does no such thing. The door opens, and a full-on house party is raging, a scene familiar from a million and one teen comedies and music videos. The girl grabs a drink and disappears into the crowd, and the initial assumption that the two had arrived at the party together subsides. Reassessing the situation as our protagonist makes his way through the crush (the camera's placement behind his head assigns our sympathies to him as a matter of course), the unfolding drama is a reversal of the stereotypical nudity dream. In the latter, a textbook expression of feelings of social panic, the dreamer appears in a social setting wearing nothing but his birthday suit, setting off anguished concern that others will discover the faux pas. In Jimmy Eat World's "The Middle," directed by Paul Fedor, our protagonist (let's call him Jimmy) suffers the misfortune of arriving fully clothed at a party attended entirely by guys and girls in their skivvies. As Jimmy passes from room to room, he is the target of two primary responses: a confusion akin to embarrassment over the social miscues of others, and the type of sneer reserved for those who cannot follow the rules.

Surrounded by tanned, hard-bodied men and women, apparently so comfortable with their bodies as to be unconscious of their near-nudity, Jimmy is an anomaly, doomed to wander the antechambers of happiness and satisfaction eternally, without ever truly arriving. Even the pasty, overweight guy, who distinctly needs to get a shirt on pronto, is standing around un-self-consciously in his tighty-whities, drinking a beer. Having maintained a near first-person point of view for the first half of the video, redemption appears close to hand in the video's center, where the girl from the video's opening scene moves toward the camera, arms open, a wide smile lighting up her face. Instead, "The Middle" has played a trick on us here, shifting perspective to Jimmy's face framed in a small window, looking in on the kitchen scene of the girl embracing some future fraternity president.

Jimmy is an outsider, prevented from even being in the same scene as the happy, sexy couple. Heading into one of the house's bedrooms, he sits on the bed as other couples make out, and dancers shimmy provocatively near him. Ignored by the other revelers, not even the tiniest speck on their unclouded existences, Jimmy has had all he can take. He sneaks into an empty room whose bed is piled high with discarded clothing and steps into the closet to strip. Cutting to a wider shot as Jimmy unbuttons his pants, we discover that the double-wide closet has another inhabitant—a girl possessed by the same logic, in the process of removing her clothes as well. In a two-shot, Jimmy, at screen right, and the girl, at the screen's far left, glance up at each other, take in the extent of the other's degradation, and pull their clothes back on. In the video's final shot, Jimmy and the girl exit the party, reversing the motion of the initial sequence. Here, though, the two have their hands in each other's back pockets.

In "The Middle," like "Smells Like Teen Spirit," a group of adolescents has gathered in one of the many rites inherent in a certain kind of American teenagerdom. Where "Smells Like Teen Spirit" hoped for a bending of teenage ritual toward greater openness and inclusivity, "The Middle" represents that dream's death. Jimmy, the Cobain-like outsider, finds himself in a position no better than before, the victim of rituals of cohesion that leave him on the outside looking in, and while he escapes, pride intact, the party rages on obliviously. Like "Smells Like Teen Spirit," the group in "The Middle" says that up is down, resetting the rules to their liking, but here the new social structure is an architecture of exclusion. Post-Kurt, in the era of Fred Durst, the assholes have taken over again, in the guise of successors to Nirvana's legacy. In the house party of alternative music some eight years after Cobain's suicide, Jimmy Eat World find themselves gazing puzzledly at a gathering of frat boys and their snooty girlfriends, high-school versions of Fred Durst, Scott Stapp, et al., and wondering: What the hell happened?

Teenage Angst Has Paid Off Well

In between those two videos, of course, an entire decade of alternative videos passed, a relatively new genre of videomaking blossoming and decaying. As at any house party, the participants congealed into groups, forming cliques and subgenres, reflecting different aesthetic outlooks by their differing attitudes to the videomaking process. Each of the genres that came to define the 90s alternative-rock video reflected on its predecessors, sympathetically continuing their work or branching out in a new direction in response to what had come before.

If "Smells Like Teen Spirit" was the source for all that followed, each of the genres that emerged, and each of the videos, was a tributary, winding its own path through the shoals of the decade's culture. Beginning with Nirvana and their immediate peers, the alt-rock video grew to encompass sallow-faced troubadours of anger and self-destruction, with disturbing imagery to match; liberal borrowers from pop culture past and present, creators of hip, postmodern assemblages; light-hearted pranksters who turned the intensity down a few notches, cracking a smile rather than cracking up onscreen; titillators, doyennes of the softcore aesthetic; and, finally, the frat boys who brought the alternative tent crashing down. At its peak, the alt-rock party had room for them all, pseudo B-boys next to grunge rockers next to fey popsters next to indie darlings next to acoustic-guitar-strumming singer-songwriters, and while the party didn't last long, it sure was fun while it did.

With "Smells Like Teen Spirit" bursting onto the scene in 1991, the stage was set for a bevy of imitators and colleagues to have their moment in the MTV sun. Nirvana was soon joined by compatriots like Pearl Jam, Soundgarden, and Alice in Chains, and later by imitators like Stone Temple Pilots and Candlebox, and grunge reigned supreme as the music of disaffected American youth. Grunge videos mostly stayed on the dark end of the street, using a palette of murky colors and elusive symbolism that emphasized, above all, two themes: grunge's place in the continuum of great rock acts past, and its special role as diviner and explicator of Generation X's anomie.

Post–"Teen Spirit," Nirvana emerged with "In Bloom" (1992) (directed by Kevin Kerslake), further affirmation of the band's unique iconography. Dressed in natty early-60s suits for this black-and-white clip, Cobain and his bandmates are introduced as the musical guests on an imitation of that staple of baby-boomer television *The Ed Sullivan Show* (a concept later borrowed by Outkast for "Hey Ya!"). After the host humorously mangles the band's name, Nirvana performs their hit single to the shrieks of lovesick teenagers. There is something inherently comic about one era's musical acts attempting to conform to the standards of another era; seeing Kurt Cobain performing in a jacket and tie is profoundly jarring in its oddness.

And wouldn't you know it, Nirvana makes the punk explosion literal, compressing the years between the wholesome moment parodied here and the ascent of punk rock into the space of one video. In an abrupt shift, Cobain and bandmates Krist Novoselic and Dave Grohl appear in some shots in dresses, and by video's end, their nice-guy blandness has been ditched once and for all; the band is seen smashing up the stage with punk-rock abandon, tearing off their frocks, and embracing homoeroticism in a fashion that the real *Ed Sullivan Show* would never have allowed. Nirvana both holds up and dismantles the traditional rock-god iconography here; they may be smashing their guitars, but Cobain is also wearing a dress while doing so. "In Bloom" exposes some of the inherent gender confusion of 80s hair metal, where testosterone-filled adolescent males were supposed to ignore the blatant fact that their musical idols were dressed and coiffed to resemble nothing so much as the overly made-up babes that starred in their videos. If "In Bloom" sets up something of a straw man here, knocking down an overly polite form of popular music that had ceased to exist twenty-five years prior, it was genuinely daring in its gender-bending panache.

The yang to Nirvana's yin, producing straight-ahead grunge bombast in opposition to Nirvana's gnarled, anguished anthems, were fellow Seattleites Pearl Jam. Fronted by Eddie Vedder, the band's videos emphasized standard rock-video imagery, establishing Pearl Jam as strait-laced inheritors of the alt-rock crown—you wouldn't catch Eddie wearing any dresses onstage. Instead, in "Evenflow" (1991) and "Alive" (1991), live-performance clips directed by Josh Taft, Vedder stalks the stage purposefully, barreling manically from side to side. Climbing to the rafters in order to bellow more dramatically, stage-diving into the crowd—"Evenflow" is practically a handbook for aspiring rock stars in how to convey the proper tone of sweaty masculine bluster. "Evenflow" stands in polar opposition to Nirvana's quirky videos, which demanded an upending of the traditional order in favor of joyous anarchy.

Both "Smells Like Teen Spirit" and "In Bloom" celebrated disruptions to everyday order, the pep rally and television program both branching out in unexpected, socially revolutionary directions. "Evenflow," while a raucous good time, could have been a Van Halen video circa 1984.

Late-blooming punk-funk superstars the Red Hot Chili Peppers split the difference between Nirvana and Pearl Jam, their cock-of-the-walk swagger tempered by the intense homoerotic subtexts of videos like "Give It Away" (1991), "My Friends" (1995), and "Scar Tissue" (1999). Frequently shirtless, and often nude, the men of the Red Hot Chili Peppers made their videos an exclusively male affair. Whether sweating off silver paint in the desert in "Give It Away" (directed by

Stephane Sednaoui), lounging around in dresses and exchanging intense hugs in "My Friends" (directed by Anton Corbijn), or bandaging their wounds in "Scar Tissue" (also directed by Sednaoui), the Red Hot Chili Peppers were simultaneously manly and man-loving, practically daring their fans to acknowledge the fairly explicit homoeroticism of their videos. "Warped" (1995) (directed by Gavin Bowden) brought the homoerotic subtext closest to the surface, wrapping the Chili Peppers in see-through plastic coats and skivvies and mixing a sex-and-drugs cocktail conspicuous for its sadomasochistic undertones and utter lack of women. Guitarist Dave Navarro flashes his nipple rings and sucks on his pearl necklace, and the video ends with two of the Chili Peppers, swathed in shadow, exchanging a long, deep embrace. "Warped" is tender, in addition to being sexual; it proposed quasi-overt homosexuality as a natural outgrowth of brotherly camaraderie.

Pearl Jam's biggest video, and easily one of the most iconic clips of the 1990s, was "Jeremy" (1992), directed by Mark Pellington. Pellington's video illustrates the song's tale of adolescent anger and violence with a dense, allusive style that required multiple viewings to parse fully. It also received an unnecessarily mysterious ending, due to MTV's refusal to air one crucial expository scene. Beginning with an ironically placid description of an average day ("3:30 in the afternoon—64 degrees and cloudy—an affluent suburb")—a nod in the direction of Alfred Hitchcock's similar opening titles in *Psycho* (1960), another tale of death's unexpected blooming amidst placid surroundings—"Jeremy" blends a familiar critique of suburban conformity with an unstinting depiction of adolescent violence. Pellington's quick cuts and scrapbook mise-en-scène intersperse newspaper headlines and Biblical allusions into the drama ("The serpent was subtil," "Genesis 3:5"), foreshadowing the tragedy to come.

Jeremy screams at his parents, desperately entreating them while they sit, utterly motionless, frozen in their inability to help or touch their son. Elsewhere, they are rendered as empty suits, simultaneously present and absent, whom Jeremy attempts to bring together, raising his arms pleadingly, attempting to weave a happy nuclear family from unfriendly cloth. Motionlessness is a persistent theme in "Jeremy," with Jeremy himself the only character in the video (outside the band) shown moving. Jeremy crouches next to a painting of a wolf—sitting figuratively in the wolf's maw from the video's outset—and poses with his head surrounded by encroaching flames. In a later scene, Jeremy is subjected to the cruel laughter of his classmates, who point, goggle-eyed, at him for unclear reasons; they, too, are rendered as mere still lifes. "Jeremy" is a modernist interior portrait, a rendering of the protagonist's subjective mental landscape rather than objective reality.

At the end of the clip, Jeremy arrives in class, tosses an apple to his teacher, sticks a gun in his mouth, and pulls the trigger. His classmates are shown (unmoving again) splashed with his blood, and frozen with shock. MTV forced Pearl Jam to remove the shot of Jeremy raising the gun, leaving it unintentionally vague as to whether Jeremy kills himself or his classmates. Pellington repeatedly cuts between Vedder singing the song's lyrics and Jeremy's descent into madness, which, together with Vedder's rocking back and forth in his best mental-patient fashion, and his half-grin, half-grimace, establishes a strong correlation between the video's two main figures. Vedder is Jeremy, in some elemental fashion, and Jeremy's anguish is Eddie's as well.

Pellington's chiaroscuro lighting renders Vedder a quasi demon, a visual trick stolen outright by Pearl Jam disciples Stone Temple Pilots in their video for "Plush" (1993). In that clip, directed by Josh Taft, lead singer Weiland is shot in profile, his head seemingly engulfed in flames, like Jeremy in Pearl Jam's video. Both Vedder and Weiland position themselves as the voice of a generation's pain, through visuals that associated them with notions of hellfire and damnation. The nascent grunge culture saw itself as spokesman for marginalized, battered youth—a generation demanding musical voices adequately soaked in pain, and familiarized with violence, to serve as their mouthpieces. Even Pearl Jam's fellow Seattleites Soundgarden got into the act with their "Black Hole Sun" (1994), half-seriously looking forward to an impending Rapture sweeping up all the freaks and outcasts of a doomed society.

In this gloomy depressive's paradise, even a mournful ballad can come to seem like a breath of fresh air. The Red Hot Chili Peppers' "Under the Bridge" (1992) (directed by Gus Van Sant) took an entire city as its stomping grounds, opening itself up to the world outside the tangled recesses of consciousness. In the video, lead singer Anthony Kiedis goes walking through the streets of downtown Los Angeles, home to the song's titular bridge, shaking hands and exchanging backslaps with bystanders. "Under the Bridge" is video as city symphony, an elegant and emotional tribute to the City of Angels from one of its foremost musical groups, with a visual simplicity later pilfered (to good use) by the Verve's "Bittersweet Symphony" (1997) (directed by Walter Stern). Split-screens and superimpositions place the band in touch with the city even while playing their instruments in close-up; Los Angeles is ever present here as backdrop and mental resting place.

Less noted at the time of the release of "Under the Bridge" was the specifically working-class nature of the imagery. Accompanying this quintessential L.A. song is not the usual dizzying array of stereotypical Tinseltown imagery—the Hollywood sign, Disneyland, Capitol Records building, and so on. Instead, it is the residents and workers of Los Angeles' decidedly scruffy downtown district who appear here—the mostly Hispanic faces an indication of "Under the Bridge's" populist yearnings. Music and image symbolically reunite the divided halves of racially split Los Angeles life—the white west greeting the brown east.

The archetypal director of this dark-hued, pain-loving era was Samuel Bayer. With his supersaturated colors (particularly a love of deep, oozing blacks), heavy symbolism, and off-putting, mysterious imagery, Bayer was a one-man hit-making machine in the early 90s, helming such clips as Candlebox's "You" (1993), Hole's "Doll Parts" (1994), and the Cranberries' "Zombie" (1994). Part of his videos' charm was in their incomprehensibility; strange touches like the dueling dancers of "You," the albinos and transvestites of the Afghan Whigs' "Honky's Ladder" (1996), the Golden Calf allegory of David Bowie's "The Heart's Filthy Lesson" (1995), or the bird-mask figures of Garbage's "Only Happy When It Rains" (1996) were notable for being unapologetic visual non sequiturs. Bayer was the quintessential alternative-rock video director because he epitomized the project of the alt-rock video: bringing high art to the masses, taking the building blocks of avant-garde film (scratched or damaged film stock, dense or nonexistent narrative, weighty symbolism, personal visual touchstones like distressed colors, masked figures, and body paint) and constructing *Alternative Nation*–ready clips. Detractors called Bayer's work prefab avant-garde, but they missed the essential point: as perhaps the quintessential postmodern art form, the music video was at the forefront of creative recycling. It struck gold in the selective reuse of cultural detritus, and a director like Bayer, who came from a background as a painter and art director, treated the video as a canvas for his own obsessions while always keeping one eye on the bottom line—was it playable? Bayer, like his colleagues Mark Romanek and Mark Pellington, thrived in this atmosphere, their quasi-avant-garde styles, heavily influenced by contemporary photography, the perfect afternoon snack for the adolescent MTV audience.

As superb as the video may have been, "Smells Like Teen Spirit," in all likelihood, would have become an enormous hit even without Bayer's influence. Considering Nirvana's enormous cultural impact, and the sheer aural wallop of their music, it is hard to imagine that Bayer's clever video was the primary reason for their rise to fame. Therefore, the Bayer video with the largest impact, the clip that managed to spin dross into gold to the largest extent, was Blind Melon's "No Rain" (1992).

Abandoning the underlit atmospherics of his work with Nirvana, Bayer floods "No Rain" with sunlight. His style here is lighter, friendlier—this could be his music-video chick flick. Nonetheless, an undercurrent of melancholy runs through its tale of a friendless, awkward pre-adolescent girl dressed in a bee costume. Pudgy, with oversized glasses and an affable manner, we first see her performing a tap dance, utterly absorbed in the moment. At the performance's close, though, there is no applause, only the vicious cackle of a single heckler cascading into mass hoots of derision as the Bee Girl tears up and runs offstage. The dark blacks and reds of this opening sequence are soon replaced by lush blues and greens, and the Bee Girl pokes her head out into the sunshine, where the band (and the song) begin to play.

Walking down the city streets, she finds companionship in the outcasts of urban life, doing her dance for passersby and striking up conversations with an African-American man walking a mangy bulldog and a grizzled older man waiting at a bus stop. Eventually, the Bee Girl makes her way to a black gate with a floral wreath, planted smack in the middle of a meadow, where, mouth agog, she discovers a whole colony of men and women dressed in bee costumes, dancing her jig. Black and white, male and female, old and young, svelte and over-weight—no one is barred from this bee's paradise.

Bayer provides a pastoralized happy ending for alienated youth, rendered not via the free-floating anger of more masculine bands like Pearl Jam, but through the heart-tugging saga of a pudgy preteen's search for her place in the world. "No Rain" clearly struck a chord; the band's album, which had been loi-tering in the nether regions of the Billboard album chart, zoomed as high as number three, and eventually sold more than four million copies. The Bee Girl, played by ten-year-old Heather DeLoach, became a cultural touchstone, if only for a minute, parodied by Chris Farley on *Saturday Night Live* and making pub-lic appearances with Madonna.

Returning with a candy-colored disturbance, crammed with rotting flesh, crows, hospital patients, and lonesome crosses, Nirvana (with director Anton Corbijn) peppered their final video, "Heart-Shaped Box" (1993), with refer-ences to death and decay, anticipating Kurt Cobain's suicide less than one year later. Far more unsettling than the *Nevermind* videos, "Heart-Shaped Box" acknowledged the harder, metallic-edged sound of their album *In Utero* and Cobain's own disappointment at cracking the glass ceiling of celebrity, only to discover himself still entirely alone, left to cope unaided with his pain and urge toward self-destruction.

Cobain and his bandmates sit vigil in a hospital room, where a large cross is painted onto the floor. An aged, worn figure, clad only in a Santa hat and ill-fit-ting underwear, shakily ascends a ladder to a wooden cross, planted in an artifi-cial-looking desert landscape filled with unnaturally blood-red flowers. Corbijn alternates between long shots, showing the band surrounded by crosses and aged, gnarled trees, and extreme close-ups of Cobain's face. The song "Heart-Shaped Box" is the soundtrack to this wasteland; even the crows mouth the words to the song. An angelic young girl dressed in white leaps into the air, grasping at a fetus growing on a tree, while a smiling, overweight woman with no skin and angel's wings, like an anatomy textbook's diagram come to life, comes toward us, arms outstretched. The girl's pointed white hat flies off, landing in a nearby puddle, and turns entirely black. In the next scene, she appears in the hospital room, her whole costume now black. She places her hands on the hospital bed, but whether she is a ministering angel or a diabolical one is ambiguous.

Cobain lies among the blood flowers, utterly motionless as a white haze seeps heavenward, his arms first crossed on his chest and then splayed on the ground—both poses strongly reminiscent of death. The young angel, now again in white, watches over him as the skinless angel gazes imploringly from a distance. In the coda, which occupies the final minute of the clip, the band plays a cramped red space decorated like a room at a chic hotel, adorned with light-emitting stars. Here, too, the stench of death is overpowering; the young angel appears, perfectly still on the bed, and Cobain, done singing, pitches forward from his chair, out of the frame and onto the floor.

One cannot help but assume that the crucified old man is a psychological extension of Cobain himself, crucified by celebrity, since at video's end it is Cobain, in his corporeal form, who lies still on the bloody ground. The angels watch, and they beckon, but even they are rendered motionless by the "real" world of the hotel and are little but spectators in the calvary of Cobain's crucifixion. Prematurely aged and stooped by the world's miseries, he nonetheless must go on wearing the red cap, a jolly Santa's outfit for an angry, bitter St. Nick. "Heart-Shaped Box" was testament that, for Cobain at least, the alternative-rock revolution had come to a premature end, nothing but a landscape of decay and deformity. Other bands, though, managed to keep the party going a bit longer.

Invisible Video

The mid-90s, from 1993 to 1996, were better defined by the videos that did not exist than those that did. During that period, one of the era's most beloved bands, Nirvana, came to an abrupt, premature end, and another chose to cease making videos, becoming the epicenter of a debate among music lovers about the nature of videomaking. Was it a simple commercial proposition, a legitimate form of artistic expression, or a capitulation to the darker forces of the music industry? After the triumphal success of Pearl Jam's debut album, *Ten*, buoyed by three enormously popular videos (for "Evenflow," "Alive," and "Jeremy"), the band soured on the entire process of MTV's perpetual popularity contest. From their second album onward, the band did not shoot a single video until 1998's "Do the Evolution," letting their multiplatinum albums *Vs.* (1993), *Vitalogy* (1994), and *No Code* (1996) speak entirely for themselves. Fans of the band were split—some endorsing Pearl Jam for their integrity and others critical of their self-serving moralizing.

What was so terrible about videos, anyhow? According to Pearl Jam and their supporters, the music video had become an overgrown behemoth, less about its original purpose (promoting the music) than its own needs as spectacle and music-channel fodder. Choosing to starve the beast, Pearl Jam cut off their connection to the music video at the height of their worldwide fame.

Post-Nirvana, grunge and its offshoots were obsessed with the idea of authenticity. The version of authenticity that 90s alternative rock groups peddled came to them whole-cloth from their 1980s predecessors, forced to tour the country in vans, playing small rock clubs in order to scrape out a living. Making an aesthetic out of their straitened circumstances, bands like Hüsker Dü, the Minutemen, and the Replacements crafted an ethic that fit uncomfortably around their descendants.

How could multiplatinum performers cram themselves into a style designed by their underground forefathers? Every band that chose to care about such matters had to reach their own accommodation with such guilt-inducing questions. Pearl Jam's answer was to turn their back on the video, taking the ideologically high-minded but ultimately rather silly tack that videos were too corporate, too commercial for them. Like any other art form, the music video was not inherently anything; it was whatever the artists and directors decided they would be. Rather than use their popularity to make challenging videos, a "Bastards of Young" for the 1990s, Pearl Jam abdicated the throne.

Kings of Pain

With Pearl Jam and Nirvana mostly absent from videomaking, a new batch of alternative stars emerged. The Goths were the inheritors of grunge rock's tendencies toward nihilism, and their videos relentlessly mined this dark vein. While lacking the saving humor of "In Bloom," clips like Nine Inch Nails' "Closer" (1994) and Tool's "Prison Sex" (1993) embody the imagination unfettered, borrowing from sources ranging from avant-garde filmmaking to contemporary photography. Like later celebrators of pastiche, such as Spike Jonze and the team of Jonathan Dayton and Valerie Faris, Goth videos searched the archaic backwaters of popular culture for inspiration, but without the self-referentiality or postmodern sense of play that define those filmmakers. They were deadly serious, and like the grunge rockers, looked to such imagery as the appropriate visual medium through which to broadcast their dirges of a generation's pain. The videos were not about what was borrowed, but rather what was made of it and how it complemented the music's tuneful brutality.

Where Weiland and Eddie Vedder sought to outcreep each other with facial gestures and the like, heavy-metal group Tool one-upped them both with their pair of spine-chilling clips for their songs "Sober" (1993) and "Prison Sex." Featuring claymation by Adam Jones, the band's guitarist, both videos penetrate a mysterious realm of portentous, ominous foreboding. The entire vision of "Sober," down to the last artfully composed paint chip, is a devilish vision from the nightmares of David Fincher, or more to the point, noted avant-garde filmmakers the brothers Quay, whose influence is felt in every frame. Employing a central visual language of high and low, inside and outside, "Sober" rapidly sketches a harsh vision of drug dependency as a brutal cycle. "Sober" is a series of addict nightmares, gnarled and freighted with symbolic weight. Addiction here is expressed through images of bodily panic—visions of the body mangled, distorted, shockingly fragile. Flesh takes on the lifeless quality of inanimate objects, and lifeless objects grow sickly, fleshy, and delicate.

Tool's next video, "Prison Sex," eliminates even the brief glimpses of the band from "Sober." Like "Sober," "Prison Sex" has an artisanal, unsettling feel, as if hand-whittled by lonesome convicts passing time during their life sentences. At the video's start, the camera whips past a small indenture running along the length of a wall, immediately suggesting "Prison Sex's" overriding motif of enclosure and imprisonment. A small creature (the Boy), lacking legs, hobbles along on his arms, while a dark figure, sheathed in all-encompassing leather, carefully hangs a pair of legs, presumably the boy's own, on a hook. His enormous shadow swamping the Boy's tiny figure as he ominously tears pages out of a book, the Dark Man is an authority figure gone rancid, a destructive force whose hold on the Boy is, like the contents of the talismanic box in "Sober," the quasi-open secret of the video.

The Boy's cracked, marbled skin, so tender and delicate, bears witness to the sufferings endured, and the helpless jerking of his legs, orphaned on their hook, is testament to the fear of future pain engendered by the Dark Man's swooping shadow and firm grasp. The Dark Man's sadistic games include swiping a paint brush along the Boy's body, leaving no mark; but in the video's final image, the Boy, huddled in a corner, paints one thick black stroke onto his chest, indicating that the scars of abuse are not invisible. Instead, they become a part of his own will to self-expression, a brushstroke of anguish that renders "Prison Sex" the symbolic artistic coming of age of one terribly damaged youth. "Sober" and "Prison Sex" are cryptic visions of a damaged generation, and of psyches brutalized by pain. They are harsh works, but necessarily so—enigmatic, Kafkaesque tales of worlds disturbing and yet familiar. In an era when teenage angst paid off as well as it did, unstinting depictions of weakness, mental and physical, were like candy to a generation that celebrated the pervasiveness of its psychic damage.

If "Prison Sex" was a noir video, a moody, character-driven work, Nine Inch Nails' "Closer," directed by Mark Romanek, took the "MTV aesthetic" (rapid-fire montage paired with a clean, coherent, immediately accessible visual style) and gave it a distinctly noir-ish twist. Strongly indebted to the work of photographer Joel-Peter Witkin, "Closer" posits NIN auteur Trent Reznor as ringmaster of a spooky menagerie of oddities, appropriately fitting his lord-of-the-underworld vibe. The washed-out colors are a primal palette of yellows, reds, and blacks, with the damaged film stock providing the distinct sensation that the video itself is in danger of imminent decay—appropriate for the video's smorgasbord of disturbing imagery, and a technique soon to be borrowed by David Fincher for his thriller *Seven* (1995).

Dressed in what appears to be an S&M aviator's costume, complete with trademark black goggles, Reznor plays host to a motley crew of frightening industrialists, crucified monkeys (edited out for MTV), and rotting carcasses. There is also a human heart pinned to a Scandinavian-modern chair, a pig's head rotating on a turning spit, a bald-headed androgyne spinning eggs on its index and pinkie fingers, and Reznor, shirtless, chained to the ceiling, an S&M ball in his mouth.

"Closer" is as coherent as any freak show can ever be, being a series of shock-value images connected primarily by their oddity. If the freak museum subtext is not literal, it is surely as good a guide as any through this nightmare world. In what would become the iconic image of this video, Reznor, dressed in a black leather jacket and black boots, levitates in the air, seemingly held in place by an invisible chair as he ceaselessly spins.

Revolution is a key visual motif of "Closer": in addition to the levitation sequence, there is the rotating pig's head and the spinning platform on which a variety of the video's figures (including Siamese twins attached by the hair, an aged executive type, and an African-American street urchin) appear. Rotation, whose motion implies a certain liveliness, is consistently paired here with images of creeping decay.

"Closer" invests each of its characters, and the animals and *mementos mori* put on display, with a grave elegance, creating a tapestry of sexual abnormality, violence, and death whose obvious visual charms offset and soothe the disturbing character of "Closer's" vision. The video's penultimate sequence confirms its aura of sexual degeneracy and its faux antique patina. The screen image sputters and burns, in imitation of a film projector's damaging a tender and aged reel of film. "Closer's" absorption of the imagery of the sexual underworld, even in the severely trimmed version deemed suitable for MTV viewers, cemented Reznor's status as dark prince of the alternative-rock world.

Nine Inch Nails' next video trawled similar ground while returning Reznor to front and center. "Hurt" (1995), directed by Simon Maxwell, is a live clip that offers a taste of the NIN concert experience, revisiting the foreboding imagery of decay and death of "Closer." Earlier Nine Inch Nails videos had similarly sought to invigorate the tired old performance video; "March of the Pigs" (1994) (directed by Peter Christopherson) was a one-take live performance that emphasized the self-destructiveness of Reznor's stage antics, and "Wish" (1992) looked like NIN headlining a show in Hell, with caged fans going apeshit and rapid cuts that shifted attention a blink faster than viewers could keep up with. Primarily filmed in long shot, "Hurt" renders Reznor a tiny figure, emoting his anthem of guilt and regeneration onstage against the backdrop of an enormous video screen. Like "Closer," "Hurt's" imagery is disturbing: atomic explosions, wounded soldiers, rotting corpses. Unlike "Closer," where he was contained entirely within the diegetic world of the video, here Reznor is explicitly outside it, a lone color figure (albeit one dressed entirely in black) posed against a black-and-white screen.

Alternating between long shots, with the crowd's pumping fists repeatedly visible against the video screen, and close-ups of Reznor's ashy-white face, his black hair matted with sweat, "Hurt" is a portrait of artist and audience communing over a shared vision of the world. And in its final image, a time-lapse reel of a dead animal's decay is played backward, implying that the cycle of collapse and despair so powerfully traced on NIN's 1994 album *The Downward Spiral*, and summarized in "Hurt," was not irreversible—a powerful image of restrained hope from a relentlessly dark performer.

Continuing where Reznor had left off, Marilyn Manson's videos embraced the 1990s hard-rock video aesthetic to the fullest: creepy, odd, distorted, and darkly beautiful. Manson was the unsettling chameleon at the videos' heart, part youth savior and part Antichrist, alternately saving and condemning a diseased world. In "Man That You Fear" (1997), Marilyn is a Christ figure harried by the boobish crowd, with even his wife, halo firmly planted on her head, ultimately consigning him to death. Taking to the other extreme, "Disposable Teens" (2000) has Manson as the Antichrist, dressed in full papal gear, overseeing a black mass Last Supper with a human sacrifice as the centerpiece. Manson owed his affinity for gross-out bodily imagery to the brothers Quay, David Cronenberg, and Mark Romanek, and his mutable video identity to David Bowie and Madonna. Manson is a dollmaker straight out of the Quays' *Street of Crocodiles* (1986) in "Tourniquet" (1996), leads a high-school marching band in full Nazi garb in "Fight Song" (2001), and wears a 1940s aviator helmet in "Sweet Dreams" (1996) like he'd had a bad crash in World War II and never been quite the same afterward. Manson's body is often under threat in his videos: attacked by the uncomprehending public and ripped apart by scientists in "Dope Show" (1998), his legs in *Crash*-like braces in "Tourniquet." In "Coma White" (1999),

Manson steps into the most famous short film of all time: Abraham Zapruder's footage of the assassination of President John F. Kennedy. Marilyn was JFK (with then-girlfriend Rose McGowan as Jackie) confronted by a Dallas of Satanists and freaks, black flags flapping in the breeze before shots ring out and Jack-Marilyn is killed, once more, for the sins of others. Looking to the same counterculture as Manson, Ministry's "Just One Fix" (1993), directed by Peter Christopherson, stars heroin guru William S. Burroughs in a drug-copping nightmare notable for its scratched frames, treated stock, and hazy imagery. "Just One Fix" intended to be not just about drugs, but to be an imitation drug trip itself, with Burroughs the one-man Greek chorus signaling to us to keep away, in order to avoid the fate of "Just One Fix's" dead-end junkies.

The Candy Revolution

With Nirvana, Nine Inch Nails, and others having taken the aura of darkness as far as it could go, a new wave of alt-rock videos blew in like a cool breeze in the mid-1990s, scattering the gloom with their self-referentiality, their casual sense of humor, and their pop sensibility. Directors like Spike Jonze, Jamie Thraves, and Dayton and Faris raided the storehouse of a century of moving images, paying homage to everything from turn-of-the-century cinematic innovators to half-remembered 70s television shows. These directors also returned to straightforward narrative, reclaiming the video's possibilities as a storytelling medium. Like the dogs that burst into the studio in Weezer's "Undone (The Sweater Song)," directed by Jonze, these videos ran wild amidst pop culture, pillaging as they saw fit, borrowing, recontextualizing, and recalibrating in order to craft new videos out of old inspirations. The pastiche videos were partially an outgrowth of slacker culture's emphasis on kitsch, and a shift away from grunge's emphasis on angst and disillusion, but they were also a response to the tragedy of Kurt Cobain's suicide. After Cobain's death, light-heartedness was the sole response to his loss that did not feel mawkish or self-serving. Even Cobain's former bandmate Dave Grohl got into the act with the downright silly videos for his new band the Foo Fighters.

If Trent Reznor was the Frank Miller of MTV, recalibrating the music video to align with his pitch-black sensibility, Green Day were comic-book artists at the opposite extreme. Picture *Archie* if Jughead were a mental patient with a raging boner, and you've got the candy-colored videos for the band's breakthrough singles "Longview" (1994) and "Basket Case" (1994), directed by Mark Kohr. Later, these clips would be closely emulated by Eminem, who made the comic-book connection more literal in "My Name Is," "The Real Slim Shady," and "Without Me," with animation, bubble dialogue, and the like. Scraping off the gloom of "Heart-Shaped Box," "Closer," and the like, Green Day replaced it with a pop-punk's cheerful "fuck you!" Made in shades strictly verboten to the lumberjack fashion mentality of grunge, these videos, bathed in fluorescent green, Day-Glo yellow, and purple, were pure eye candy after all the gloomy, avant-garde-inspired videos, like a Slurpee after six straight months of fine dining. Both "Longview" and "Basket Case" make out adolescence to be a form of low-grade insanity, with Billie Joe bouncing off the walls in the former like a wild monkey, and the trio rocking their local mental institution in the latter. "Longview" takes up arms against boredom, with Green Day turning lead singer Billie Joe's cramped apartment into the scene of an assault on domesticity. Billie Joe, fed up with the slim pickings on afternoon television, takes to riding his coffee table like a surfboard, rips his couch to shreds, and then sits back placidly amidst the carnage, content to let his now-deceased sofa's feathers adorn him like a paper crown. "Basket Case" moves to an insane asylum, with the band as mental patients coaxed into performing their anthem of post-adolescent anomie. Skewing to an older, wearier audience, "When I Come Around" (1995), also directed by Mark Kohr, turns Hitchcock's *Rear Window* into a minor-key romance of broken dreams, its geometry of exchanged glances defining a world of dissatisfied souls, all hopelessly wishing to find themselves anyplace other than where they were.

Another wing of the candy revolution took root in southern California, where postmodern folkie Beck Hansen shot out of obscurity on the wings of his effervescent single "Loser" (1994). Much like the song itself, the video, directed by Steve Hanft, is slapdash, jury-rigged, and ultra-low-budget, entirely lacking the glossy sheen of Romanek, Pellington et al. Shot in grainy black and white and washed-out color, "Loser" looks like every cent of the approximately $17 spent on producing the video made it onscreen.

Slow-motion footage of Beck energetically leaping around in Indian headdress is intercut with a plain wooden coffin's passage through a wooded landscape and a film-negative image of cheerleaders in knee socks doing exercises in a cemetery. "Loser" is rock as standup comedy, a California kid with blond bangs looking at hip-hop in a funhouse mirror, and the video for "Loser" is a similarly surreal mishmash of silliness. If Beck circa 1994 was like the Beastie Boys' younger, cuter little brother, "Loser" was like a Beasties video made for peanuts, motivated by a winning sense of play. The Angel of Death washes windshields, and Beck mans a leaf-blower onstage before doing a spectacularly inept breakdance. The Angel of Death joins a pair of cheerleaders in a cemetery, shirtless but with mask carefully affixed, and Beck himself washes windshields, flames shooting out of his squeegee. After a quick glimpse of him performing onstage, Beck is then on the beach, seen from the waist up in a wetsuit. As the camera pans out, we see it is in tatters, and that he is wearing a pair of shorts to cover his legs.

The resident genius of cut-and-paste made videos that imitated the aesthetic of his songs, jumbling together genres, themes, and images until the surreal and the strange came to feel perfectly normal. Collaborating with Steve Hanft and Mark Romanek, and directing on his own, Beck, whose grandfather Al Hansen was a member of the Fluxus art movement, crafted a visual analog to his musical output—a sample-heavy set of disjointed parts held together by good humor and charisma. "Where It's At" (1996), directed by Hanft, is a series of witty juxtapositions, with Beck in a variety of predicaments that required an MC-like line of patter. Playing a host of characters, from used-car salesman to tuxedoed lounge lizard to jumpsuit-clad prisoner picking up trash on the highway, Beck finds himself in unexpected situations, only to learn that everywhere he went, his two turntables and a microphone still carried the day.

Like Dave Meyers' later work with Missy Elliott, "Where It's At" teaches viewers how to hear the music, the video's narrative collision of antithetical musical sensibilities unified by Beck's slacker charm emphasizing the triumphant stylistic mashup of Beck's music. Having ransacked all genres, "Where It's At" transcends genre; even Beck's incarnation as a country-music line caller instigates a slew of boot-clad feet to stomping and twirling. "The New Pollution" (1997), directed by Beck himself, also serves up a heaping portion of genre soup: Mormon singing groups cohabiting with swinging 60s hepcats, James Brown imitators, and spandex-clad metalheads. "The New Pollution" looks the way it sounds—an effortless mash-up of styles held together by Beck's own shambling charisma, and a spot-on knack for getting to the heart of its parodic subjects' silliness.

"Devil's Haircut" (1996), directed by Mark Romanek, casts Beck as a cowboy lost in the New York City of Francis Ford Coppola's *The Conversation* (1974). Employing a directorial palette straight out of the American New Wave, Romanek uses zooms and freeze-frames of Beck adrift in New York (at Coney Island, surrounded by birds in flight at Astor Place, in a Chinatown parade) for an aesthetic both numinous and menacing. The freezes, checking in at regularly scheduled intervals, suggest the presence of an unseen, watching figure—an implication confirmed at video's end, when Romanek returns to each of the locales where Beck has been and zooms in on hidden corners of each frame, revealing mysterious figures in black, taping and recording his every move. Romanek's video echoes Coppola's famous film of surveillance and Brian De Palma's similarly themed *Blow Out*, reminiscent in both theme and style of those masterpieces of free-floating paranoia. Romanek twists the unsettling quality of those New Wave classics and makes it into a condition of the musical idol's daily existence, with Beck unwittingly recorded at every step of his journey.

Perhaps the most unexpected participants in this movement toward light-heartedness were the Foo Fighters, the new project begun by former Nirvana drummer Dave Grohl. Their video for "Big Me" (1996), directed by Jesse Peretz, was literally candied. A Jonze-esque parody of the Mentos commercials that had become popular among advocates of kitsch, "Big Me" is surprisingly feather-light and comic, considering that Cobain had died only eighteen months prior. Playing burly workmen who help a woman lift her (absurdly tiny) car out of a tight parking spot, and soccer players who venture across a busy street by climbing through a limousine, the Foos' video cobbles together the plots of the European oddities that had pleased/plagued watchers of late-night television. The band has fun at their own expense, too; during the first sequence, guitarist Pat Smear looks like he's about to plotz while lifting the car, and Grohl, mugging shamelessly for the camera, mocks his own boyish good-naturedness. "Big Me" was a reminder that, as short films, music videos were so compact that one joke would suffice to carry an entire clip.

The Foos returned to comedy with "Learn to Fly" (1999) (also directed by Peretz), which sensibly adopts an airplane motif, with Grohl and his bandmates taking on a variety of roles (overweight female passenger, starstruck teenager, swishy flight attendant, wisecracking pilot, chic rock star) in their own version of *Airplane!* (1980). Grohl, being one of the few passengers not to drink the tainted coffee planted onboard by a pair of nefarious cleaners (Tenacious D's Jack Black and Kyle Gass), steps in to guide a commercial airliner to safety, quickly studying an instruction manual on flying before taking the wheel. The objects of ridicule of "Learning to Fly" are wearily familiar, picking on the overweight, the geeky, and the nonheterosexual, but with the Foo Fighters themselves playing nearly all the roles, the humor is gentle, not vicious. The best Foo Fighters video, though, and undoubtedly one of the most astounding clips of the decade, was "Everlong," directed by Michel Gondry (see chapter 7).

Equally unlikely comedians Yo La Tengo made one of the decade's funniest videos, the rock-school parody "Sugarcube" (1997) (directed by Phil Morrison). The trio, notorious for their lack of affect onstage, screen their latest video, a particularly emotionless rendition of their song, before being interrupted by a label executive. "Are you scared of making money? Cause with a video like that, you don't have to worry about it! Young band, you are going to rock school!" Co-lead singer Georgia Hubley takes to rock school like a fish to water, assiduously taking notes on hot-button issues like hobbit-themed songwriting and the Foghat Rule (a band's fourth album should be double-live). Her husband and bandmate Ira Kaplan does not fare as well, jeered by their teacher for taking out a poster of Lou Reed in class, and sniffed out secretly playing his clarinet in the boys' room. Georgia is hit on by a hair-metal casualty with a pink shag, and the band are taught how to smash up their hotel rooms. (Ira, gamely trying his best to be a badass, jumps on the bed.) Four weeks later, the band screen their new, improved video—which is exactly the same as their first stab. Crowing, their boss announces, "Gentlemen, you've just made your first number 1 video," and the band toss their gold caps in the air, having officially graduated from the School of Rock. Yo La Tengo and Morrison wrap their fans in the cocoon of a shared joke, made at the expense of rock-star profligacy and stupidity.

Nerd-rock seemed to spawn its own brand of nerd-rock videos—inside jokes about the band, sophisticated I-paid-attention-in-school humor, and sophomoric clowning. Pavement's "Cut Your Hair" (1994) is a shaggy-dog story of shaggy locks, its structure little more than a series of non sequiturs. One band member sneezes out a bunny rabbit, another gets a trim wearing a gorilla mask, and lead singer Stephen Malkmus is handed a crown, scepter, and cocktail before sitting in the barber's chair. The Rentals' "Friends of P" (1995), directed by leadman Matt Sharp (already familiar with big-time videomaking from his day job as Weezer's bassist) and Jason Russio, imagined what a Communist music video would look like (echoing the Eisensteinian Soviet propaganda of Test Dept.'s "Total State Machine" of 1985, which employed a socialist-realist film language of Constructivist geometry and heroic workers ascendant). The band, filmed in black and white, play their instruments motionlessly, and emotionlessly, the only movement in the frame the straight up and down of Sharp's arm as he strums his guitar. Russian subtitles run at the bottom of the screen, ostensibly translating the song's lyrics, and after the song is over, the band stands (almost) stock-still for another thirty seconds, as if waiting for some offscreen presence to inform them that the video has come to a conclusion. Never cracking a smile, or even intimating that its joke might actually be funny, "Friends of P." is brilliant cultural pastiche, imagining music video cultivating eras and cultures distinctly foreign (to say the least) to its sensibility.

Hall of Mirrors

Like Spike Jonze and Mark Romanek, the husband-and-wife directing team of Jonathan Dayton and Valerie Faris often looked to other, older sources for initial inspiration, playfully subverting and adapting their influences. Unlike Jonze, though, Dayton and Faris were mostly unconcerned with being funny or clever; rather, they preferred to look for nodes of untapped emotion in the unlikeliest places, locating the beating, bleeding heart at the center of heretofore stolid bands like Smashing Pumpkins and the Red Hot Chili Peppers.

Their clip for the Pumpkins' "1979" (1996) tips its cap to *Dazed and Confused* (1993) and other paragons of 1970s teenage nostalgia (as well as their own video for Jane's Addiction's "Been Caught Stealing" [1990]), following bored teenagers over the course of an average day. A teen comedy in four minutes, taking in the backseat of a car, a raging house party, and the aimless, testosterone-filled hijinks of teenage boys and girls, "1979" is replete with the humor, anxiety, and pathos of adolescence. Teens drive around in circles, pause in an empty field to give their town the finger, and run wild through a Kwik-E-Mart. Throughout it all, lead singer Billy Corgan sings from the back seat of a car, smiling benevolently at their dead-end delinquency. Corgan has returned, as it were, to the scene of his adolescent crimes, bearing witness to the agony and the ecstasy of youth. Dayton and Faris' camera work provides a throbbing, buzzing first-person point of view, injecting the mundane with a tinge of the dream-like—an aesthetic they would use again for the teenage-fantasy dream sequence of Janet Jackson's "Go Deep" (1998). Dayton and Faris were seeped in nostalgia for a past of their own imagining, cobbled together out of memory, imagination, and stray fragments of pop culture. "1979" and R.E.M.'s "Tongue" (1995) are both pickled in fond recollections of the 1970s, with the latter a layman's ode to shag carpets, tacky clothes, shlocky hairstyles, and garish colors.

Dayton and Faris' clip for Smashing Pumpkins' "Tonight, Tonight" (1996) is equally self-aware, borrowing extensively from Georges Melies' legendary 1903 short *A Trip to the Moon*. *A Trip to the Moon* was one of the earliest films to embrace cinema's capability for fakery, its utterly unrealistic lunar sets silly enough to bring childish expressions of glee onto the faces of the most hardened cinéastes. Partially shot with a silent-era, hand-cranked camera, "Tonight, Tonight" reanimates the spirit of Melies' work, which, reemerging in the cultural arena ninety-three years after its first appearance, feels like a transmission from another era of human existence.

In addition to serving as a remarkable act of cinematic appropriation, "Tonight, Tonight" pinpoints a Victorian-romantic visual form that matches the Pumpkins' bittersweet sound, giving their lovelorn ballad an aura of timeless transcendence. Dayton and Faris are master cultural manipulators, conjoining a turn-of-the-century French cinematic visionary and a mid-1990s American rock band with aspirations to baroque grandeur in order to craft a unique melding of sound and vision, as if the music video were one enormous cultural warehouse from which any sound and any image from all of recorded history could be summoned at will.

Their video for Scott Weiland's "Barbarella" (1998) pays homage to the classic Nicolas Roeg film *The Man Who Fell to Earth* (1976), while the Red Hot Chili Peppers' "Otherside" (2000) borrows the fractured perspective and chilly landscapes of German Expressionist cinema, looking like an outtake reel from *The Cabinet of Dr. Caligari* (1920). (Other music videos made the link between music-video directing and hip-hop DJing present in "Otherside" yet more explicit; witness the world-as-turntable metaphor of Lauryn Hill's "Everything Is Everything" [1999], or the matching aural and visual loops of Roni Size and Reprazent's "Brown Paper Bag" [1997]). This spirit of inspired appropriation is also present in Dayton and Faris' clip for Oasis' "All Around the World" (1997), which lifts large chunks of the animated classic *Yellow Submarine*; an appropriate choice for a band with so enormous a debt to the Beatles. Dayton and Faris assemble a pop-psychedelic children's emporium of fantasy, a video pop-up book that flattens London, the planet, and the entire universe into panels of a glorious children's storybook. The directors' taste for dense mise-en-scène, also evident in "Tonight, Tonight" and "Californication," crams each frame full of constant activity. No sooner does one set of images appear than it begins to mutate, transforming into its successor. Like Romanek, Dayton and Faris were among the culture-savviest videomakers around; their videos abound with references to everything from Cubist painting (Porno for Pyros' "Pets" [1993]) to graphic novels (Korn's "Freak on a Leash" [1999]).

Spanning a century of popular culture, Dayton and Faris went from Melies to the Beatles to *Grand Theft Auto*, tapping into the dynamism of video games for the Red Hot Chili Peppers' "Californication" (2000). Dayton and Faris ape both the content and the style of a video game, from the "Now Loading . . ." graphic which begins the video to the Player Select screens, in which each of the Chili Peppers is a potential character. Because this is a music video, though, and not a game, the grounding rules of gaming coherence are not fully respected, and "Californication" melds together four different adventures, one for each member of the band, cutting regularly between them. "Californication" soars on its endless energy, its extreme-sports buzz, and its playful sense of possibility. Lifting the you-are-here camera work of video games, "Californication" is dreamlike in its seamless melding of multiple adventures. "Californication" is the best video game that never was, all endlessly propulsive motion without the encumbrance of joysticks and keypads. Dayton and Faris' editing is so artful that it takes multiple viewings just to parse out who does what, and how each band members' game coagulates into the other, and the shared finish. Finally, "Californication" is a video about brotherhood, one of the Chili Peppers' favorite topics. A band as a community; the metaphor stretches to encompass the band's fans and the entire fraying canvas of alternative rock. "Californication" was so successful it spawned a live-action semimake, "By the Way" (2002), in which the whole band leapt to the defense of Kiedis when he is kidnapped by a mulleted, mustachioed taxi driver with a jones for *Flashdance* moves.

Rallying the Troops

With hip-hop taking an ever-bigger bite out of the traditional rock demographic of white teenagers every year of the 1990s, putting a serious dent in alt-rock's dreams of communal representation and commercial domination, it was past time for a figure to emerge that would stanch the flow, holding the fort for rock bands yet to come. That man, taking his place in the pantheon of great video figures, was the Fly Guy, and his home was the 1998 clip for SoCal punk rockers the Offspring's satirical jab at wigger culture, "Pretty Fly (for a White Guy)," directed by future *Charlie's Angels* helmer McG. Having tried flattery in their attempts to cajole white listeners into sticking around, Offspring and their alt-rock homies were relegated to desperate measures in an attempt to prevent the last white suburban teenager from dropping that Sum 41 CD, and picking up 50 Cent instead.

Since "Pretty Fly" was a satire of the very audience the band hoped to maintain, the video's jabs were fairly gentle—satire mild enough that white hip-hop lovers themselves could embrace it. With his backward baseball cap, goggles, and thick gold chain, flashing wannabe gang symbols while rolling in his 6-4, the Fly Guy (played by the marvelous Guy Cohen) is the embodiment of a certain strand of emulatory American adolescence, looking to fit in by becoming someone else. Flashing a W (for West Coast) to a posse of homeboys, pumping his hydraulics while a pair of Hispanic vatos shake their heads in dismay, the Fly Guy is the white kid as eternally clueless outsider, hell-bent on emulating his cultural betters without ever understanding how or why.

"Pretty Fly (for a White Guy)" is soft-pedal satire, and even after the Fly Guy thoroughly embarrasses himself with a pitiful attempt at breakdancing, he remains as ebullient as ever, slouching his way up the path to his family's home in the suburbs in the video's final shot. The Offspring had their cake and ate it too, bashing the potential rock fans who had flown the coop while also getting to make a fun video like the hip-hop guys knew how to, with honeys in hot pants, souped-up cars bopping up and down, and the like. As with most music-video satire, "Pretty Fly" pokes fun at the very aspects of its video that would also attract an audience.

The post-Nirvana rock video had so fully embraced the visual aesthetic of obscurity, employing tangled symbolism as a matter of course, that it was easy to forget that music videos could also simply be short (narrative) films. Telling stories became another way of taking a stance—of indicating where, in the ever-proliferating continuum of aesthetic possibility, a performer stood. For videos like "1979" and Radiohead's "Just" (1995) the film metonymically stood in as a representation of the band's full musical-spiritual aesthetic. "Just" was a meditation object for the burgeoning cult of Radiohead, its opacity rendering it a suitable talisman of the band's buried truths.

On a crowded thoroughfare, a slightly harried man in a suit and tie, clearly a lawyer or businessman, trips over another man, lying prone on the sidewalk, half-curled into a fetal ball. Since the man looks neither mentally ill nor impoverished, the white-collar man offers his assistance in getting up off the pavement. "Just," like R.E.M.'s "Everybody Hurts," employs subtitles, a strategy that allows it to avoid the silent-film theatrics otherwise necessary to communicate plot developments in the music video. Reaching a crescendo of impatience, the increasingly flustered white-collar man demands to know, regardless of consequence, precisely why his anguished compatriot has chosen to perch himself on a public thoroughfare. In response to the man's slightly hostile question ("Do you want to know? Do you really want to know?"), he hurriedly nods his head, desperate for an answer that will resolve this frightful impasse.

Encountering this phenomenon in conjunction with our guide, viewers, tormented by the video's teasing intimations of great knowledge, clamor equally for an answer. As "Just" heads into a squalling, dissonant guitar solo, the prostrate man unleashes a great torrent of words, a verbal counterpart to guitarist Jonny Greenwood's streaming, fluid solo. As the white-collar man listens stunned to his compatriot's unleashed truths, the audience is left out of the loop, with no subtitles provided. Like a word earthquake, his speech fells everything in sight, culminating in the stunning final image of the same London sidewalk, now populated entirely by individuals, each curled into a fetal ball.

"Just" is a mystery video in two senses. In the first, it is a video about a puzzling occurrence, one that demands resolution: Who is this man? Why is he lying down on the sidewalk of a busy London street? What does he *say*? It is also an induction into a mystery in the sense of Greco-Roman cult religion—"Just" is the story of an absence to puzzle over, obsess about, and, finally, to create one's own answers for.

T&A Parade

Growing savvier to the high-gloss possibilities of the video, and its longstanding relationship to portrayals of female sexuality, some mid-to-late-90s alt-rock videos waxed conventional, looking more like Madonna than the Minutemen, embracing titillation in the hopes of winning viewers over. The results are mostly crass, pseudo-high-minded work that looked to push product on the backs of (unclothed) women. The videos lack the decency to admit their prurience, dressing up their risqué sexual content in high-art fabric.

Alanis Morissette's "Ironic" (1996), directed by Stephane Sednaoui, is a clip of the Canadian wunderkind singer-songwriter driving a clunker sedan down an empty highway. "Ironic" favors tight close-ups, with four different Alanises filling every seat of the car, alternately shrieking and freaking, each by turns cuddly, anguished, serious, and playful. Everywhere you look, there she is—a suitable metaphor for Morissette's enormous overexposure in 1995 and 1996, when her debut, *Jagged Little Pill*, became the best-selling album ever by a female artist, and of a certain narcissistic self-absorption. In "Ironic," there is no world outside the car's windows, just the different sides of Alanis—a set of imagery that suited her self-help-language damaged songs. Morissette may have kept her clothes on for the video, but "Ironic" embraces a brand of emotional nudity and self-absorption distinctly out of tune with alt-rock's affinity for irony and self-deprecation. "Ironic" was among the first shifts away from the dark content, themes, and imagery that had dominated the alt-rock video from Nirvana on, and the beginning of its replacement with carefully crafted facsimiles. "Thank U" (1998) took the whole emotional-nudity thing a bit too seriously, with a naked Alanis (her unmentionables digitally blurred) wandering the streets of the big city, her pain occasionally assuaged by the healing touch of compassionate strangers.

Taking T&A to the next level, with a facile attempt at justification via embracing female empowerment, is Prodigy's notorious "Smack My Bitch Up," which was relegated to the post-midnight wastelands of MTV when first released in 1998. Directed by Jonas Åkerlund, "Smack" is a first-person exploration of the seamy urban underworld, rife with the sex-and-violence cocktail familiar from countless Hollywood endeavors. The camera is positioned at eye-level, with jutting hands extending into the frame to provide a you-are-there feel. "Smack My Bitch Up" begins in the bathroom, where our protagonist showers, towels off, and attends to toilet before heading out for the evening.

Åkerlund's video intentionally seeks to implant in viewers the assumption that the protagonist is male, from the dingy, spartan accommodations, to the shaving cream and razor used after the shower. Out at a club, chain-smoking and downing shot after shot, our protagonist pinches a woman's butt on the stairs, attempts to fondle a miniskirted lovely, knocks down a dance-floor lothario, smashes a DJ's records, pukes blood, pulls an unfortunate bloke bodily off the toilet, pukes again on the street, heads to a strip club, buys a bottle, sprays champagne on strippers, gets a personal lap-dance, takes the dancer home, and shags her silly. As the stripper leaves, our protagonist's reflection is seen in a mirror, giving a glimpse of our alter ego for the first time; lo and behold, it is a woman, blond, rail-thin, with a slash of dark red lipstick for a mouth. Åkerlund's camera work gets progressively more distorted over the course of the clip, as if in imitation of our protagonist's increasing inebriation.

Åkerlund's use of first-person point of view, and his tweaking of technique to make what we see onscreen subjective, makes the video a subjective expression of one individual consciousness—music videos for modernists, if you will. To a more cynical eye, though, "Smack My Bitch Up" was just a highfalutin excuse for tits and beatdowns on MTV.

Another adaptation of the softcore aesthetic that similarly raised a ruckus, with supporters and detractors divided over whether it was art or filth, was Fiona Apple's "Criminal" (1997). "Criminal" is a copy of a copy, a video version of the controversial Calvin Klein commercials that were themselves imitations of homemade amateur pornography, featuring teenagers in forthright, lascivious poses. Apple, a twentysomething singer-songwriter whose narrow frame and long, dark tresses give her the look of an angry, articulate teenager, poses on the laps of shirtless hunks, in bed amidst rumpled sheets, and taking a bath, with a stranger's legs propped by her head. "Criminal" is by no means as graphic as "Smack My Bitch Up," but the intimation, oozing out of every frame of the video, is of sweaty, illicit sex, with Apple as an underage vixen. Seeing her in her underwear, lying on the living-room carpet amidst an array of other similarly attired girls and boys elicits a mixture of sexual magnetism and taboo voyeurism, creating the overwhelming desire to simultaneously look and look away.

Director Mark Romanek makes the CK connection, and by extension the link to amateur pornography, concrete with a consistently overlit frame, like a first-time director overcompensating for dark interiors with floodlights, exposing glare in practically every shot. Apple is glimpsed in a closed loop on a television screen, as if some unseen presence was playing back previously shot footage. Both "Criminal" and "Smack My Bitch Up" leave similarly sour aftertastes, as if art-school M.F.A.'s had chosen to take the same salacious objectification of women that had always been the province of videos, and update it with a sprinkling of female empowerment and a taste of avant-garde experimentalism. In neither case is the experiment wholly successful; while both videos remain eminently watchable, neither achieves the perfect melding of sound and image that is the imprimatur of a great video. Instead, one is left with the distress that arises from being hoodwinked, of buying the same ideological garbage of woman-as-object in a shiny new package.

Not all 90s women bought into the sexualized self-promotion of "Criminal" and "Smack My Bitch Up." Performers like PJ Harvey, Portishead's Beth Gibbons, Tori Amos, and Jill Sobule shied away from the relentless, quasi-pornographic prurience of the average music video, choosing instead to explore other genres, other forms of expression. Harvey's videos with photographer Maria Mochnacz featured her as a nightclub diva ("Down by the Water"), a brokenhearted lover ("C'mon Billy"), and a spooky hotel guest ("A Perfect Day Elise").

Mochnacz's videos capture something essential to Harvey's raucous, elegant music: its air of continuous self-invention, of knowingly, constantly taking on new roles. Portishead, makers of elegant, anxious trip-hop, made a James Bond film to go along with their faux-Bond theme "Sour Times" (1994), with Gibbons as a grieving widow with a few secrets of her own. Director Alexander Hemming's video references Costa-Gavras' *Z* (1964) and Cold War thrillers, its fractured narrative ultimately revealing Gibbons as less victim than *noir* femme fatale. Sobule's "I Kissed a Girl" (1995), a peppy ode to casual lesbianism, is set in a Day-Glo suburban paradise—adulthood as imagined by a daydreaming preteen, complete with Fabio as adoring husband. Tori Amos' "Silent All These Years" (1993) is stripped-down in comparison, just Amos, a white backdrop, and a plain white box, with director Cindy Palmano using a slight time-delay effect that heightens the video's dreamlike aura. For Amos, as for Sobule, Harvey, and Gibbons, being true to your art did not necessarily mean keeping to the straight and narrow.

Frat Boys and Altar Boys

Ultimately, it was a series of hand gestures that did in the alternative-rock video, voiding "Smells Like Teen Spirit's" dream and leaving a fractured set of subgenres in its place. Grunge and its immediate followers had always been about voice and performance; its archetypal symbols were the testosterone-heavy howl of singers like Soundgarden's Chris Cornell and Pearl Jam's Eddie Vedder and the populist stage dive (best practiced by Vedder in "Evenflow") affirming a direct relationship of trust and affinity between audience and performer. A new wave of performers, though, elevated gesture above voice and performance, their attention-grabbing mechanisms symbolic of alternative rock's being wrenched off the course set by Nirvana. Limp Bizkit's Fred Durst and Creed's Scott Stapp each claimed a portion of the mantle once held by Kurt Cobain; Durst as the voice of disaffected youth, and Stapp as the latest successor to Kurt's barbaric yawp. The hands gave them both away, though, and what had begun as the rebellion of the high-school losers ended as the faux rebellion of the faux losers and secret frat boys (and altar boys).

Stapp's baritone may have owed a great deal to Vedder and Cornell, but watch the video for Creed's "My Sacrifice" (2001) (directed by Dave Meyers), and after soaking in the Rapture–End of Days atmosphere of the clip's floods and blind wise men, note Stapp's favorite pose while barreling out the song's chorus. Again and again, he returns to a similar stance: arms held straight out, head tilted back, eyes closed. The Creed frontman has a serious Jesus jones, and his band's videos betray no intention of hiding it. Embracing the Jesus Christ pose, Stapp is less poet than savior, and unlike Cobain, Vedder et al., he does not blush at intimations of his anointed role as leader. Stapp is the alt-rock leading man having shed his cocoon of self-doubt, and the results are unswervingly self-righteous and pompous. The tunes are catchy, and the videos watchable if bland, but Creed's narrowed vision of a youth culture is one distinctly limited to the faithful.

Meanwhile, Limp Bizkit's Fred Durst was the Fly Guy come to life. Like that joyriding hip-hop wannabe, Durst, clad in his trademark backward red baseball cap, is a walking joke who does not quite realize he himself is the punch line. Durst's band Limp Bizkit were the foremost of the rap-rock bands of the late 90s, which in their case meant a metal sound joined to hip-hop attitude. And so we have Durst, in his band's video for "N2Gether Now" (1999) (a duet with the Wu-Tang Clan's Method Man), accentuating his verses with arms held above the head, thumb and index fingers forming an L and reverse L, or the sidearm version of same, as if in imitation of some crime-film baddie pointing his Glock. Durst was a metal mook who wanted to be Ice Cube, and his band provided a rap-dusted version of metal to suburban kids who were too afraid of real hip-hop to give it a go. Durst was a kabuki imitation of a hip-hop star, whose awkward, forced hand gestures gave the game away. With all those Ls being tossed up like gang symbols by Durst, any valley girl would have seen them for what they were: a self-branding L for Loser.

Stapp and Durst were not the causes of alternative rock's going awry, merely symptoms. With their ascendancy, it became clear that the meek of "Smells Like Teen Spirit," the sons and daughters of the Replacements, the Minutemen, and Hüsker Dü, would not inherit the earth. Rather, crafty, skin-deep imitations ruled the roost, and by the time Jimmy made his way to the house party of "The Middle," he found that Kurt, Eddie, and the rest of the gang had left long ago.

CHAPTER 6

Spike and Michel

Spike and Michel

MTV may have created its own subculture, and its own notions of artistry, but it had fallen short of feature filmmaking in creating its own geniuses—artists who fully grasped, and embraced, the peculiar possibilities and limitations of the music video. Throughout the 1980s, the music video was a hotspot for experimentation and innovation, with directors like Godley and Creme, Russell Mulcahy, Steve Barron, Jean-Baptiste Mondino, and Danny Kleinman breaking out as exemplary short-filmmakers. However, the notion of director as auteur did not truly reach the music video until the early 90s, and the rise of two film-makers who would come to dominate the form as no directors before them had done: Spike Jonze and Michel Gondry. (MTV had laid the groundwork for greater recognition of directors by posting directors' names in the credits of every video they showed, beginning in 1993.) Jonze and Gondry would later rise to Hollywood prominence as the directors of *Being John Malkovich* (1999) and *Eternal Sunshine of the Spotless Mind* (2004), respectively, but their apprenticeships were served in the music-video factories. Brothers beneath the skin, both directors tugged playfully at the genre conventions of the music video, crafting hip, self-aware clips that rewarded multiple viewings and marked the beginning of a new era in videomaking. Jonze, a TV brat at heart, sought solace in the half-remembered joys of the culturally fleeting, choosing the ephemeral, and the simulacrum, over the lasting and real, creating something fresh out of culture's stale leftovers. Where Jonze was more pop-culture savvy, sticking collective cultural memory in a blender and hitting "puree," Gondry mostly avoided the familiar thickets of pop, preferring to cobble together an alternate world of the unusual and alluring. Never satisfied with simplicity where complexity would do, Gondry's music-video work embraced the tangled, gnarled aesthetic of modernism, alleviating that form's fatal seriousness with a soupçon of Gallic humor and a twist of sheer oddity.

French Twist

Gondry, a Frenchman born in Versailles in 1963, was an art-school graduate who entered the world of the music video through the back door, directing videos on a shoestring budget for his band Oui-Oui. His later French work includes two videos whose bravura technical mastery and charming wit are precursors to his American videos. His video for Jean-Francois Coen's tender ballad "La Tour de Pise" (1993) is a small masterpièce, turning itself into a combined sing-along and lecture on graphic design. Beginning with a screen set up like a panel of cards, Gondry establishes a rhythm of opening the panels from left to right, top to bottom. It takes a minute, though, to realize that the panels, a mélange of natural imagery and snippets of the French landscape, also contain commercial signs, and that those signs spell out, in bits and fragments, the lyrics to "La Tour de Pise." Some of the signs from which the lyrics are snatched are highly familiar (the "La" of the song's title is taken from the end of a Coca-Cola logo), while others are delightfully one-of-a-kind. Gondry provides a playful answer to the age-old music-video question "How do you turn music into image?"

During the song's closing guitar solo, Gondry offers the comic coup de grace: a sign that says "guitar," followed by a series of musical notes. "La Tour de Pise" is a dream for post-structuralist music buffs seeking to deconstruct the music video, but Gondry is less concerned with theory than praxis. Enjoying the challenges he set for himself, Gondry creates little worlds with every video, each one complete with its own unique composition and rules. Part of the joy of watching a Michel Gondry video lay in determining just what those rules might be.

Gondry's clip for IAM's "Je Danse Le Mia" (1993) likewise adopted a rigorous structure that paradoxically left room for a great deal of playfulness and spontaneity. Using the technique known as zoom-morphing, Gondry's camera unceasingly penetrates further and further into its established space. This was no mere trick of beginning with a wide-angle long shot and zooming closer; Gondry starts fairly close in to his subjects, making you wonder just how he can possibly maintain this wire-walk for the clip's entire length. Going from a performance at a smoke-filled club to a street scuffle to a series of middle-aged guys chanting the song's chorus, "Je Danse Le Mia" is a perpetual-motion machine that never appears bored with anything in its sights. In the video's most remarkable magic trick, Gondry zooms into the sunglasses of lead MC

Akhenaton as he scuffles with a bystander. Reveling in having seemingly painted himself into a corner, Gondry zooms deeper into the shot of his sunglasses until he is focused on their reflection, managing to zoom his way into a reverse shot of his original shot. Like a restless, gifted child who can only summon the interest for a project when challenged beyond his capabilities, Gondry delights in making the impossible possible.

His French videos having attracted her attention, Gondry set to work in 1993 on his first clip for a non-French audience: the Icelandic chanteuse Björk's "Human Behaviour." A twisted take on the classic fairy tale, "Human Behaviour" turns Björk into a Little Red Riding Hood manqué. Since "Human Behaviour" is a surrealist fairy tale, its governing theme is that actions lack consequences; therefore, although Björk falls hundreds of feet to the ground, in the next sequence, she floats in a river, the moon bathing her face with white light. In the topsy-turvy atmosphere of "Human Behaviour," the bear, not mankind, is king, and his reign is a return to environmental wholeness. Gondry runs wild inside the fairy tale, twisting it into both a visual extension of Björk's dotty, fanciful imagination and a Sierra Club–friendly cartoon (much like the subtle environmentalism of his video for Oui Oui's "Le Caillou" [1989]).

Here, as in much that would follow, Gondry tinkers with differing levels of reality, establishing one baseline of reality only to immediately snatch it away. Gondry's videos render it nearly impossible to establish what is and is not real; instead, they must be taken on faith, their illogic accepted as logic. Never content to leave us content, Gondry unceasingly tampers with his product, his wizardry poking and prodding our senses. Fundamentally dreamlike, Gondry's videos follow the irrepressible logic of reverie—objects shrink and grow without warning, perspectives suddenly shift, and, most essentially, the fundamental rules of reality are subtly tweaked.

Like the ideal collaborations of architect and client, in which the client's well-articulated desires and the architect's technical know-how and artistic savvy meld to create a superior final product, the pairing of Gondry and Björk has been one of the most fruitful in the history of the music video. Let loose by her music's avant-garde daring to dream freely, Gondry's work for Björk is among the most unfettered work in his oeuvre. It is also a pitch-perfect visual complement to Björk's music, composed of a similar blend of humor, beauty, and sheer oddity. Björk has been Gondry's best client because her music already exists on the borderline between fantasy and reality. Is Björk real, or does she merely play herself on TV? Gondry, fascinated by exploring the liminal regions where dreaming and waking hours, the real world and the imagined world, mingle, found the perfect collaborator in Björk, whose songs are practically Gondry videos all on their own.

Björk and Gondry collaborated on five more videos, each of which elaborated on her kooky-chanteuse vibe. "Army of Me" (1995) features Björk as the driver of a three-story-high tank, so large that regular-sized cars drive underneath it. Her body contains wonders as well: her legs magically extend so she can reach the tank's engine, and a dentist extracts a gleaming diamond from her mouth. Needless to say, since this is Gondry, the dentist is a gorilla, and Björk must tie him down to retrieve her treasure. Tossing the diamond into her vehicle's engine, it rumbles back to life, and she steers her way to a nearby museum. Wearing a black karate outfit, she steps past some Damien Hirst-style color-field paintings and sets a stick of dynamite next to a sleeping statue. Running out just seconds before the museum blows up, she returns after the smoke has cleared to find the statue, now flesh and blood, awake and unscathed, and the pair hug, surrounded by broken artworks and dead bodies. Is Björk an art-world avenger, literally blowing up in the face of the mediocre and the careerist? Is it a touching futuristic love story à la *Blade Runner* (1982)? Or is it her lyrics' promise that "if you complain once more, you'll meet an army of me" brought to Technicolor life? With "Army of Me," as with the majority of Gondry's work, the meaning is less in interpretation of individual segments than in their all-over sensation. Like certain paintings of the Pop Art era, they are meant to be ingested all at once, not broken down into their constituent elements. "Army of Me" is funny, bizarre, imaginative, and a touch frightening—a formula that appears time and again in Gondry's work.

A recurring theme in Gondry's work is the attempted reconciliation of nature and technology, lending to nature some of technology's solidity and to the man-made some of nature's essential mystery and beauty. In seeking to unite diametric opposites, Gondry looks to the imagination for inspiration. In "Isobel" (1995), a set of lightbulbs with miniature airplanes growing inside bloom in the ground, and a small metropolis sprouts in the dirt of a garden. Björk is enveloped by the tiny airplanes, each buzzing and emitting light like mechanical dragonflies. Gondry enjoys keeping his viewers on their toes, denying the comfort of steady values or stable measures. "Hyperballad" (1996) includes video-game-like footage of Björk dashing past electricity towers and diving into a ditch, but midway through the video, Gondry reverses course: the video game imagery becomes real, and what had initially been dismissed as obviously fake becomes something neither here nor there, caught between the real and the unreal. His video for the Chemical Brothers' "Let Forever Be" (1999) is a similarly dizzying closed loop of reversals promulgated through sleight-of-hand, with digital effects and clunky, handmade faux effects dueling for supremacy.

Above all, Gondry revels in blurring boundaries, crafting puzzle boxes where fantasy and imagination take precedence over logic and narrative. This is most evident in his video for Björk's "Bachelorette" (1997) where layer after layer of complexity piled onto an initially simple premise. Like "Je Danse Le Mia" and the Foo Fighters' "Everlong," "Bachelorette" is an extended riff whose power partially derives from Gondry's remarkable expansion of its seemingly limited capabilities. "Bachelorette" begins with Björk's voiceover: "One day I found a big book buried deep in the ground. I opened it, but all the pages were blank. And to my surprise, it started writing itself." Mixing grainy, flickering images of Björk in the big city with archival urban photographs, "Bachelorette" evokes a bygone era in the life of the metropolis, and in the history of the musical. Enthused about the book, her publisher accompanies her to the office of a theatrical impresario, who agrees to put on a show based on the book. Opening night, the curtain rises, and wouldn't you just know it—the show we see onstage bears more than a passing resemblance to the story we've already seen. Except that the mise-en-scène has grown even more stylized and outlandish—the book has grown man-sized, the train heading to the city is one solitary car whose side flips up to allow for the protagonist's egress, and Björk's path to the publisher's door is lined with words. Ourobouros-like, the play swallows the staging of the play itself, moving to a smaller stage concealed at the back of the stage. The train grows smaller, the skyscrapers shorter, and the show's audience is similarly miniaturized. Gondry has set up a hall of mirrors in which Björk's Great Adventure with the Book can be endlessly retold. Only at this point, Björk and her publisher beau part ways, and the story begins to disappear as mysteriously as it appeared. Her book's ending is erased, and key elements of the stage set start to vanish as well: her ex-boyfriend, sitting in the audience, turns into a shrub, a similar fate befalls his theatrical counterpart, and nature in general takes its revenge on this urban tale, a frightening leafy beast consuming everything in sight.

Gondry can never quite settle the tension between nature and society, neither here nor elsewhere, so he abandons "Bachelorette" on this ambiguous note of threatened destruction. There is a similarly unresolved tension swirling around the notion of art and artistic fecundity. Here, as in "Army of Me," sterile or clichéd art is punished with destruction—there by terrorism, and here by the revenge of Mother Nature. Gondry sets up a straw man, depicting a particularly airless brand of creativity in order to knock it down. It is almost as if Gondry, as a young artist on the upward curve of his career, feels the need to wield his scythe and slice up a few easy targets, just to prove he could. The rhetorical violence may feel a bit over-the-top and unnecessary, but it is part and parcel of Gondry's mission to crown himself Something New. In his passion to reimagine the possibilities of the music video, Gondry took the occasion, Godzilla-like, to swipe with his giant paw at the pretensions of the rival arts as well.

The theatricality of "Bachelorette" is evidence of Gondry's persistent fascination with performance, a trait that bears full flower in his Busby Berkeley-esque clip for Daft Punk's "Around the World" (1997). Gondry sets in motion an ingenious rotation of figures, like the movement of an infinitely complex watch. Five separate groups of individuals move around a central platform, each marching to the beat of their own drummers in sync with the rhythms of the song. B-boys with tiny shrunken heads appended to their track suits, skeletons, space explorers, mummified hospital patients, and bathing beauties move to the beat, with Gondry's camera alternately close up and swirling above the dancers, lifting Berkeley's camera angle of choice. Gondry's DIY musical provides no context, although it clearly takes place on a soundstage. It merely is, as if the camera had stumbled on the event *in medias res*. Gondry synchronizes his dancers' movement with the different sounds of "Around the World," each group of dancers representing one discrete instrument: the B-boys bounce up and down a flight of stairs in time with the bass line, the bathing beauties dance to the synthesizer's beep and burble, and the space explorers circle the stage as a visual representation of the vocal track. Gondry is summoning the ghost of the Hollywood musical past, but it also aims for a quasi-scientific process of alchemization. "Around the World" seeks to turn music into motion, directly translating sound into vision.

Straight-faced absurdity is also the order of the day in Gondry's video for Beck's "Deadweight" (1997), ostensibly meant to promote Danny Boyle's *A Life Less Ordinary*, the film from whose soundtrack it is taken. Gondry lifts a good deal of footage from *A Life*, but he uses it to spin an entirely different yarn. (Likewise, his video for Polyphonic Spree's "Light and Day" [2004] borrows from Gondry's own film *Eternal Sunshine of the Spotless Mind*, snipping out and replacing the characters' mouths to turn scenes from the movie into a comically amateurish attempt at lip-syncing.) On a golden-hued beach where children frolic and couples soak up the sun, we spot a traditional-looking office setup straight out of a 1950s movie: metal desk, file cabinet, coat rack. Beck sits behind the desk, dressed in a conservative black suit, fussing with his papers, entirely oblivious to his idyllic surroundings.

"Deadweight" is a testament to the powers of shot and reverse shot, with Gondry cleverly cutting between small doings on the beach and larger-scale scenes from the film itself. A man tosses a matchbox car into the water, and the next shot shows a truck tumbling over a cliff; Beck falls into the sand, and *Life* star Ewan McGregor hits the ground in a similar position, pummeled by a posse of thugs. Gondry, relishing the prospect of taking the familiar and rendering it unfamiliar, slaps a traditional American office smack in the middle of a traditional American vacation. After that parlor trick, what could be better than to follow the joke to its logical conclusion? Packing a suitcase full of Hawaiian shirts and a framed piece of wallpaper (his family photos cover the walls), Beck puts on a white leisure suit and heads to an average-looking office. Setting up a beach chair in the middle of the office floor, he soaks his toes in the now-liquid carpet. In the final scene, Beck heads to a movie theater, where he watches himself relaxing on the beach and working at the office, and laughs heartily at the ludicrous absurdity of it all. A gloss on the classic scene in Luis Buñuel's *The Phantom of Liberty* (1974) where a bourgeois family and their guests sit around a table, each perched atop a toilet, with individuals occasionally excusing themselves, entering a small room, and eating, "Deadweight" provocatively jumbles the stuff of our everyday lives and shows us the world afresh.

Gondry's recurring interests culminate and consolidate in his masterpiece, the Foo Fighters' "Everlong" (1997). "Everlong" is an irruption of irrationality within the orderly confines of comforting, safe space. It also features Gondry's most detailed disquisition on dreaming (succeeding his darkly humorous video for Cibo Matto's "Sugar Water" [1996]), a full-on philosophical exploration of the dream state in which it ultimately becomes impossible to say which part of "Everlong" is "real" and what is merely dream.

"Everlong" begins in black and white, with two fearsome-looking strangers lurking in the bushes of a suburban street. Slipping inside one home, the camera crawls up the stairs, past a wall of photos of the man of the house and his wife (played, respectively, by Foos leader Dave Grohl and drummer Taylor Hawkins, in drag) and into their bedroom, where the happy couple slumbers. Zooming in on Dave's face, washes of water pour over the screen (a traditional signifier for the beginning of a dream sequence), and the placid suburbanite is transformed into a punk rocker, with black leather jacket and bleached spiky hair. Black and white also switches to color for the dream, in a reversal of cinematic convention. Striding past a pair of out-of-place lumberjack types (played by his bandmates Pat Smear and Nate Mendel) at an 80s-themed party, Dave struts into a room full of New Wave revelers to find his wife being hassled by the very same rednecks. Back at home, Dave's wife also slips into a dream, in which she reads a romance novel while sitting on a rocking chair in a rural cabin. Suddenly, a trapdoor creeps open in the floor and a hand pokes out from underneath. Back to Dave's dream, where his rage at the offending miscreants causes his hand to grow to superhuman size. First smacking them around with his outsized appendage, Dave grabs one by the lapels and bashes his head repeatedly against the low tin ceiling in time with the song's pounding drums. Dave, still in bed, punches the air in his sleep. The would-be assailants vanish from Dave's dream, only to transfer themselves over to his wife's dream, lurking outside her cabin. In Dave's dream, the couple leave the party and end up in a room filled by a giant rotary telephone. The phone rings, and Dave and Taylor cover their ears, shielding themselves from the ear-splitting noise. Dave awakes and discovers that the phone is ringing in their bedroom.

Gondry, deliberately laying out his cards openly here, is setting up his audience for a major fall with this supposed return to normalcy. Picking up the phone, Dave immediately looks over at his sleeping wife. Taylor, trapped in her cabin by the backwoods types, bars the doors in a desperate attempt to keep them out. Meanwhile, Dave chops wood, blithely oblivious to the mounting crisis. In bed, Dave desperately tries to shake his wife awake (which registers in her dream as one of the intruders knocking her around) and, gritting his teeth, struggles to fall asleep once again and join her in her dream. He first finds himself in a different bed, caressed by a bevy of lovely ladies, but he shakes that dream off and the women fall away like a disused backdrop, the only evidence of their presence the red shoe attached to one of the pieces of wood in his hand. As the baddies get set to wield their comically oversized chainsaw and hatchet, Dave pierces the membrane of his wife's dream, his hand grows to enormous size again, and he proceeds to smack the living daylights out of them then dump them in the lake (where they appear to be mere mannequins). We return to the bedroom, where the two intruders lie in wait by their bedside. Have they come to wreak yet more havoc? As it turns out, they've come to rock, and they strip off their costumes, their entire bodies popping out through their engorged mouths, simultaneously shedding their skins and playing their instruments as if possessed of four hands. Jamming on their instruments, the song returns front and center, and the preceding events become nothing more than—well, a bad dream.

Where the realm of sleep elsewhere in Gondry's work is rendered with soft-focus delicacy, "Everlong" is infected with a malevolence that is difficult to shake off. Dreams are not just real, they are potentially deadly, and while "Everlong" is humorous, there is also something genuinely frightening about its danger. Like Richard Linklater's film *Waking Life* (2001), "Everlong" is an extended series of interlocking dreams whose force often exceeds that of the waking world. The world of "Everlong" is unsafe, unstable, fraught with anxiety; even ensconced in their beds, deep in sleep, its middle-class couple is tormented by elusive, hideous demons. Although perhaps Gondry is satirizing Americans' obsession with violence, finding even placid-seeming suburbanites' dreams wholly devoted to violence and danger? "Everlong" subscribes to a logic familiar from our own dreams, not to mention the dream states created by cinematic masters like Buñuel and Linklater. Tools magically appear and disappear, limbs grow to enormous size in a matter of seconds, and unassuming individuals take on superhuman powers as a matter of course. Reality is always a step out of reach, leaving us struggling to piece together the logic of what we see. "Everlong" is the pinnacle of Gondry's videomaking, achieving the dual miracle of appearing wholly unfamiliar and instantly recognizable.

Gondry found another willing client in Detroit rock duo the White Stripes, whose aesthetic (red and white color scheme, faux legendary background story) was already a Gondry fever dream. For each of their four videos, Gondry set himself a back-breaking task to accomplish, with results ranging from the humdrum (the underwhelming "Dead Leaves and the Dirty Ground" [2002]) to the astonishing ("Fell in Love with a Girl" [2002]). Returning some of the whimsical charm of early music videos to an increasingly computerized, FX-laden genre of filmmaking, Gondry is an artisan of the short film, painstakingly hand-crafting his own works. In "Fell in Love with a Girl," the bulk of the video is dedicated to the band straightforwardly bashing out their tune, with one crucial caveat—rather than their flesh-and-blood selves, singer-guitarist Jack White and drummer Meg White are constructed from thousands of tiny Lego pieces.

With so much contemporary filmmaking, music video and otherwise, devoted to computer wizardry, it was refreshing to see a video so thoroughly dependent on the homespun and hand-crafted. Like studying a medieval fresco, though, it is difficult to watch "Fell in Love with a Girl" without simultaneously marveling and agonizing at the sheer amount of labor required to make it. With no CGI assistance, every single frame of the video required a different Lego configuration, and, considering the breakneck pace of "Fell in Love with a Girl," the work involved is simply staggering. Pulling the curtain back from his often effortless-seeming work, Gondry presents "Fell in Love with a Girl" as the Agony of the Director. Of course, "Fell in Love with a Girl" is also a remarkable example of extracting beauty from inexpressive material, but it is near-impossible to separate any enjoyment of its splendor from a similar appreciation of its awe-inspiring difficulty. Using what must have been about a million red and white Lego pieces, "Fell in Love with a Girl" intersperses "performance" footage with Lego-assisted décor—spirals, arrows, and walk signs. The video is evidence of Gondry's fascination with the childlike, being only one of the two clips the director has dedicated to iconic toys of middle-class childhood: Radiohead's "Knives Out" (2001), which celebrates the game Operation, being the other. Gondry is a childlike director, embracing wide-eyed wonder over cynicism, and children and icons of childhood play a substantial role in his work, from the urchins that accompany Kanye West on his nighttime romp through Macy's in "Heard 'Em Say" (2005) to the fairy-tale bear of "Human Behaviour."

Gondry's taste for the artisanal and the handmade finds expression in a different medium in his video for Steriogram's "Walkie Talkie Man" (2004). Like

"Fell in Love with a Girl," "Walkie Talkie Man" goes to absurd lengths to fulfill the requirements of its underlying principle—here, to knit an entire video out of yarn. Even more so than that Lego-heavy video, the labor of "Walkie Talkie Man's" production is a part of the video itself, at least in symbolic form, with a young woman (herself made out of yarn) furiously knitting guitars, drums, and microphones for the band to play. As always, Gondry sees his scenario through to its logical conclusion, and so we have a studio floor covered with thread instead of wires, a knit camera whose film is a clump of yarn, and a screening room where the screen is attached to spools of yarn. This retro clip also has a knit King Kong attacking the Capitol Records building where the band is recording, only to be foiled by a masterful counterattack: one of the band members pulls some string off the end of Kong's fingers and attaches it to a reel-to-reel tape recorder, slowly unraveling the ferocious beast.

Gondry's video for the White Stripes' "The Hardest Button to Button" (2003) also employs unusual material, making the instruments themselves the building blocks of its visual scheme. "Hardest Button" emphasizes the song's persistent beat with an initially simple visual formula: every time Meg presses her kick drum, the number of drum kits multiplies exponentially (2, 4, 8, etc.), and she moves farther away from the camera. Soon Jack appears as well, and he walks down the steps of an urban park playing his guitar, with the drums following closely behind. "Hardest Button" renders physical all the hoary rock-crit clichés about singing in front of or behind the beat. Gondry enjoys intensifying or complicating his initially simple formula, and as in "Around the World," "Hardest Button" grows steadily more and more convoluted until it is a veritable blur of action. Gondry increases the speed of the action, drums and amps piling up to fill the frame, and vanishing just as quickly. Going from a walk to a trot to Mach 3, "Hardest Button" is a speed demon, gobbling up time and space under cover of its voracious beat.

"The Denial Twist" (2005) is constructed out of neither Legos nor yarn, but shot on film with flesh-and-blood actors. Nonetheless, Gondry's most recent video with the White Stripes fits comfortably into the director's aesthetic of artisanship, being a one-take clip with a dizzying array of shifts in perspective. Jack and Meg pay a visit to *Late Night with Conan O'Brien*, then get in their car, drive home, and watch the show. Stretching and compressing effects wreak havoc on our sense of perspective, with people and objects growing impossibly large, or shrinking to infinitesimal size. The narrative itself also messes with perspective, with doublings and repetitions clumping the entire video into one dense interlocking unit. After the band visits *Conan*, Conan visits the band, stopping by their house and making awkward small talk in their living room. The video is crammed full of echoes, and in some unexplained sense, the two spaces, talk show and living room, are inverses of each other, each subtly and mysteriously affecting the other. Jack and Meg are blessed with supernatural gifts in "The Denial Twist," and Gondry's video leaves us with the impression that we are seeing only the tip of the iceberg. There is also the distinct sensation that the video's spaces are themselves magical, capable of bending the laws of time and space to their own unexplained needs. As with all of Gondry's video work, the true magician remains offscreen, casting his spells for three-minute periods, invigorating the stultifying music video with traces of the uncanny, the dreamlike, and the wondrous.

The Joker

Spike Jonze, born Adam Spiegel, in 1969, has long claimed to be an heir to the Spiegel magazine fortune. In reality, while distantly related to the actual heirs, Jonze did not grow up fabulously wealthy, but his straight-faced biographical deception speaks to his love for pranks, practical jokes, and all forms of trickery. Getting his start as a maker of skateboard videos, Jonze became a known figure among skaters for his work, which featured all manner of spills and marvels. Jonze first broke into music videos working for the Beastie Boys, the musical group who most share his bratty, jokey sensibility, and assisting video vets Tamra Davis and Kim Gordon (of Sonic Youth fame). With a few clips under his belt, Jonze's first MTV success came with the video for the Breeders' "Cannonball" (1993), codirected by Gordon. While lacking in the sustained visual innovation that marks Jonze's later work, "Cannonball" is notable for its MTV-friendly take on experimental filmmaking, taking that subgenre's deadpan outlandishness and creating a bite-sized, juniors version.

A savior to good but ephemeral alt-rock singles, Jonze developed entertaining, accessible, and delightful accompanying videos that brought them their share of glory. Nineteen ninety-four was the year MTV was first taken over by Jonze's oddball, brilliant creations, playing them again and again in a closed loop of incongruous humor and surprising elegance—rampaging dogs, meandering golf carts, Vegas swagger, and 70s television pastiches.

It was his second video for the Beastie Boys, released one year after "Cannonball," that would prove to be the most memorable, MTV-beloved of Jonze's work. Crowned in 2002 by VH1 as the second-greatest video of all time (topped only by another Jonze production), "Sabotage" chooses as its source material the credit sequence of an imaginary TV cop show of the 1970s, starring the three Beasties in costume, excessive facial hair, and heavy makeup as tough guys kicking ass and taking names. Opening with a shot of a flashing police siren, "Sabotage" engages in the single-minded pursuit of every police-related cliché it can track down, simultaneously paying homage to a lost era of unsophisticated cop shows and mocking them for their ludicrous earnestness. And like character actors sinking their teeth into particularly juicy roles, Mike D, Ad Rock, and MCA ham it up here, clearly loving every second of their transformations into urban warriors. "Sabotage" is a video in motion, with nearly every shot filled with speeding cars and running cops. The Beastie cops kick down doors, climb buildings to conduct surveillance, leap across rooftops, and go undercover as hotel staff to bust a drug dealer. The clichéd nature of the action in "Sabotage," and its lack of dialogue, play directly into Jonze's hands; like an episode of your favorite old cop show on mute, the plot is so familiar, so shopworn, that no words are necessary for comprehension or appreciation.

Undercovers dressed as bellboys chase after a drug dealer (played by "guest star Sir Stewart Wallace," better known as MCA in a fright wig) and fall into a pool while grappling with him; they disarm a Scandinavian man on a bridge, who proceeds to fall headfirst into the water; they tackle a perp headfirst into a mountain of garbage bags on an urban street; they run full speed toward the scene of the crime. Jonze's video is note-perfect parody, a Tarantino-esque blendering of pop culture past and present into a frothy milkshake. "Sabotage" only mocks what it loves, and thus every detail is just right, down to the garish 1970s-relic red-and-yellow logo that appears onscreen mid-video. Jonze lets the Beasties mug to their hearts' content in "Sabotage," hitting on the common factor between the New York City hip-hoppers and small-screen cops: a tendency to gesticulate wildly and engage in rounds of quasi-meaningless hand signals. "Sabotage" jabs lovingly at the self-inflated pompousness of its source material, ending with a freeze-frame on each of its cops before a slo-mo shot of the trio walking their turf, just three officers of the law doing their job. "Sabotage" is a masterpiece of the form for its ability to synthesize client and idea, bringing together the Beasties' own pop savvy and hipster humor with Jonze's concept. Jonze has done his best work for artists with the ability to take the piss out of themselves, possessing enough confidence to know that mocking themselves via Jonze will be a mutually beneficial act.

Jonze's follow-up with the Beastie Boys, "Sure Shot" (1994), similarly allows the group to run free in a campy, quasi-surreal wonderland, to enjoyable but less triumphant result. The trio, joined by sidekick Biz Markie, wanders through the casinos and alleyways of Las Vegas, at times dressed in tuxedos, at times in B-boy gear. There is a single moment when the Beasties exchange elaborate hand signals before entering a casino that feels like a "Sabotage" outtake, but the bulk of the video is a performance clip, with few added bonuses. As is appropriate for such a name-check-heavy song, Jonze cut in inserts of each of the icons "Sure Shot" references: Lee "Scratch" Perry, Rod Carew, John Woo. Jonze used a camera poised at ground level and equipped with a bar to grab onto; each MC bends down to rap, taking hold of the bar when the camera ascends, and flying through the air together.

Jonze's pair of videos for power-poppers Weezer follow a similar formula: one offbeat performance clip, and one TV-damaged piece of Zelig-esque cultural japery. Jonze is a director attuned to the immediately accessible, indelible image, and "Undone (The Sweater Song)" (1994) is "the video with the dogs." Mid-video, as Jonze shows drummer Pat Wilson sighing while playing, with a "just another day at the office" look on his face, a herd of dogs pounce from off-screen, hurtling themselves toward the band and then across the stage. Jonze injects some levity into the oft-stone-faced proceedings of the performance video, taking "Undone" from the strained seriousness of its opening black-and-white footage (admittedly shown upside down) to the low comedy of Wilson wiggling his butt while playing, running around his drum kit as the song surges into its finale, and heading partway up the blue backdrop before collapsing as the dogs dash offstage.

Both parody and homage, "Buddy Holly" (1994) implants Weezer's members, Forrest Gump-like, into the real world, or the real world of fondly remembered television shows at least. Unlike Robert Zemeckis and Tom Hanks' vision of post-WWII American history, "Buddy Holly" is uninterested in jacking into the front-page past of wars and presidents, just the collective fantasy realm of lowbrow television programming. "Buddy Holly" plants a big sloppy kiss on the face of Happy Days, the semi-beloved sitcom about a 50s family, creating a unique cultural wormhole: a 90s video nostalgic for a 70s TV show nostalgic for some bygone myth of 50s teenagerdom, a pastiche of a pastiche. "Buddy Holly" literally inserts the band into the show, seamlessly placing them inside Happy Days hangout Arnold's, where they perform for Richie and the gang. Jonze, a connoisseur of credit sequences, opens "Buddy Holly" with a piece of the show's credits, appropriately crediting himself as the director, and a prototypical TV announcer declares an "exciting event" in the making. Inside, Al, the restaurant's proprietor, introduces "Kenosha, Wisconsin's own . . . Weezer!" but won't leave the stage before pleading with patrons to "please—try the fish," to hoots from the laugh track. The band, in sweaters and ties, appear onstage, their performance superimposed on a shot of dancers taken from the show, blending past and present, reality-pastiche and pastiche-pastiche. Sitcom drama takes place at the fringes of the video, with Richie Cunningham (Ron Howard) slamming the bathroom door in disgust, and the Fonz (Henry Winkler) walking in to Arnold's to the cheers of the studio audience. Jonze blends the band into the sitcom action as well, with guitarist Brian Bell mouthing "I love you" to a swooning girl in time-capsule-worthy catgirl glasses. "Buddy Holly" has a laugh at the expense of bygone television traditions, pausing midperformance (right after the Fonz's entrance) to announce "TO BE CONTINUED," to the audience's groans. In appropriate sitcom fashion, and continuing in the vein of "Undone (The Sweater Song)," the band engages in shameless winking, mugging, and preening, adopting the broad comic tone of *Happy Days*, and by extension all the middlebrow sitcoms of the era, and making it their own. Returning for part two ("stay tuned for more *Happy Days*," the announcer beseeches us), the band finds itself in a predicament wearily familiar to any *Happy Days* character: upstaged by the Fonz, who steals the scene by doing a vaguely ethnic-looking dance. At song's end, he gets all the applause, forcing even the band members to clap for him as he makes a triumphal exit, a lovely lady on each arm. In a postscript, Al congratulates the band, then asks for a verdict on his fish special. Imitating the less-than-positive response he receives, Al exits to a huge laugh and thunderous applause as he turns out the lights.

"Buddy Holly" finds Jonze zapping his own work into the television set, creating a bizarro cultural universe where contemporary bands engage in dialogue with the television shows of their youth. Jonze is like a DJ here, not content to merely love his favorite cultural artifacts, but wanting to make them his own. Like a far funnier, wiser version of the film *Pleasantville* (1998) (which was heavily influenced by "Buddy Holly"), Jonze implants a contemporary sensibility on the ghost of television past, with decidedly hybridized results. Borrowing a page from Woody Allen's famous chameleon Zelig, and from 1994's omnipresent Forrest Gump, Jonze inserts his clients into the culturally mediated past of their (and his) choice; the perfect parlor trick for the irony-afflicted, hipper-than-thou aura of the mid-90s.

For bands with a less noticeable funny bone, Jonze made an odd choice of a video director. Grunge godfathers Dinosaur Jr and Cali one-hit wonders Wax both employed Jonze's services, with mixed results. The former's "Feel the Pain" (1994) made a small MTV splash, garnering the underappreciated postpunk pioneers some long-overdue acclaim, but the video is at odds with their mopey dirge. Band members J Mascis and Mike Johnson tool around the streets of New York in a golf cart, playing a round of urban golf. Teeing off from the Flatiron Building, their balls fly over the Empire State Building, land near Lever House, jet through Central Park, and land on a rooftop with an unencumbered view of the World Trade Center. While a pleasant tour of the city's architectural sights, and laced with some of Jonze's trademark humor (the golfers beat the crap out of some suits who make the mistake of touching their ball), "Feel the Pain" is a misfire, matching Jonze with performers whose aura does not sit right with his own.

Wax's "California" (1995) has a similar handicap, although Jonze's clip for the song does not contain the band at all. Taking the time limitations of the music video and making hay of it, "California" is a slow-motion epic, expanding ten or so seconds of full-speed footage to fill an entire video. Opening in close-up, and slowly zooming farther and farther out, "California" moves out from a shot of black boots to an image of a man in a baseball cap, silver jacket, and jeans sprinting at top speed, while on fire. The first indication that things are not quite what they seem, though, is when he checks his watch. Bystanders pay him no attention whatsoever, and he hardly pauses as he passes a puddle and a fire hydrant. Waving his hand in the air, and flailing wildly, we see that he is attempting to flag down a bus, his flame-engulfed clothing no real concern of his, possibly just an expression of his haste. "California" is clever, but its cleverness wears thin quickly, nothing more than one silly joke expanded to epic length. Jonze is at his best when he has personalities to work off, some source material to reference from his clients, but Wax give him little, and the result is work devoid of his signature cultural wizardry.

Not content to work with only one of the masters of the form, Björk hired Jonze to shoot a video for her single "It's Oh So Quiet," from her 1995 album *Post*. Seeing the song as a showstopper from some lost French musical, Jonze cast Björk as the star of his slightly demented song-and-dance number. "It's Oh So Quiet" is Jonze's attempt at re-creating the aura of classic Jacques Demy musicals like *The Umbrellas of Cherbourg* (1964) and *The Young Girls of Rochefort* (1967), with Björk as the kooky, perky leading actress. The video begins with Björk in a filthy bathroom, washing her hands, with the song's opening chords kicking in as she exits. These opening shots are so underlit that it is difficult to decipher the surroundings, and the camera keeps its distance, letting a constant stream of people, tires, and tools get in the way of our view of Björk. When "It's Oh So Quiet" kicks into high gear, with Björk's scat-singing, and a big-band orchestra as backup, Jonze lets in the sunshine, flooding the shot with light. Mechanics step in as background dancers, and Björk does a soft-shoe with a soda delivery guy and the store's mascot, a giant wrench. Later in the video, she kicks a newspaper machine, which sets a bystander off on a series of backflips and a posse of old ladies in sundresses to twirling their parasols. Jonze uses a Busby Berkeley-esque overhead shot of the ladies spinning their umbrellas in unison, before splitting them apart into separate components. In the finale, Björk mopily hugs a mailbox, and when the musical number returns, the mailbox itself sprouts legs and arms, and begins to dance. Even the Doric columns on a nearby building do a little jig before a crane shot lifts Björk high above the dancers still cavorting in the street.

"It's Oh So Quiet" continues Jonze's interest in pillaging the cultural past for inspiration, even if this time, he headed all the way back to an era and style that most of the MTV-watching audience would be dimly aware of at best (much like the *Godzilla* references of Elastica's "Car Song" [1995]). Once again, Jonze pays homage by poking fun, creating a dizzyingly ditzy tribute to the musical by borrowing its conventions to create a delirious, bizarro-world spin on them. "It's Oh So Quiet" finds a side to Björk that Gondry had never tapped into, casting her as a zany analog to Gene Kelly or Catherine Deneuve, the glamorous cutup, and providing some of the inspiration for her later starring role in Lars von Trier's *Dancer in the Dark* (2000). The video is also proof of Jonze's restless artistry; not content as a mere pilferer of half-remembered television shows, with "It's Oh So Quiet" he exhibits his own exquisite eye for what goes into a good video. Perhaps one of the reasons that artists like the Beastie Boys and Björk came to depend on Jonze was because his own taste was just as impeccable as theirs. Watching Jonze videos was like getting a sneak peek inside Spike's brain, and seeing what got him jazzed.

If "It's Oh So Quiet" is Jonze doing the musical, with Daft Punk's "Da Funk" (1997) he reaches the previously virgin shores of drama. As with "California," Jonze enjoys tweaking his audience, building videos centered on lumbering, unmentioned elephants. There it was a man on fire; here it is a twentysomething new to the big city with a dog's mask for a head. Rather than that disability, or his broken leg, being a primary concern, what actually comes to haunt the video's protagonist is his ever-present boombox (blasting "Da Funk," of course), which he is leery (or perhaps incapable) of turning off. Dog-boy Charles wanders the streets of Manhattan, having only recently arrived in the city. He is taunted by some streetwise teenagers (who pause momentarily to concede, "Yo, that's a good song!"), rejected for a survey of New Yorkers for not being a permanent resident, and ticks off a street vendor for his boombox's blast. Lonely and unappreciated, he steps into a bodega, following a blond as she does her shopping, and we fear the worst—that Charles, despondent, is set to take out his hostility on this unsuspecting young woman. All fears are alleviated, though, when he goes over and says hello, gently reminding her when she evinces a blank look that he is Charles, her next-door neighbor from adolescence. Thrilled, too, at the reminder of home, she lets loose a steady stream of gab about the folks from back home, and offers to take him downtown to her apartment and cook him dinner. About to board the bus with her, Charles freezes, spotting a "NO RADIOS" sign, and lets the doors shut with him on the outside, leaving his friend, confused, to make the trek home alone.

"Da Funk" takes a commercial gamble by forcing the video's content upfront, and the song into the background. "Da Funk" believes so thoroughly in its drama that it refuses to yield to the song, its supposed purpose for existence. While ever-present, the Daft Punk song is ultimately little more than mood music for Jonze's portrait of urban anomie. In so doing, Jonze violates the first commandment of videomaking: Thou Shalt Sell the Song. Playing off the unsettling city symphonies of the New Hollywood 1970s, Jonze sketches a disheartening portrait of urban alienation but caps his work with a comic exclamation mark, like Duchamp drawing a mustache on the *Mona Lisa*.

Another of Jonze's preferred clients is the electronica artist Norman Cook, better known by his nom de turntable, Fatboy Slim. Perhaps drawn to the egolessness of electronica, which avoids the video hero-worship inherent to rock and hip-hop, Jonze made two celebrated clips for Fatboy Slim, which, while having little to do with the artist, capture something of his lager-lad, musical standup vibe. "Weapon of Choice" (2001) has become legendary, taking first place in the 2002 VH1 poll of the all-time greatest music videos, but their earlier collaboration "Praise You" (1998) is its superior. In a guerrilla-video setup that would *not* have been out of place on *Jackass*, or *TV's Bloopers and Practical Jokes*, Jonze and a herd of acolytes swoop down on a West L.A. movie theater, performing an original interpretive dance for unsuspecting moviegoers. Jonze even credits the video to the "Torrance Community Dance Group," and its erstwhile lead dancer, Richard Koufey (played by Jonze). Jonze, wielding a boombox, leads his troupe of suburban moms and overweight guys in 80s hot pants in their seemingly long-rehearsed performance and, having set off the music-video equivalent of a Happening, records the inevitably hilarious results. Part of the comic punch of "Praise You" is its capturing the caught-on-the-fly, cinema vérité responses of the moviegoing crowd to this outbreak of homegrown goofball. The theater's manager comes by and shuts off the boombox (prompting Jonze to leap into his arms), and another employee takes it away entirely, but a round of (spontaneous?) booing allows the Torrance Community Dance Group to finish what they have started. Jonze/Koufey, the most athletic of the bunch, makes an attempt at breakdancing that closely resembles, in its spastic lack of coordination, an epileptic fit. Koufey may be an exceedingly poor dancer, but he is undoubtedly a vigorous one.

The troupe gathers into line for its final number, kicking their legs into the air and swinging their arms over their heads in a wave motion before bowing to applause at song's end. In a post-song interview, Koufey/Jonze hilariously notes that "a lot of people tell us that we have a very hip-hop vibe. Growing up in Manhattan I performed with several B-boy posses and different groups, so that's . . . some of our inspiration." "Praise You" understands that a joke is funniest when its teller doesn't even crack a smile. Its vérité-style shaky camerawork is also a huge departure from the bulk of the director's own work, and from the glossy MTV aesthetic, with its sheen of affordable luxury.

Jonze, intuitively understanding the rules that govern the music video, repeatedly seeks to undermine them, here and elsewhere. "Praise You" violates the unstated rule of videomaking that a video should always look and sound as alluring as possible, a gorgeous neverland of beautiful people, lovely commodities, and ravishing settings. "Praise You" is shot on a video camera, features washed-out sound, and generally avoids any gussying-up of its locales and characters, and still works; and as such, serves as an inherent rebuke to the glossy fakeness of most videomaking.

Fatboy Slim's "Weapon of Choice" is an unremarkable song from an unimpressive album, but Jonze's video has immortalized it. In the video, a weary business traveler (Christopher Walken) sits, half-dazed with exhaustion, in the overstuffed chair of a hotel lobby. One shudders to think what type of unremitting drudgery could possibly have caused such a sapping of spirit. After a number of seconds of immobile repose, the traveler glances up, as if having heard a far-off sound, too faint to decipher. And indeed, the video's sound track features a distant clatter that takes some seconds to amalgamate into the song in question. Walken begins to move his head robotically to the faintly sensed song, then is propelled into standing up and busting a move. His dance step is unfamiliar and lovely, a heretofore unfamiliar mixture of jazz dancing's elegance and the raver's solo bustle. Steadily building steam as his dance progresses, he rings the bell at the front desk, dances up, then down, then up the up escalator. Standing at the foot of a typically soulless, repetitive postmodern hotel corridor, the same the world over from Los Angeles to Lisbon to Kuala Lumpur, his response to the ugly design is to unleash a killer cartwheel. If, as Elvis Costello once said, writing about music is like dancing about architecture, then "Weapon of Choice" is some killer rock criticism. As if he knows what a bravura performance he is in the midst of turning in, Walken pauses here, slowly extending his finger to call the elevator. Jonze, subverting the set of expectations he has established as this video's ground rules about what may or may not happen here, injects a wholly surprising and fantastically apropos surrealism, with Walken diving off the ledge of the hotel's interior hallway, overlooking the lobby, and gracefully flying through the air, swanning his way over to an oversized painting of a nautical scene. He takes a breath there, as if gearing up for even more, and then swoops down to the lobby, landing on his feet and walking over to the chair he had initially been sitting in, returning to the pose of unrelieved exhaustion with which the video had begun. As if the song was a clarion call to action, the video's protagonist demands action, even in defiance of gravity, during the song's duration, before returning him unchanged at its end. While on its face a celebration of the musical impetus to change (to dance?), the song ultimately has no long-term impact; the traveler is returned to literally the same pose he began with.

Jonze could straddle both sides of the glossy-versus-vérité debate, and his pair of videos for the Bad Boy royal family of hip-hop are a return to glossiness, although with goofy, satirical intent. If kings know that sometimes the best way of maintaining power is hiring a jester to poke fun at your foibles, allowing harmless steam to be let off, so too does Bad Boy CEO Sean "P. Diddy" Combs, who commissioned videos from Jonze for his own "It's All About the Benjamins (Remix)" (1997) and his star Notorious B.I.G.'s posthumous "Sky's the Limit" (1997).

Both a biting parody of the hip-hop video and a shrewd business maneuver, Jonze's video for "Sky's the Limit" offers one potential solution to a problem that dogged hip-hop videomaking in the 90s: how to make a clip for a deceased or otherwise engaged performer? A number of Tupac Shakur's posthumous videos feature outtakes and other old footage, along with snapshots and other personal memorabilia. "Sky's the Limit" adopts an entirely different tack, casting dead-on middle school ringers for Biggie and his sidekick Puff Daddy, and setting them loose in the stereotypical world of privilege and consumption that is the hip-hop video. Parodying the way that the 90s hip-hop video was seemingly obsessed with its own wealth, "Sky's the Limit" opens with a green-tinted shot of a Mercedes pushing its way through a tunnel and joining a posse of luxury cars pulling into the front driveway of a McMansion, complete with faux Greek sculpture on the lawn. Attendants rush up to open the car doors, out step Biggie and Puffy, and the joke becomes clear: everyone here is between ten and thirteen years old. The posse even sit down to watch television, and discover a pint-size Busta Rhymes rapping onscreen. "Sky's the Limit" takes place in a series of familiar spaces: the Jacuzzi, the club, inside a luxury car. "Biggie" is dressed in note-perfect clothing, imitating his dead mentor in well-tailored pinstripe suits and garish collared shirts. Walking into the club, Jonze positions the camera at floor level and, for a moment, Biggie and Puffy look almost real. Intent on piercing the illusion of reality, Jonze cuts to eye-level, and the push of screaming fans becomes what it is: a bunch of tittering middle-schoolers surrounding a pair of their contemporaries. There is even a juniors-version Lil' Kim, complete with red fur hat and red sunglasses, getting dolled up for the big show and telling a friend that she's "going to get my groove on."

Jonze, always an astute student of conventions, sends up the hip-hop video with dead-on accuracy in "Sky's the Limit," echoing the stinging catalog of the genre's foibles found in the Roots' "What They Do." Jonze's affection for the occasionally silly excesses of the genre is genuine, but "Sky's the Limit" is also a concession to the business necessities of the music world couched as a soft critique of the industry. Biggie was dead, but the show must go on, and videos must continue down the assembly line toward MTV rollout. Jonze may have offered the most light-hearted solution to Bad Boy's conundrum, but the result, if studied too closely, remains more than a little ghoulish, like tossing off one-liners at a wake.

"All About the Benjamins" crosses genres like Michael Jackson rocking out to "Dirty Diana." The Bad Boy posse crash a high-school prom and put on a raucous, impassioned performance for a crowd of tight-assed adolescents in tuxedos and cocktail dresses. The best part of "Benjamins" is seeing well-established hip-hop stars relax and play against type, if only momentarily: Puff Daddy as a pomaded crooner warbling "Everybody Hurts," Lil' Kim slow-dancing in a frumpy lavender dress before grabbing the mic and ripping her dress off to reveal a leather bustier and matching pedal pushers. For Jonze, the oft-humorless expanses of the hip-hop video were ripe for an image makeover and an injection of absurdist energy.

Gondry and Jonze were the bridge that connected their moment of arrival—the *Alternative Nation*–friendly confines of mid-90s MTV—with the blighted, video-unfriendly television landscape that followed. Jonze and Gondry's restless spirit of innovation would be the inspiration for a cadre of up-and-coming filmmakers who would keep the spirit of the music video alive in the face of a culture no longer fascinated by the form. In that heroic effort, Jonze and Gondry helped lead the way to the contemporary re-emergence of the music video as product of the Internet, virally weaving its way into inboxes and browsers worldwide after being unceremoniously booted from television screens everywhere.

CHAPTER 7

No More Stars

I f you turned on MTV anytime starting in the mid-1990s, a striking thing would have happened: in all likelihood, the channel was probably not showing a video. To fans of the early MTV, and the postmodern theorists fascinated by its fragmentary flow of decentered imagery, it may have come as a shock to find *Singled Out, The Real World, Daria,* or *Laguna Beach* in its place. MTV had grown up, and left its adolescent infatuation with music behind, as did, to slightly lesser extents, its colleagues VH1, BET, and CMT—all owned by media giant Viacom, and all homogenized and diluted by the impact of ownership by the corporate behemoth. While MTV expanded its reach worldwide, starting channels in Australia, Africa, Brazil, Canada, China, Russia, and Taiwan, among others, the original American channel had almost entirely divested itself of its original purpose for existing—the music video.

With all the airtime formerly given over to music videos now the province of reality TV, animated programs, game shows, and the like, the music video business shrank accordingly. Record labels realized it was no longer in their interest to spend upward of $100,000 on a video that might never be played. Instead, they chose to adopt a wait-and-see attitude reminiscent of the early years of music video, shooting a video only if a single had already taken hold on radio. Without the support of specialty shows like *120 Minutes* (dedicated to alternative music), *Headbangers' Ball* (heavy metal), and *Amp* (electronica), video became the province of stars, established acts, and hopeful debut artists.

Like Hollywood, music video in the late 90s and onward was a polarized affair, with big-budget blockbusters starring big names surrounded by a handful of scrappier upstarts. Music video's middle ground was lost, as was something in sheer numbers. In the absence of a built-in television audience, music videos had to resort to ever-intensifying attempts to keep eyeballs from stray-ing: more aggressive sexual content, higher production values, or indie attitude. But just because the big television players were less interested than ever in showing them did not mean that artists weren't still making them. Music video remained vibrant in the post-MTV era, but its energy existed in a vacuum, caught between its television past and a broadband future.

TV Nation

Perhaps the defining artist of the post-MTV era, and for the television-drenched generation he came to represent, was Eminem. The Detroit-bred great white hope of hip-hop became the most familiar face on MTV post-2000, because of his shock-jock antics and his uncanny ability to make videos that softened his sharp edges and lightened his darker moods, leaving a playful Eminem ready for his close-up. His videos are award-winning raspberries, indiscriminately machine-gunning a host of enemies real and perceived, from his then ex-wife to his rivals in the multiplatinum gallery, but they succeed by sanding his edges down, making him more kid-friendly. The videos are like his songs—brash, col-orful, and a bit ragged. With a few exceptions ("Mosh" and "Stan" foremost among them), Eminem's video work was a clown's face painted on a tragic mask. Presenting a cartoonish Em in cartoonish situations, acting in cartoonish fash-ion, videos like "My Name Is," "The Real Slim Shady," and "Without Me" were custom-built for the short attention spans of a generation raised on MTV cuts.

This was made literal in his first video, "My Name Is" (1999). Em hugs his core constituency close by tearing Middle America a new one. In a fairly accu-rate account of his future media ubiquity, "My Name Is" finds Eminem on every station as we channel-flip along with a corpulent white-trash couple. He plays the stolid dad on the "Beaver"-esque "Slim Shady Show," a lowest-common-denominator talk-show host, President Clinton, and the entire cast of "The Shady Bunch," where nine smiling Marshalls fill the tic-tac-toe boxes of the iconic family show. Em-as-Clinton leaves his presidential podium, and a Mon-ica Lewinsky look-alike, beret and all, steps out from underneath and wipes her mouth. "My Name Is" depicts a landscape familiar to any daytime television-watcher, composed of one part talk-show debasement, one part television nos-talgia, and one part current events, all tarred with the same brush of dead-end inanity. Eminem makes this TV world his home, luxuriating in its tawdriness and embracing its mindlessness.

Knowing he had hit on something, Eminem's next videos pick up on the theme, each ambushed by television in its own way. "Guilty Conscience" (1999) features *America's Most Wanted*–style reenactments of criminal moral dilemmas. As in the song, Eminem and Dr. Dre serve as onlookers and instigators, with Eminem alternately watching and egging on the video's three blue-collar protagonists toward criminal hooliganism. Television-show parody became Eminem's video mode of choice, finding it so felicitous a strategy that he brought it back for his Video Music Award–winning "Without Me." Before that, though, "The Real Slim Shady" (2000) (directed, like its predecessors, by Dr. Dre and Philip Atwell) tinkered with the other source material for Eminem's visual scheme (and world outlook): comic books. A catch-all clip painted in loud, primary colors, "Slim Shady" is even more slapstick than "My Name Is." Eminem cements his role as MTV's class clown, poking fun at icons like VJ Carson Daly, Christina Aguilera, and Pamela Anderson in this freewheeling video. Living in a candy-colored psych ward straight out of Green Day's "Basket Case," Eminem is surrounded by muttering, drooling mental patients, and hounded by look-alikes—a legion of bleached-blond drones, referencing the slew of Caucasian-rap imitators that emerged in Eminem's wake. "The Real Slim Shady" is a half-hearted dis of his imitators, proving more effective in cementing Eminem's role as cultural critic, kneading the dough of pop culture into amusing shapes.

Laughing at his reputation as a demon preying on the unformed, "Without Me" (2002) (directed by Joseph Kahn) stars Eminem and Dr. Dre as a hip-hop Batman and Robin whose mission is to stop a preteen boy from listening to the Parental Advisory–stickered Eminem album he has illicitly purchased. Eminem plays Robin, the overenthusiastic sidekick in the silly costume taking the passenger seat of the Batmobile to Dr. Dre's Batman, paying tribute to his own scrappy persona and his relationship with his mentor Dre. "Without Me" shifts between this plotline and a new batch of TV parodies, uniting the comic-book and television motifs of earlier Eminem videos. Eminem plays an infomercial host, Elvis Presley (enjoying a hero sandwich he's conveniently stored in the toilet), Moby (reclining in a yoga pose before receiving a beat-down from sidekick Obie Trice), a Puck-like gross-out king on *The Real World* (where he makes out with an inflatable doll until his housemates run out, horrified), and a contestant on *Survivor* (floating on a log of Elvis' shit). Funniest of all, and firmly establishing Eminem's role as hip-hop's successor to Lenny Bruce, is his appearance as none other than public enemy number one Osama bin Laden. Em-Osama, dressed in a camouflage outfit, does a jig in a grainy video reminiscent of the real bin Laden's filmed messages. A thought bubble appears over his head in illegible Arabic, with a small asterisk indicating a translation at the bottom of the screen—"Oh, no! D12!—Editor." Surrounded by Eminem's sidekicks in D12, Osama gestures to them to momentarily cease hostilities, and waves a white flag. They all pause and then engage in a nifty running man dance. "Without Me" did not make Eminem an intellectual

heavyweight, but its willingness to move beyond the boundaries of his previous videos' *Us Weekly* material marked an increasing interest in matters
beyond his doorstep, or his television set. Eminem as Osama was just a silly, if
hilarious, prank, but the political content of "White America" and, especially,
"Mosh" would be far more assured and serious.

Can't Stop Won't Stop

The hip-hop video made extensive use of the cultural shorthand of pastiche,
grafting elements of well-known films and other cultural artifacts to itself as a
form of rapid-fire communication. Little X's clip for Mystikal's "Shake It Fast"
(2000) borrows liberally from Stanley Kubrick's swan song *Eyes Wide Shut*
(1999), and the notorious orgy scene at its center. Taking only what it desired,
"Shake It Fast" is all come-on, yanking the Kubrick film's aura of rampant, law-
less sexuality and leaving the free-floating paranoia behind. Busta Rhymes'
"Turn It Up/Fire It Up," directed by Hype Williams, borrows from the borrowers, ripping off *Mad Max* by way of "California Love." Busta's retrofuturistic
garb is reminiscent of nothing so much as George Clinton's getup in the "California Love" video, and the *1984*-esque plot of Big Brother authoritarianism
run amok, and guerrilla warfare led by rebel leader Busta, is deeply familiar, but
nonetheless entertaining. Williams' video for Busta's "What's It Gonna Be?"
(1999) took things one step further, borrowing strictly from other videos.
Rhymes' duet with Janet Jackson swipes the futuristic look of her 1995 duet
with brother Michael, "Scream" (directed by Mark Romanek). Like "Scream,"
"What's It Gonna Be?" has the sheen of a big-budget blockbuster set aboard a
spaceship, every shot caressed by Williams' immaculate formal technique.

Other hip-hop icons used their videos to burnish their own personae, polish-
ing the plaques in their personal shrines to themselves. Their videos were extensions of their fan clubs, presenting idealized, larger-than-life versions of
themselves to a putatively adoring public. This was not different in any substantial
measure from their predecessors, but these hip-hop videos increasingly took place
in an airless zone of joyless fantasy and mindless conspicuous consumption.
Hype Williams and Paul Hunter had been crowned hip-hop king through their
elegant, upwardly mobile videos, but their followers blindly worshipped the commodity value of luxury cars and McMansions to the exclusion of any reality principle, or much sense of a good time. Ja Rule, Ludacris, T.I., and other hip-hop
royalty all fell prey to this video commodity—and self-worship, but no other MC
could quite match 50 Cent's absorption in the splendors of his own self.

50 Cent's smash "In Da Club" (2003), directed by Philip Atwell, takes place
in the "Shady/Aftermath Artist Development Center," a secret bunker in an

undisclosed location. The video's setup, in which Dr. Dre, Eminem, and a team of professionals took 50's measure in the categories of pumping iron, pimping, and MC'ing, made jokes about the factory aesthetic of Dre's empire tangible. Dre and Eminem, clad in white coats and carrying clipboards, lurk in the background of every shot, peering through one-way mirrors as their protégé 50 Cent whoops it up and taking notes on his progress.

"Candy Shop" (2005), directed by Jessy Terrero, has 50 partying in a mansion full of beautiful women, with the hulking rapper grinning like a kid in the titular establishment, enjoying the parade of riches on display. Pulling up in a stunning red sportscar (barring full-frontal male nudity in music videos, the presence of luxury cars will have to suffice as testimony to male performers' purported physical prowess), 50 Cent struts through a Gothic mansion whose every room is occupied by another lovely. In one room, he plays doctor with a nurse in shiny pink vinyl; in another, he watches as one woman drizzles chocolate onto another as she lounges in the bath. A third woman, carrying a whip, flicks her wrist and yanks 50's shirt off. The video ends with a stereotypical "but it was all a dream" twist, with 50 daydreaming in front of the takeout window at the Candy Shop fast-food restaurant, but the attempt at man-of-the-people grit fails to stick. 50 is the glammest thug around, and no amount of Queens realism could erase his million-dollar scent.

Hip-hop's single-minded devotion to its established video tropes made the experience of watching rap videos a far more uniform and less pleasurable experience in the late 90s. There were a number of exceptions to this orthodoxy, though. Besides Eminem, two other major hip-hop artists embraced the oddball as a video career move. One (Missy Elliott) went in whole hog, and the other (Outkast) skirted the boundary between hip-hop's mainstream and its avant-garde. Elliott made her debut with "The Rain (Supa Dupa Fly)" (1997), directed by Hype Williams, which borrowed the director's fish-eye aesthetic from Busta Rhymes' "Woo-Hah!" and "Put Your Hands Where My Eyes Could See," and something of those videos' taste for sci-fi absurdity. "Get Ur Freak On" (2001), her first video directed by Dave Meyers, embraced the template established by "The Rain (Supa Dupa Fly)," with its recipe of arresting, off-kilter imagery and Elliott's trademark dance moves, relying on disorientation for effect. Meyers' casually surrealist enterprise placed Elliott in a haunted, mud-drenched warehouse choked with weeds. Shirtless men, their chests painted black, hang upside down from the rafters, Elliott's head comes unhinged and detaches from her body, and her torso swings from a chandelier.

Elliott embraced FX because the primary avenue for female artists to reach a mass audience—the sexy come-on—was closed to her as a less-than-svelte woman; and by doing so, helped open up the narrow-gauge world of hip-hop videomaking, and videomaking by female artists in general. Meyers' videos teach viewers how to listen to the music, providing a visual analog to the surprising samples, unusual textures, and off-kilter splices of producer Timbaland's sound beds and Elliott's mix of ghetto grit and feminist urgency. Meyers' videos and Elliott and Timbaland's musical endeavors share a patchwork assemblage and an interest in finding beauty in the surprising hook or image. Having splintered into fragments, each then reassembles themselves haphazardly, with unexpected shards surging to the forefront, whether a stray vocal sample or the image of a miniature Missy wearing a giant dunce cap.

"Work It" (2002), featuring a newly slimmed-down Elliott, is the strongest of her collaborations with Meyers, its palette a mélange of textures, including bleach-outs and black-and-white footage, along with his trademark delirious FX. Backup dancers spring up from the ground like plants, a Prince look-alike mimics giving Elliott a tongue bath, and a thug wannabe slaps the living daylights out of an Uncle Tom in a powdered wig. The effects take a substantial step forward as well; Missy kicks game to a guy sitting in his car while standing at a precarious forty-five-degree angle, and her jaw expands exponentially to swallow a Lamborghini whole.

Outkast, another champion of the avant-garde within the mainstream, embraced a more cautious brand of videomaking, but one no less vibrant when juxtaposed with the carbon-copy world of their peers. "Ms. Jackson" (2000) is Southern-fried storytelling, video-style, with Big Boi and Andre 3000 patching the holes in their shotgun shack's leaky roof, a potent metaphor for their song's elegiac tale of a failed relationship. "The Whole World" (2001) reaches back into the wilds of prewar, pre-televisual pop culture for an archaic, dusty, mystical-magical vibe, with the Outkast boys the stars of a traveling carnival sideshow.

"Hey Ya!" (2003), Andre 3000's smash single from the *Speakerboxx/The Love Below* double album, was accompanied by a video that took off from that launching pad of yore for musical acts of the 50s and 60s, *The Ed Sullivan Show*. What was, after all, the seemingly endless music-video obsession with Ed Sullivan? For Nirvana's "In Bloom" and the Strokes' "Last Nite" (2001), the show served as a reminder of epochal moments in musical history—Elvis' first televised performance, the Beatles'—in the hopes of reclaiming some shreds of lost authority. Taboos were not worth smashing without their possessing significance, and "In Bloom" and "Last Nite" look to rebuild the once-magnificent power of the live television performance so they could break it down again and have it mean something. "Hey Ya!," however, was on a different nostalgia trip. For Outkast, the bygone era of live musical performance was about a lost moment in black music. "Hey Ya!" is nostalgic for tight bands, efficient performers, and huge JB's-P-Funk-style extravaganzas of a type no longer mounted in the era of the sleek, efficient solo performer. Andre 3000, as a solo artist, manically attempts to recapture this vibe, multiplying himself ad infinitum to fill all the roles in his imaginary band, from beret-wearing keyboardist to backup singers in riding outfits. There is also nostalgia at work for a bygone era in youth culture. Dre and Big Boi play rival gang leaders who face off after the performance, and their *West Side Story*-esque choreographed fighting speaks volumes about the relative innocence of the era, at least in their recollections. Their past is a bit jumbled, lumping in anything that says "not contemporary"—Big Boi rocks a circa-1989 oversized cell phone—but "Hey Ya!" is forthright in its love for an earlier, more jubilant, less violent era in black music. The video also allows Dre and Big Boi to wink at their roles within the group, with the latter playing a gruff, outspoken tough guy, and the former a virtuoso weakling, secret leader, and all-around showman.

Likewise looking to a half-remembered, half-invented past for inspiration, Ol' Dirty Bastard's "Got Your Money" (1999) (directed by Hype Williams, Scott Kalvert, Nzingha Stewart, and D'Urville Martin) borrows liberally from 1970s blaxploitation pictures, going so far as to superimpose ODB's head on the body of a stereotypical bandleader from some half-forgotten film of the era. "Got Your Money" aligns Ol' Dirty Bastard with the ever-popular tropes of blaxploitation redux while simultaneously poking fun at the genre's inherent absurdity. ODB is transformed via cut-and-paste into an African-American nationalist hero, becoming the "man done more for the blacks than anyone"—a particularly humorous alteration to his unhinged public persona.

Perhaps the best of the new breed of hip-hop-friendly directors, providing the class-clown yin to Dave Meyers' surrealist yang, was wunderkind Marc Klasfeld. Getting his start during the spit-shine heyday of Hype Williams and Paul Hunter, Klasfeld first came to prominence with his grimy clip for Juvenile's "Ha" (1998), which resembles an episode of *Cops* set in New Orleans' Magnolia Housing Projects. Rather than buff each video to within an inch of its life, Klasfeld's videos are deliberately ragged. Alien Ant Farm's "These Days" (2003) records the band's guerrilla performance across the street from the BET Awards, surprising the hip-hop luminaries on the red carpet. Echoing U2's "Where the Streets Have No Name," "These Days" pokes fun at hip-hop royalty ascendant with a backhanded swipe of punk attitude.

Funniest of all is Klasfeld's clip for Sum 41's "Hell Song" (2002), which perfectly encapsulates his slapdash, goofball aesthetic. Sum 41 is represented onstage by a set of action figures with the band's faces haphazardly pinned on, while action figure stand-ins for celebrities like the Osbournes, Destiny's Child, Snoop Dogg, Ludacris, and President Bush cavort in the crowd. The

Statue of Liberty arrives with two tickets to the show, W. spins on his head, a dog pisses all over the band, and AC/DC's Angus Young shows up to play the guitar solo. It all ends with a climactic showdown between Jesus and Marilyn Manson, followed by the band hopping onto the Spice Girls' helicopter, which ignominiously crashes (read: is dropped out a window) to the hoots and hollers of the video's crew. "Hell Song" is willfully amateurish, looking like a video cobbled together by a Sum 41 fan with far too much time on his hands, and both despite and because of this, it was one of the funniest videos to ever appear on MTV.

Scarface's "On My Block" (2002), though, shows off Klasfeld's dramatic gifts, a bravura single pan (much like Klasfeld's other faux one-take video, Jay-Z's "Girls, Girls, Girls") across a generation's struggles in the ghetto. "On My Block" surveys births, deaths, riots, basketball games, new sneakers, memorial services, and petty squabbles. Klasfeld matches the elegiac, despairing tone of Scarface's song with a calm but unceasing camera movement, its refusal to pause an echo of the steady ghetto march of "On My Block." With "On My Block," Klasfeld proved himself able to do what only the best videomakers could—tailor-make videos to fit a song's, and a performer's, sensibility.

One of the few artists capable of breaking hip-hop video out of its artistic doldrums was a relative newcomer, Chicago producer and MC Kanye West. Violating the unspoken rule "Every hip-hop video must have a posse of backup dancers in skimpy clothing," his clips for "All Falls Down," "Jesus Walks," and "Diamonds (from Sierra Leone)" breathed new life into the moribund body of the hip-hop video. "All Falls Down" (2004), directed by Chris Milk, borrows liberally from the film noir palette for its clever first-person structure. Taking off from the you-are-the-hero conceit of 1940s films like Robert Montgomery's *Lady in the Lake* (1947) and Delmer Daves' *Dark Passage* (1947), "All Falls Down" casts the viewer as Kanye, escorting his lady friend to the airport for her flight. West's face is only seen when spotted in reflective surfaces, so the first glimpse of our hero is in the mirrored windows of his limousine. West attempts to clean his soiled shirt in the bathroom, and when his reflection in the mirror is at first blurry, he blinks and rubs his eyes and the shot comes into focus. Going through security, he is repeatedly stopped, and has to remove his gold chain, then his watch. Tiring of the routine, Kanye sticks himself bodily into the X-ray machine, and the X-ray Kanye raps as the machine's green lines pass over his outline, inspecting him. Rejoining his girlfriend, and returning to first-person point of view, the couple spin around together briefly, then he lifts up her sunglasses to see the tears running down her face. She pushes them back down over her eyes and boards her plane, and we return to our car. Sitting down and gazing through the open sunroof, we see her plane taking off and flying away.

"All Falls Down" is a simple tale, yet its clever conceit and superb craft make it superlative, an offbeat idea rendered with style and panache. Borrowing from the traditions of noir, "All Falls Down" was not about violence or revenge or death, but it nonetheless gathers some of the genre's retro stylishness for its own purposes. The video was secret pastiche, a kind of cultural borrowing edging out beyond the frontiers of the obvious, crafting its takings into an alluring new pattern.

If "All Falls Down" was West's noir, then its follow-up, "Jesus Walks" (2004), directed by Michael Haussman, is his religious film, starring Kanye as a charismatic preacher riling up his parishioners by riffing on Jesus. The video introduces three characters in rapid sketches, each attempting to flee their increasingly constricted, desperate existences: a streetwalker, a homeless man, and a gang member. The prostitute walks away from her perch and her johns; the homeless man abandons his cardboard-covered spot and his meager few possessions; and the gangbanger leaves his cat-calling crew behind. "Jesus Walks" cuts between these lonely souls and Kanye in church, where his rousing sermon has the choir swaying and parishioners testifying, their hands waving in the air. Escape is not always possible for these characters; the gang member, victim of a shooting, lies dead in the street. But even for those who have not made their way out of suffering, there is assistance. An angel swoops down and lifts up the dead man, and the others eventually make their way into West's church.

"Jesus Walks" belongs to the same category of videos as Bone Thugs-N-Harmony's "Tha Crossroads": vaguely New Age-y religious parables of death and redemption. "Jesus Walks" stars West as a preacher, an unusual enough role to play for a twenty-first-century hip-hopper, but it also has the intellectual honesty to engage with both the value and limitations of faith. Religion cannot save everyone, at least in this world, and "Jesus Walks" reflects seriously on faith without resorting to treacle. "Jesus Walks" summons some of the enormous energy and passion of traditional African-American Christianity, mingling the church and the street in an effort to make religion hip.

Having made one video that summoned all his powers of moral authority, and another that cast him as an avatar of contemporary hip, West's next video splices the two strands together, to distinctly odd effect. The two halves of "Diamonds (from Sierra Leone)" (2005), directed by Hype Williams, have little to say to each other, but the mere presence of its activist half is so shocking, so out of step with the average music video, that it forces viewers to reckon with its unusual, disturbing content.

The video begins in the diamond mines of war-ravaged Sierra Leone, where an eight-year civil war, and the scuffling over the country's diamond wealth, has cost hundreds of thousands of lives. Over glossy black-and-white images of the dank tunnels where they work, diamond miners testify to their unbearably harsh existences: "We work in the diamond rivers," "We are the children of the blood diamonds." A white-bread American couple appears onscreen, with the man kneeling down and proposing. He puts a diamond ring on his fiancée's hand and the ring hideously oozes blood all over her fingers and arm as one of the diamond-mining children watches, sadly but impassively.

Strangely, these scenes, and others like them, are intercut with Kanye West driving around Prague in a tricked-out coupe with gull-wing doors. West dances in church, plays the harpsichord, and dives out of his car in slow motion before it crashes into a storefront. What this might have to do with the enormously affecting imagery of the Sierra Leoneans is left unstated. "Diamonds (from Sierra Leone)" is an incoherent video, but its first-person testimony is nonetheless haunting. Like Green Day's similarly politicized "Wake Me Up When September Ends," "Diamonds" has the element of surprise on its side. One burly middle-aged man tells his offscreen interviewer, "Some of us were enslaved by rebels and forced to kill our own families for diamonds." "Diamonds" must be honored for its willingness to bring such harsh, unfiltered truths to our attention, even if it ultimately cannot commit to what kind of video it wants to be.

Leaving even "Diamonds" behind for sheer oddity, R. Kelly's twelve-part "Trapped in the Closet" (2005) turns music video into dinner theater, with Kelly starring at the center of a psychosexual three-ring circus of half-suppressed secrets. Codirected by Kelly and Jim Swaffield, the epic-length video was released serially, each part ending with a new revelation. Functioning like a video soap opera, "Trapped in the Closet's" bland mise-en-scène and indifferent acting indicate a clip with other things on its mind, focused more on the bit-by-bit visualization of Kelly's highly detailed story-song than striking out on its own. Nonetheless, the video's suspense-melodrama is pointedly effective, with each revelation (R.'s cheating with a pastor's wife! The pastor's gay! The men want to marry! R.'s wife is cheating too!) adding a layer of complexity to the mix. The relative lack of edits, and emphasis on acting, make "Trapped in the Closet" among the most narrative-heavy videos of its era, a story of Dickensian proportions when compared to its surface-heavy peers. That it veers dangerously close to self-parody in its wave upon wave of surprises does not concern it in the least, focused as it is on untangling the sexual and emotional allegiances of its characters. Like a beach-reading novel, "Trapped in the Closet" impels viewers to watch until the end in order to assimilate its shocks in their entirety, but few would voluntarily choose to go back for a second helping. For a medium so dependent on repeat views, this front-loaded lack of subtlety was effectively a kiss of death.

Madonna or Whore?

The idea of winking at, or altering, one's persona through a video was a common one, especially for women, who often used video as a way of shifting from slutty to serious (seemingly the only two poses available for most female performers) and back again. For no one was this duality clearer than the former Mouseketeer partners turned teen-pop idols Christina Aguilera and Britney Spears, and VH1 neo-folkie Jewel, but its either-or dialectic held true for any female star butting her head against the silicone ceiling of the pent-up cultural demand for unbridled sexuality. High-profile women in music were required to sell their bodies as part of the package, or, if choosing not to (like Alanis Morissette), to explain their reasons for shirking their duty. The cultural appetite for young, beautiful female flesh was endless, and its demands were unstinting: more, more, more.

Jewel had emerged as a star with hits like "Who Will Save Your Soul?" (1995) and "Foolish Games" (1997), songs accompanied by stolid, unassuming clips that managed to casually reference the Alaskan singer's snaggle-toothed, earth-mother sexiness. It was with her video for "Intuition" (2003) (directed by Marc Klasfeld) that Jewel attempted to have her sexiness and eat a big slice of moral superiority as well, casting herself as a fantasy figure à la Madonna or Britney while also castigating her fellow female performers for the blatant commodification of their bodies. A rip on the rampant commercialization of the music video, "Intuition" casts Jewel in a series of sexy faux commercials, dressing her in sexpot outfits, letting her stomp around in knee-high leather boots, and ending with her sprayed down by the fire department. The unstated message here is that Jewel, sensible and prim singer-songwriter she is, would never make so blatant, so shabby a video as the ones she has just made.

"Intuition" was part of her never-ending, record-selling tease with her audience, toggling between sensitive folkie and sex goddess. Jewel, like many of her female compatriots, wants to be both, and because her video is good-natured fun, and skewered some major business-world icons (Sprite, Corona, Nike, Levi's), she gets away with it. But on the whole, "Intuition" was the erotic equivalent of the "antiviolence" films that let viewers sate themselves on a heaping plate of gore before tacking on their message.

Among the younger generation, Christina Aguilera chose not to play any such games with her audience, accelerating from teenypop icon to outré sexuality in the blink of an eye. "Genie in a Bottle" (1999) has her pining wistfully for the high-school heartthrob in the convertible, but by the time of "Dirrty" (2002), from her second album, directed by David LaChappelle, Christina, or her video persona, had grown up. In opposition to Spears' tease with her audience—innocent versus "I'm not that innocent"—Aguilera adopts the most extreme position she could find and staked it out for herself. Teenage sexuality had long been a video selling point, from Aerosmith's Alicia Silverstone fixation to Russian faux-lesbian duo T.A.T.U.'s "All the Things She Said" (2002), but "Dirrty" lacks the faux wholesomeness of her contemporaries' efforts.

Drastically tarting up her persona, "Dirrty" deposits Aguilera in a maelstrom of sex, motorcycles, kickboxing, and Asian otherness, like extreme sports and illicit sex meeting in a dank pit straight out of *The Deer Hunter* (1978). "Dirrty" opens with Aguilera riding into a boxing ring on a motorcycle, getting in the ring with some sweaty, shirtless men. Christina also beats the living daylights out of a masked woman, dances in a naughty-schoolgirl outfit, and sings while sitting on a stool and flashing her crotch. While undoubtedly sexy, there was something off about so shameless a video (especially considering the Thai-language signs clearly visible in the background, which read "Young Underage Girls" and "Thailand's Sex Tourism"). Half the fun of Britney Spears' numerous videos was her alternating between playing her original role, that of virginal pop star, and her new role, a twentysomething in full sexual heat. Aguilera skips the tease, and all the intermediate levels, going directly to the straight-to-video softcore film, and the effect was something like accidentally seeing your sister naked.

In its embrace of the sexually insalubrious, "Dirrty" owes more to other videos attracted to pushing the envelope regarding nudity and sexual content, like Fatboy Slim's "Slash Dot Dash" (2004), Eric Prydz's "Call on Me" (2005), T.I.'s "Let's Get Away" (2005), and Kevin Lyttle's "Turn Me On" (2004). With music videos' cultural footprint shrinking annually, the dose of shock value necessary to make a splash grew. Blurring the line between music video and softcore porn, these videos drastically ramped up their sexual content. They played the same sexual shell game of old, promising ever so slightly more than they delivered; the difference now was that sexy videos delivered full-frontal nudity, casual lesbianism (for the enjoyment of male viewers), and intimations of further sexual debauchery, stopping just short of actual pornography. Even fairly tame videos made reference to the sexual thrill of spectatorship. In Jennifer Lopez's "If You Had My Love" (1999) directed by Paul Hunter, a boho buppie grins like a kid on Christmas morning when he illicitly accesses streaming video of J.Lo posing lasciviously. The hilarious premise of Fountains of Wayne's "Stacy's Mom" (2003), in which the video's protagonist only has eyes for Stacy's gorgeous mother (Rachel Hunter), and not for teen Lolita Stacy, owes a great debt to the raunchy hijinks of 80s teen comedies like *Fast Times at Ridgemont High* (1982) (to which "Stacy's Mom" pays explicit tribute) and the frisson of danger implicit in looking. Shakira's "La Tortura" (2005) has costar Alejandro Sanz reprise the Jimmy Stewart role from *Rear Window*, watching the action from his window like it was a feature film; except here, instead of a murder mystery, we are presented with the sight of Shakira thrusting her powerful hips and summoning Sanz with her prodigious sexual magnetism. Even Weezer got into the flesh-peddling business, setting their video "Beverly Hills" (2005) within the famous confines of Hugh Hefner's Playboy Mansion, with Playboy bunnies filling the frame in nearly every shot. Knowing the audience's predilection for voyeurism, Air's "Cherry Blossom Girl" (2003) punishes those who liked to watch, implicating them by extension in the pornography industry's vicious exploitation of women.

Aguilera's main competitor in the teenypop field grasped the nature of the tease more intuitively. Britney Spears, whose early videos show her engaging in risky behavior like playing on swings, riding a bicycle, and throwing a pajama party, effectively plays the flirt, offering up ever so slightly more of her sexuality in each new video. Spears' nascent sex appeal is never far from front and center in these clips; in ". . . Baby One More Time" (1998), she is a Catholic schoolgirl sexual-fantasy cliché, and in "Oops—I Did It Again!" (2000) Spears is a slinky Martian dancer enrapturing a hunky astronaut. "I'm a Slave 4 U" (2001), directed by Francis Lawrence, takes a further step in sexing up Spears, featuring Britney as a silver-painted teen queen strutting through a party, well aware of her sexual magnetism. Spears was following Madonna's "what-will-she-do-next?" version of image management, teasing her audience with her sexual allure while simultaneously drawing back from its implications.

"Toxic" (2004), directed by Joseph Kahn, serves as the final stage in the sexualization of Spears, and is by far her most entertaining video. In it, Spears plays a retro heroine, blending two of the preferred fantasy lifestyles of the 1960s—James Bond-esque secret agent and high-flying stewardess. Spears is a flight attendant by day who battles international intrigues by night. Kahn uses supersaturated colors and sharp, bold contrasts for that graphic-novel look, only begging the question—Why haven't they made a movie of "Toxic"? It would make for a terrific *Austin Powers* spin-off—call it *Tinker, Tailor, Stewardess, Spy*. "Toxic" hits up every cliché of the John Woo/John Frankenheimer school of international intrigue films (masks, car chases, high-tech headquarters, security laser beams, magic drugs) along with an equally hefty helping of the clichés of the half-forgotten air-travel genre pioneered by *Coffee, Tea, or Me?* Spears abandons the half-girl, half-woman dialectic of earlier clips for an older, more dramatic persona, playing a fully adult heroine for the first time. "Toxic" is enormous, unabashed fun, like watching someone play dress-up in their mom's clothes, inventing elaborate stories to justify the outfits.

Spears' mentor Madonna got into the act as well, playing Austin Powers' lust-object in "Beautiful Stranger" (1999), and getting the most out of her collaboration with directorial flavor of the moment Jonas Åkerlund (who also helmed Aguilera's "Beautiful" and Prodigy's "Smack My Bitch Up"). Åkerlund directed her award-winning clip for "Ray of Light" (1998), in which Madonna hosts a light-speed version of the environmentalist documentary *Koyaanisqatsi* (1982). "Ray of Light" journeys through a day in the life of the United States from sunrise to sunset with its hand on the fast-forward button, treating American life as a perpetual-motion machine. The video opens with the sun rising over Manhattan's towers, followed by an average-looking guy opening his bedroom blinds, putting on his shoes, and speeding away from home. His exodus sets in motion an onslaught of cars, trains, and buses, followed by imagery of America at its business: in schools, at the Stock Exchange, directing traffic, at the races. A guy attempts to catch his last bite of salad before lunch ends and is immediately, symbolically followed by a hamster on a wheel.

Rather than find it depressing, "Ray of Light" is enamored with the speed of American life. Madonna dances in front of a blue sky and is superimposed, larger than life, against a whizzing shot of highway traffic, ducking bridges and shimmying amidst the gridlock. Night falls, and playtime begins—supermarket shopping, bowling, game shows on TV, carnivals, Manhattan again. Madonna bobs up and down, a smile on her face like America is a never-ending amusement-park ride. She ends her day cutting a rug on the floor of a club; in a tip of the cap to another classic video, Michael Jackson's "Billie Jean," colored blocks on the dance floor light up as dancers make their moves.

Madonna may have lost some of her cutting-edge caché in the third decade of her superstardom, but her string of music videos with their collective fingers on the zeitgeist continued unabated. Gathering together a disparate series of influences ranging from ancient Jewish mysticism to avant-garde British comedy, Madonna adapted to a new generation of music fans, and video-watchers, by adeptly spotting (and influencing) cultural trends just ahead of the masses. In a way, the main thesis of "Beautiful Stranger," her pas de deux with Austin Powers, was to show just how well-preserved Madonna remained on the far side of her fortieth birthday; the rest of it is dedicated to sticking her in as many shots as possible with Austin, in the hopes that some of Mike Myers' youth cred would rub off on her and keep her young for another cycle of adolescents. "Music" (2000), directed by Åkerlund, stars a pre-HBO Ali G as Madonna's driver, who insists on sharing with her the fact that "your babylons don't look as big as they do on the telly, but I still definitely would." "Die Another Day" (2002), directed by Traktor, pits Madonna against herself in a battle royale, wrapping fencing competitions, North Korean torture chambers, phylacteries, and Kabbalah tattoos together into a neat package. "What It Feels Like for a Girl" (2001), directed by husband Guy Ritchie, co-opts the masculine aggression of Ritchie's films *Lock, Stock, and Two Smoking Barrels* (1998) and *Snatch*

(2000), with Madge cruising by the Ol Kuntz Ladies Home in a yellow muscle car (license plates "PUSSY CAT") to pick up her aged grandmother and take her out for a night she likely won't forget. Tasering men at ATMs, shooting cops with water guns, instigating head-on collisions in her car, stealing a rocker's Camaro—Madonna and her grandma are like a bizarro-world Thelma and Louise, sucking as much enjoyment as possible out of one last night of utter debauchery, recklessness, and anti-male aggression before going out in a blaze of glory, wrapping their car around a pole in sensuous slow motion.

Embracing Performance

The Beastie Boys were never ones to say no to dressing up, having played mustachioed cops in "Sabotage" and Vegas lounge lizards in "Sure Shot," so starring in their own version of Godzilla hardly seemed a stretch. "Intergalactic" (1998), directed by Nathaniel Hornblower (Beastie Adam Yauch's nom de cinema), outfits the Beasties in funny wigs and beards that give them the look of mediocre Groucho Marx impersonators. In this guise, the Beasties pose in fish-eye stop-action shots, freezing them in motion as they run, kick, and jump their way through a subway station battling the malevolent robot terrorizing Tokyo. Where most pastiche tended to stick with the obvious, for fear of losing their audience in the backwoods of pop culture's past, the Beastie Boys, longtime connoisseurs of the unique and strange, were trendmakers, seeing nothing odd with their video's delving deeply into the conventions of Japanese horror films.

Taking the notion of performance literally, and turning their video into a Goth coming-out party/funeral for glam teenagers, New Jersey emo stalwarts My Chemical Romance treated "Helena" (2005) as an opportunity to put on the high-school play they never had the chance to star in. Outfitting band and mourners in suits and dresses, "Helena" is a rock-and-roll funeral for the emo generation, embracing Catholicism and swing dancing in equal parts. Lead singer Gerard Way plays the preacher, guiding the congregation through a distinctly untraditional set of mourning rites. Director Marc Webb sprinkles "Helena" with Goth Catholicism, all swinging censers and signs of the cross. Way alternates between the pulpit and the floor in front of the coffin with his band behind him. Getting down on his knees, Way cry-sings the chorus, with mourners wailing behind him next to the coffin. Helena's eyes pop open, jarred loose by all the commotion, and she tentatively puts one ballet slipper down on the parquet, as if testing her own abilities. Waxy of pallor, with heavy purple eyelids, like a makeup artist's notion of death, she dances through the church's aisle, gracefully pirouetting before collapsing back into lifelessness. Out on the church steps, mourners open their black umbrellas, and the pallbearers shoulder the burden. Ready, at last, for his close-up,

Mr. DeMille, Way wails as if his very stardom was dependent on it. Way's own sun-deprived skin, black uniform, and intensity of demeanor make him a vampirish heartthrob for the high-school set, and "Helena" a melodrama of religious transformation for adolescents. "Helena" posits a musical sound so powerful, a dedication so all-encompassing, it raises the dead, if only momentarily, with Way the sorcerer capable of raising the audience/congregation to the heights of frenzied transportation. Webb would start a cottage industry in Goth melodrama, later helming AFI's tip of the cap to Fascist authoritarianism, "Miss Murder" (2006). And "Helena" itself would instigate a bevy of imitators, including Panic! at the Disco's "I Write Sins Not Tragedies" (2006), which took Webb's fondness for church scenes and supplemented it with its own taste for Stanley Kubrick and the dress-up videos of Adam Ant.

Making a more uncomfortable transition to video performance was boy band 'N Sync, whose "Bye Bye Bye" (2000) (directed by Wayne Isham) turns the group famed for their robotic, synthetic music into marionettes in the grip of their female fans. Freed from their bonds, the video has lead singer Justin Timberlake and his bandmates fleeing their overzealous followers, who chase them in their cars, sic the hounds on Justin, and loom comically large over the helpless boys. 'N Sync choose an odd way to show love to their supporters, to say the least; "Bye Bye Bye" contains one of the ugliest portrayals of fans ever in music video.

Timberlake uses his own life, and his relationship with ex-girlfriend Britney Spears, as fodder for his biggest video as a solo artist, "Cry Me a River" (2002), which expresses a similar brand of gynophobia. On a commando mission with his musical partner Timbaland, Timberlake breaks into a house, smuggles a slinky brunette into the master bedroom, and films them making out. Lurking in the shadows when the lady of the house, a Britney look-alike, returns, he sneaks into her bathroom as she showers, haunting her with the distinct sensation of his presence. When she pops out to check, though, there is no one there, only Justin's makeout tape playing on the television screen. "Cry Me a River," directed by Francis Lawrence, casts Timberlake as a semicreepy stalker on the loose, viciously slapping his ex-girlfriend in public with this ugly prank. Much like "Bye Bye Bye," the gloss of the high life was only a wispy garment covering an undercurrent of adolescent anger and woman-hatred. In both videos, Timberlake does whatever he can to avoid letting women pull his strings.

High-Gloss Country

More conservative than their pop, rock, and rap compatriots, country videos came into their own in the late 90s, finding a middle ground between roots nostalgia and high-gloss modernity. New stars like Faith Hill, Shania Twain,

Toby Keith, the Dixie Chicks, and Brad Paisley made videos that conflated urban and rural, male and female, macho and sensitive, white-collar and blue-collar—in short, staying true to country music's roots while expanding its appeal to a new audience uncomfortable with an unapologetically down-home ethos. In the early 90s, country videos still waxed rhapsodic for unbroken expanses of plain, clear blue skies, and rural living. Clips like Dwight Yoakam's "A Thousand Miles from Nowhere" (1993), Alabama's "I'm in a Hurry" (1992), and LeAnn Rimes' "Blue" (1996) were nostalgic for a shimmery, mostly unreal past, with Rimes channeling the ghost of Patsy Cline, and of 1950s culture; "I'm in a Hurry" warning harried city folk to take it easy; and Yoakam's video a paean to sensuous loneliness capped by beautiful landscape shots straight out of a John Ford film. At the same time that Dolly Parton and her friends were rhapsodizing over a barroom hunk in "Romeo" (1993), a new kind of country video was being born: a savvier, more sophisticated, and more urban style infused with sex appeal and stabs at social significance. Billy Ray Cyrus' "Achy Breaky Heart" (1992) was the epitome of the former, with Cyrus as a down-home Elvis mobbed by fawning women; and Garth Brooks' "The Thunder Rolls" (1991) the prime example of the latter, tackling domestic violence in its tale of a cheating bastard who gets his comeuppance from his long-suffering wife. Martina McBride's "Independence Day" (1994) also deals with spousal abuse (a perennial country-video narrative staple as a universally loathed domestic crime), its celebration of Americana punctuating a battered woman's own declaration of independence.

Faith Hill and Shania Twain were ideal paragons of the new country's upwardly mobility, their videos celebrations of country life couched in VH1-friendly terms. Hill's videos are like moving picture postcards, starring the maddeningly perky diva in a series of scenarios designed to emphasize her girl-next-door sex appeal. "Let's Make Love" (2000), with husband Tim McGraw, is a tourist's-eye-view of Paris, displaying a taste for swirling 360-degree shots and an unstudied narcissism. "Breathe" (1999) tangles Hill up in her bedsheets, bathed in desert light—a golden-hued earth goddess for the SUV set.

Twain seemed to derive more enjoyment from her videos, treating each one as an opportunity to take on a new role. "From This Moment On" (1998), directed by Paul Boyd, transforms Twain into an Arabian princess sheathed in white; "That Don't Impress Me Much" (1998) strands her in the desert in a leopard-print catsuit, rejecting an array of unsuitable suitors; and "Man! I Feel Like a Woman!" (1999) casts Twain as Liza Minnelli in *Cabaret*, making love to the camera with her patented onslaught of winks and smiles. Twain's upfront sexuality and high-maintenance persona distinguish her from the often prim presentation of female singers in country videos—an impression only partially tempered by the reassuring presence of the regular-slob truck drivers, motorcyclists, and working stiffs who populate her videos.

Playing a working stiff of sorts, Toby Keith is a clownish man's man, his videos unabashed displays of testosterone moderated with comic flair. Representing embattled masculinity everywhere, Keith flies the flag of unreconstructed guyness in videos like "Getcha Some" (1998), "I Want to Talk About Me" (2001), and "How Do You Like Me Now?" (1999). His videos are an impressive amalgamation of traditional values and locker-room pranks. Keith plays a professor of love in "Getcha Some" who teaches his hapless male students how to get some . . . babies; in "I Want to Talk About Me," he takes a stand for men everywhere overwhelmed by their women's motor mouths; and "How Do You Like Me Now" is a chipper screw-you to the girl who rejected him in high school, inviting her to an intimate concert at the fifty-yard-line of the football stadium only to tell her off once and for all, riding back to stardom in his stretch limousine. And then there is "Beer for My Horses" (2002), featuring Willie Nelson, which is essentially *CSI: Redneck*. Keith's persona was an implicit rejoinder to the sensitive hat acts of the early 90s, embracing guydom in all its unwashed rankness and rakish charm. In that sense, he was a close cousin to Alan Jackson, whose videos all seemed to take place in tropical paradises composed of equal parts mixed drinks, yachts, and jet skis. Jackson appears as the master of ceremonies in such videoparties as "Chattahoochee" (1993) and "It's 5:00 Somewhere" (2003), leading the revelers once more into the breach, daiquiri firmly planted in his right hand.

Most prestige country videos of the late 90s and early 00s never stray much from the template of romantic yearning, domestic drama, and social problemsolving already in place as country video's bedrock agenda. Country videos, like the songs they accompanied, often wrestle with knotty social and emotional affairs, their story-songs a jumping-off point for imaginary solutions to their very real problems. Kenny Chesney's "That's Why I'm Here" (1997) is underlit, its heavy blacks and deep shadows particularly unusual for the typically brighthued country video. Its story of alcoholic stupor and partial redemption is dramatized by slow-motion shots of Chesney and his wife sloppily swigging vodka, and Chesney passing out on a bathroom floor, before the pair reunite for a joint testimonial to their renewed commitment to each other and to sober life. Brad Paisley's "He Didn't Have to Be" (1999) is a heart-tugging ode to a caring stepfather, delivered from the maternity ward where an expectant young father awaits the birth of his own first child. Strangest of all, the Dixie Chicks' "Goodbye Earl" (2000) is a deliriously cheerful kiss-off to an abusive husband murdered by his wife and her best friend.

Domestic violence, broken homes, alcoholism; country videos tackled them all, and many other social problems just like them, but always with the uplifting, values-affirming twist it was known for, even when (as in the case of "Earl") it seems entirely inappropriate. And if the videos often look interchangeable, there is good reason for that: directors like Michael Salomon, Paul Boyd, and the team of Robert Deaton and George J. Flanigen IV made an impressive percentage of prestige country videos, their (fairly undistinguished) sensibilities coming to define the look of country music onscreen.

Get Ya War On

Politics had long played an occasional, supporting role in videomaking. The music-video networks had always embraced a vague social liberalism, concentrated in efforts like MTV's "Choose or Lose" voter-registration push. Having to keep their advertisers satisfied, though, meant that politically outspoken videos were few and far between. Never as big a presence as sex or violence in the music video, politically astute artists had occasionally used videos as a soapbox of sorts. Videos had long been opportunities to introduce pet causes to a wider audience, or jump on a trendy bandwagon to look sensitive. Aerosmith's "Janie's Got a Gun" and a slew of country videos had all tackled domestic abuse; Rage Against the Machine's "Freedom" (1993) protested the incarceration of Native American activist Leonard Peltier; and Soul Asylum's "Runaway Train" (1993) solemnly informed us in an opening title that "There Are Over One Million Youth Lost on the Streets of America," pondering the plight of lost children, complete with names and snapshots of actual missing persons. Spike Lee's sensitive, deeply moving video for Prince's "Money Don't Matter 2 Night" (1992) contrasted the effortless comfort of fat cats like then-President George H.W. Bush and Donald Trump with the struggles of one African-American family to keep their heads above water. As the war machine cranks into high gear, life on the home front turns dire, with soup kitchens and urban homelessness (explicitly compared by the video to the travails of the Great Depression) the signs of a nation that has turned its back on its strugglers. Sarah McLachlan's ingenious "World on Fire" (2004) takes a page out of the how-we-spent-our-video-money routine of Too Much Joy's hilarious "Donna Everywhere" (1992), cataloguing just how much relief the money that would have been spent on a video managed to bring to the world's needy.

In one of the better, and lighter-hearted, intrusions of politics into music video, rap-rockers Rage Against the Machine teamed up with satirist Michael Moore for their 2000 video "Sleep Now in the Fire." Predating Moore's *Fahrenheit 9/11* (2004) anti-Bush crusade, "Sleep Now" takes on Wall Street in the prosperous moments before the Internet bubble burst. Opening with the sound of newspapers clattering hot off the presses, the opening titles read, "Monday—

Wall Street announces record profits, record layoffs," followed by "Tuesday—New York City decrees Rage Against the Machine shall not play Wall Street." "Sleep Now in the Fire" pegs Rage as the nemeses of two of American liberalism's favorite whipping boys: Wall Street archcapitalism run amok, and then-mayor of New York Rudy Giuliani. The rest of the video follows the template of U2's "Where the Streets Have No Name": band plays song while cops and other authority figures do their utmost to shut down the shoot. Pissed-off police officers mill around as Rage plays outside the New York Stock Exchange, with Moore eventually arrested and the video shoot coming to a halt. As always, Moore crowns himself (and Rage by extension) in a victory wreath, but this one comes with a welcome dose of humor. The closing title reads, "At 2:52 PM, in the middle of the trading day, the Stock Exchange was forced to close its doors. No money was harmed." Moore and Rage make their stand, and even emerge momentarily triumphant over the massed forces of capitalism. Moore's next video, for System of a Down's "Boom!," was even more outspoken, documenting the worldwide antiwar protests of 2003 and giving average citizens the (very brief) opportunity to express their anger about the impending war in Iraq.

Putting computer graphics to the work of mimicking the corporate and consumer world, amplifying their inherent absurdity, the video work of Pleix, a French collective of digital artists, adopted an anticorporate, antimilitaristic progressive stance. Plaid's "Itsu" (2002) takes place at a board meeting of Pork Corp., with charts and graphs multiplying in unending profusion onscreen. As executives applaud the latest numbers, the song kicks into higher gear and "Itsu" grows sexual, and gory, with rutting, pig-faced corporate officers, a female employee suggestively stroking a sausage, and a woman riding a pig-man with an apple stuffed in his mouth. Charts show profits spiraling as the pigs' sexual frenzy produces ever more pork products, and a crazed worker with a meat cleaver chops up his fellow employees, stuffing them into meat grinders as blood spurts everywhere. The corporation, in search of ever-larger profits, willingly sacrifices its own in the name of money. Profit and pornography grow interchangeable, the pursuit of revenue setting off an orgy of sexual desire for filthy lucre.

Basement Jaxx's "Cish Cash" (2003) takes on two other sacred cows of Western life, sport and militarism, creating a deranged halftime-show spectacle. Like an outtake from an LSD-stoked socialist musical, or the Super Bowl gone wild, "Cish Cash" pays homage to the glories of militarism. After a baton-twirler takes the stage, an array of tanks, helicopters, parachutists, fighter jets, and missiles spin, cross paths, and make Busby Berkeley geometric patterns: squares, circles, stars, and concentric circles. The tanks raise their turrets and charge in unison, fighter jets leave dazzling trails in the sky, and the explosion of missiles provide some genuine fireworks. Not content with this show-stopper, "Cish Cash" ends with a real grand finale: the mushroom cloud of a nuclear explosion, followed by the baton-twirler's proud curtsey.

"Cish Cash" conflates the inherent one-upsmanship of the football halftime show and global military appropriations, with the former's urge toward ever-bigger spectacles compared to the militarists' infantile desire for an even bigger blast. Pleix's video, by amplification, critiques the militarization of sports, and the aestheticization of war, with the enormously destructive fighting machines rendered objects of aesthetic pleasure. "Cish Cash" positions its viewers as passive spectators, forced to watch this aesthetically beautiful and morally repulsive exhibition, its poker-facedness containing a silent condemnation.

Equally horrified by the stifling of genuine political discourse, W.I.Z.'s video for the Chemical Brothers' "Out of Control" (1999) attacks the commodification of dissent via guerrilla operation. Set in an unnamed Spanish-speaking metropolis, "Out of Control" depicts workers and students taking to the streets against the police, in classical leftist imagery familiar from a thousand and one films, photographs, and news stories. From the outset, though, there is a lurking sensation that something is not quite right here; among the dark-hued shots of gathering hordes of faceless soldiers and bloody demonstrators are repeated close-ups of a beautiful protester in designer jeans (played, we soon come to realize, by Rosario Dawson). After comforting her bloodied friend, she proceeds to the front line, shakes up a can of soda, and pours it all over herself, the sexually deprived soldiers losing it at this display of unbridled sexuality. "Is this a soda commercial?" we wonder, disbelieving, sure that the hidden messages have been misinterpreted, but moments later, we see a sign for "Viva Cola," and a motto pops up onscreen—"In the Heat of the Moment—Serve Chilled."

The revolution has been televised, commodified, and sexualized, turned into yet another product bought and sold on the open market. After destroying its initial illusion, "Out of Control" takes back the reins of power with a brown-tinted shot of a "real" street fighter tossing a brick through a store window where a television playing the commercial rests. Greenish, night-vision shots of masked demonstrators battling police follow, along with protesters smashing a Viva soda machine and a woman spray-painting "Give Me Some Substance" on a wall. "Out of Control" finds hope in the post-Seattle antiglobalization activist movement, seeing in it an opportunity to combat the relentless appropriation of progressive ideals by big business. That it celebrates a violent struggle against the violence it perceives in corporate practice is an irony beyond the video's ken. "Out of Control" forces viewers to viscerally experience the sensation of corporate commodification, articulating and embodying the problem before laying out a proposed solution. Less rigorous, but similarly politicized, is W.I.Z.'s video for Leftfield's "Dusted" (1999), a fake Soviet newsreel of Chinese workers fighting off capitalist aggression via kung fu. Even less rigorous was Jonas Åkerlund's video for Jane's Addiction's "True Nature" (2003), a slab of riot porn with anarchist bikini models smashing windows and spray-painting walls. As the video proceeds, the revolution recedes, replaced fully by cheesecake shots of dancing women. Fuck the revolution, indeed.

After September 11, and the American invasion of Iraq, politics returned to the forefront, with multiplatinum artists like Green Day and Pharrell Williams taking advantage of music video's relative cultural obscurity to make impassioned, artful statements on the state of the world. A video that accidentally took on political overtones in the aftermath of September 11 was Ryan Adams' "New York, New York," directed by James Minchin. Filmed just four days prior to the attack on the World Trade Center, "New York, New York" poses Adams performing his song against the enormous, looming backdrop of the Twin Towers. Appearing on television in October of 2001, "New York, New York" was accidental history, serving as a mourning video, or a post-9/11 rallying call. Made before the disaster, the video bears no marks of the overplanned, the mawkish, or the politicized. "New York, New York" is like a home video of the happy family taken moments before the fatal car crash, weighted with poignance in light of what we all knew came next.

John Vanderslice's "Exodus Damage" (2005), directed by Brent Chesanek, burrows deep into the heart of post-9/11 American trauma. "Exodus Damage" is an assemblage of snapshots and shaky handheld footage of apartment towers, hotel lobbies, and subway trains. Airplanes and industrial plants, along with a lone young man with a video camera, prompt increasingly serious questions: just what are we watching? Shots of buildings are interspersed with cars, vans, and airplanes, and the sensation of watching a clandestine terrorist scouting video grows stronger. "Exodus Damage" backs away from literalism, ending with a zoom on a series of freeze-frames of clothes tumbling from a great height. Chesanek's video references the all-too-familiar iconography of September 11 without crossing the line into tastelessness or disrespect; instead, it teases the edge of our collective trauma, raising memories of the destruction of the World Trade Center without explicitly mentioning it.

The 2004 election, a bitterly divisive struggle, prompted Eminem to weigh in on political affairs, with a video intentionally released with less than a week to go before Election Day. Intended to sway fans toward voting for Democratic challenger John Kerry, "Mosh" (directed by Ian Inaba of the leftist Guerrilla News Network) is a dagger pointed directly at the heart of President Bush and his cronies. Like the flipside to "The Real Slim Shady," "Mosh" depicts an animated army of Ems taking to the streets to protest the vicious inequities of their American experience. Where the Shady factory in the earlier video symbolized the biters' lack of originality, here slipping a black hoodie over your head represented joining Eminem's army of the dispossessed. "Mosh" shows a nation of millions of angry young men (along with a few women), white and black, left out and left back, pumping their fists in rage. The video limns a parade of social ills—police harassment, eviction notices, military understaffing, cross-burning—with Bush present as smirking demon, egging things on. "Mosh" depicts the President as fatally out of touch with the realities most Americans face, and while this narrative did not manage to win the election for Senator Kerry, Eminem's video is a reminder of the roiling undercurrent of anger felt by many liberals toward the Bush administration. "Mosh" is unabashed propaganda, ending with Em's hoodie brigade, now thousands strong, breaking into the Senate, interrupting President Bush midspeech, and confronting both him and those bogeymen (and women) of the liberal agenda, the Supreme Court. They are assisted in their task by one wing of the Senate, who stand and clap, and in case the message is not quite clear enough, the video ends with smiling Democratic nominees Kerry and John Edwards marching with the "Mosh"-ers.

"Mosh" encroaches on territory that Eminem had approached once before, with his video for "White America" (2003) (directed by Guerrilla News Network's Stephen Marshall). In this precursor to "Mosh," America's Main Street is a battleground of cops, buzzing Army helicopters, and menacing American flags fluttering ominously from every building, with Eminem as the voice (and parent) of America's disaffected, possibly homicidal, youth. Even former Bad Boy MC Jadakiss found politics, making like Eminem in "Why" (2004) and lazily flipping channels in his living room, finding nothing but war all the time. Making his way inside the screen, Jada (now in natty suit and tie) gives frustrated Americans the *real* news, his testifying prompting television watchers across the country to nod their heads and slap hands, jazzed to finally hear the truth coming out of their idiot boxes.

Another mostly light-hearted performer, similarly dependent on comedy for the bulk of their clips, took a foray into political waters in 2005. Green Day had been MTV staples for over ten years, with comic videos about disaffected youth, masturbatory impulses, and out-of-touch rock stars. From the outset, the tone of "Wake Me Up When September Ends," directed by Samuel Bayer, and starring Evan Rachel Wood (*Thirteen*) and Jamie Bell (*Billy Elliot*), was so serious, so un-Green Day, that the question was whether the video was a marked change of pace or a particularly brutal send-up of overly serious art videos. As it turned out, it was the former, and the combination of Bayer's assured direction and the video's unexpected turn toward political candor would mark "Wake Me Up" as one of the more astounding music videos of the new decade.

The dialogue (affecting despite its hokiness), the glorious lighting, and the overwhelming beauty of the natural landscape in "Wake Me Up's" early scenes call to mind Terrence Malick's *Days of Heaven* (1978) (in particular, Nestor Almendros' glorious cinematography) and the work of David Gordon Green (especially the lovers' babble in *All the Real Girls* [2003]). As the song begins, the lovers watch TV, kiss, and play-fight, basking in the glow of each other's company. The band appears on a stage covered in black and red bunting, playing with unusual grace and calm. Billie Joe, often antic in his flailing attacks on his equipment, makes a bid for rock statesmanship here, even bowing at the song's close.

Bayer interrupts the song approximately midway through, with Wood blowing onto the porch of their house to confront her boyfriend. She is hysterical about his betrayal, tearing into her boyfriend with impunity as Bell sits impassively, allowing the torrent of abuse to rain down on him. Finally losing patience, he responds forcefully, telling her that of all people, he thought she would understand why he had done it. Having made the logical assumption that the nature of his betrayal is an emotional, sexual one, this is the first indication that we may not have grasped the entirety of the situation.

The next shot is jarring—a match on action from Bell getting a haircut to him, in Army uniform, patrolling an Iraqi city. His girlfriend, with tears on her cheeks, looks off into the distance, as if able (like we are) to see him across the ocean. His unit comes under heavy fire, and Bayer makes another visual match, between the lights that shower down on Green Day onstage and the explosions that light up the night over there. "Wake Me Up" goes from echoing Malick and Green to a very different kind of film—Ridley Scott's *Black Hawk Down* (2001), with its jagged, you-are-there battle footage. As Wood looks up to the sky again, we hear an echo of her earlier message of unbending loyalty to her lover, and we see him one last time, gun poised, alert, crouching behind a tank.

Adopting a different tone from Eminem's politicized anger, or the jingoistic militarism of 3 Doors Down's "When I'm Gone" (2002), "Wake Me Up When September Ends" brought the war home to MTV. A good deal of its power derived from sheer shock value, of the type that derives from one genre abruptly lurching into another, but its authority did not dim on repeat viewing. With the war in Iraq stretching into its fourth year, and with so little of it making its way onto Americans' television screens and into their consciousnesses, "Wake Me Up When September Ends" was a dramatic reminder of what was taking place overseas as we all slumped in front of our TV sets. Bayer's video existed in a realm beyond simple for-or-against positions; in its world, the war simply is, and it must be reckoned with on its own terms.

Not taking matters quite as far as "Wake Me Up," N.E.R.D.'s "Provider" (2003) tells a substantially different soldiers' tale—one with a more explicitly partisan political message. Echoing the narrative of the song, "Provider" (directed by Diane Martel) is the story of a teenage burnout who takes to cutting class and hanging out in front of a convenience store with a cast of shady, drug-dealing characters. Kicked out of school, presumably for dealing, he becomes a full-time associate of the 7-Eleven crew, with the promise of easy money winning out against the continual threat of violence. Hoping to effect a reconciliation with his estranged girlfriend, and patch up the disaster zone that is his life, he comes back to her, and she hands him a military service application in response.

On the soundtrack, the song seamlessly segues into a live performance, where N.E.R.D. leadman Pharrell Williams sings the song's original line "Someday, this will be over" as "Someday, the war will be over." Both Williams and the video's protagonist appear in fatigues, the latter marching down the road, presumably toward military duty overseas. As the offscreen crowd roars, Pharrell shouts, "If you want to live another day, put your peace signs up." "Provider" is more explicitly antiwar than "Wake Me Up When September Ends," which assiduously conceals its politics, but both videos use the element of surprise to render a well-rounded character before abruptly depositing him in uniform. As both videos made clear, the MTV audience and the soldiers fighting overseas were one and the same, and their aesthetic daring, especially when compared to the bloodless coverage of the war in Iraq on the news channels, brings the reality of the war's sacrifices home.

Also weighing in on current events with a swipe at President Bush, the Decemberists' "16 Military Wives" (2005) tackles current events with a caustic embrace, recasting *Rushmore* (1998) as an Iraq-war fable of Model United Nations intrigue and American imperialism. Even oddball director Harmony Korine (whose only other video effort had been the sensuous slow-motion tableau of Sonic Youth's "Sunday" (1998) (starring Macaulay Culkin) leapt into the fray, turning W. versus Osama into a women's track meet showdown between Islam and Christianity in Cat Power's "Living Proof" (2006). Adding to the sheer weirdness of it all, "Living Proof" ends with its medalists holding up their fists in the Black Power salute.

The other defining calamity of the decade, the devastation wrought by Hurricane Katrina, makes its first explicit music-video appearance in Ben Mor's clip for Juvenile's "Get Ya Hustle On/What's Happening" (2006). Standing on a storm-ravaged front lawn, the New Orleans MC is surrounded by evidence of the horror: wrecked houses, burned-out cars, and ever-present debris, even (for comic effect) an SUV being pulled by a team of horses. Survivors hold up signs that read "Still Here" and "You Already Forgot," while kids in Bush and Cheney masks (along with a third member of the villainous triumvirate, New Orleans

Mayor C. Ray Nagin) pretend to have the situation under control, dropping packages of food and water off a bridge into uninhabited mud. Mixing satire and mournful testimony, "Get Ya Hustle On" is true to the second-line tradition of New Orleans musical culture, testifying firsthand that death is not the end and throwing one hell of a party on the back end. "Get Ya Hustle On" made an earlier video from another New Orleans artist, in the aftermath of a different American disaster, look downright prescient: Mystikal's "Bouncin' Back" (2001) envisioned a full-on New Orleans second-line, hip-hop style, with Mystikal at its head, marching triumphantly over the massed forces of neoconservative warmongering, anthrax terror, and urban poverty. In their videos, New Orleans hip-hop artists tied themselves explicitly, and meaningfully, to their home city's deep musical roots, finding optimism in music's ability to turn tragedy into hope.

The Center Cannot Hold

Not every video could be as ballsy as Green Day's, but even as the star of mainstream music video began to dim, at least in its TV incarnation, there were still artists who bothered to craft worthwhile clips. These included two unlikely contenders for biggest rock band in the world: a pasty-faced bunch of English softies and a SoCal ska group. Both Coldplay and No Doubt looked to Hollywood to shore up the ever-diminishing hold of the rock video, borrowing liberally from sources mainstream and otherwise in the hopes of preserving some shred of their antecedents' authority. The mission was ultimately hopeless, but of all their compatriots in the rock multiplatinum club, No Doubt and Coldplay fought hardest to preserve the video as a forum for aesthetic innovation.

No Doubt viewed videos as opportunities to wrestle with the band's demons, which included the failed romantic relationship between lead singer Gwen Stefani and bassist Tony Kanal, and the inordinate share of attention garnered by Stefani. Like bite-sized versions of dysfunctional-band doc *Metallica: Some Kind of Monster* (2004), No Doubt's videos are tangled, self-reflexive takes on the band's odd dynamic. Rather than glossing over the band's tensions, No Doubt choose to shine a spotlight on them, and the effect is alluring.

In "Don't Speak" (1996), directed by Sophie Muller, the three boys glare as Gwen, all dolled up, is moved to front and center at a photo shoot. The band watches her pose, and whisper among themselves, their faces cast in shadow. Tony, standing in an enchanted forest, pulls down an apple and discovers it to be full of writhing worms. The Garden of Eden has been poisoned by success, and by the machine that demands one easily identifiable star per band. Later videos play off the tension exhibited in "Don't Speak," depicting the band as either a fun-loving bunch of troupers or an angst-ridden collective. "Sunday Morning" (1997) (directed by Muller) has the band cooking Sunday dinner together, and culminates in an all-out food fight. "Simple Kind of Life" (2000), though, returns to the bittersweet side, with Gwen fleeing Tony at the altar, dashing away from the pursuing groomsmen. Gwen drops to her knees to gather up the remnants of the wedding cake, smashed in the heat of the chase.

No Doubt's videos engaged Stefani in a dialectic that it made part of their explicit content, between her persona as just one of the guys, and an emerging, sexualized temptress that she sometimes plays in the videos. In "Simple Kind of Life," the video ends with her returning to her trailer, handing her (fictional) baby off to her mother, and wiping the glam makeup off her face. In "Underneath It All" (2002), Gwen appears in two guises: first, as a seductress provocatively undressing in a room dominated by dark, heavy furniture; and second, lounging on her bed in a sun-drenched room, wearing a simple tank top. The video asks you to prefer her in the latter pose, burnishing her role as Girl Next Door, even as she poses in temptress' garb. Her solo effort "Hollaback Girl" (2005) only solidifies this persona, dressing her up as a high-school cheerleader leading the gang in a shout-along of her absurdly peppy quasi-feminist anthem.

"It's My Life" (2003), directed by image-maker extraordinaire David LaChapelle, borrows from Best Picture winner *Chicago* (2002) for its iconography, but its band dynamic was already very familiar. Stefani stars in an omnibus clip, playing a woman who resorts to murder to get rid of her three lovers (played by bandmates Kanal, Adrian Young, and Tom Dumont). In the first scene, which pays the most direct homage to *Chicago*, Gwen and husband Tom reside in a dingy set of rooms with a neon sign blinking outside the window. Inspired in the midst of preparing his food, she pours a hefty dose of rat poison into his dinner. In the second, she runs over wealthy businessman Tony, crushing him against the gate of his house with his own car. In the last, having apparently seduced housepainter Adrian, he leers at her, and she responds by tossing her hairdryer into his bath and electrocuting him. LaChapelle's video takes the form of a courtroom confession/plea to a jury of disbelieving blue-collar women. Gwen cries, her makeup running down her face, as she sings, and police officers come to drag her away, apparently toward the gas chamber. Stefani may have killed her male tormentors, but the men have the last laugh; the trio, all still clad in their period costumes, watch on television as Gwen in led to her death, and toast each other, laughing.

Taking a page out of the Hollywood playbook as well, Coldplay borrow liberally from *Memento* (2000), and Gaspar Noé's French shocker *Irreversible* (2002), for their reverse-motion clip "The Scientist" (2002) (directed by Jamie Thraves). Zooming out from a close-up of his sleeping face, the camera reveals lead singer

Chris Martin lying prone on the street, and then follows him as he jerkily trots backward, away from the city center, across the train tracks, and back into the forest. His time in the forest, gazing up at trees as leaves fall, is a momentary irruption of peacefulness, but the narrative continues onward, inexorably drawn backward, literalizing the song's refrain, "take me back to the start." Chris puts his shirt back on, gets back into his car, and appears to fall asleep, only to suddenly be joined by another presence, a woman, who flies up off the ground, along with a pile of broken glass that reconstructs itself into a windshield. The car makes its way back up the mountain, and through the guard rail it pierced, ending with a single moment of calm. Chris smiles lovingly at his girlfriend as she puts on her jacket, and their car recedes into the distance, safely ensconced in the past. Like Radiohead's "Just," "The Scientist" is a mystery video at heart, rendering mundane tragedy mysterious and beautiful by running the tape backward, and making each discrete action a miracle unto itself.

"Trouble" (2001), directed by Tim Hope, is lighter-hearted, adopting a more playful, magical tone. The song's opening piano chords become the soundtrack to nature's bounty, with plants sprouting in the forest and pollen flying through the air. Martin and the rest of the band ride a horse-cart through this landscape, watching the rapid-fire growth proliferate. Martin plays his piano, cunningly made of fireflies, each tinkle of the keys sending another bug flying off. The band are cast in their own fairy tale, where the world has taken on magically benevolent new powers and the whole of nature is dedicated to the promulgation of Coldplay's "Trouble."

Incredible Shrinking Video

With the music video increasingly absent from television screens, the action shifted away from superstars and blockbuster videos, and toward quirky, low-budget videos for indie-rock and electronica acts. These videos found new life on the Internet, where a host of video-hosting and streaming music-video sites offered access to a remarkable array of clips past and present. This new generation of videos was far less attuned to the selling of celebrity—appropriate for a medium reinvented for cult heroes and unknown artists.

A new, post-grunge wave of indie-rock and alternative performers ushered in a new generation of directors dedicated to celebrating and adorning their self-effacing personae. Videomakers like Chris Cunningham, Chris Milk, Jon Watts, Pleix, Jonathan Glazer, Brent Chesanek, and Garth Jennings shifted the spotlight from performer to video, shooting clips that owed less to the lifestyle-aspirational mode of mainstream video and more to avant-garde filmmaking and installation art. These videos were discrete artworks appended to the song, intended to stand on their own merits. With their arrival, the music video ushered in a new golden era of artistic fecundity, albeit one that went unseen by the overwhelming majority of video watchers.

Electronica and dance-music artists, operating under different generic rules than rock and hip-hop performers, were generally content to skip out on their videos, handing directors a blank canvas to paint on. In the absence of stars, these videos depended on unusual narrative setups and a renewed emphasis on texture, playing with damaged film stock, obsolete-looking graphics, and effects that re-created the feel of worn or distorted video tape. Much like Spike Jonze, their directors saw the entire repository of recorded images as a massive warehouse, to be raided at will for their own needs. Their efforts even bled into the mainstream, evident in such unlikely pairings as rock scion Kelly Osbourne's "One Word" (2005) and director Chris Applebaum's *Alphaville*-biting video, which featured trench-coated noir castaways pondering questions like "What is the privilege of the dead?" From *The Osbournes* to Jean-Luc Godard in one step; the cultural gaps breached were mind-blowing.

Coming closest to the mainstream among the newcomers while still playing a starring role was Milk, whose work adapted already-familiar narratives and tweaked them, turning out adult fairy tales comprised of captivating imagery. Courtney Love's "Mono" (2004) features the unpredictable rock icon as Sleeping Beauty adrift in America, besieged by paparazzi, and seeking to lead her army of lost little girls back to the peaceful, silent forest; Mellencamp's "Walking Tall" (2004) stars actor Peter Dinklage as the hated outsider in a 1950s America viciously biased against short folk; Audioslave's "Doesn't Remind Me's" (2005) little boy lives out his *Rocky* fantasies (complete with the famous jog up the steps of the Philadelphia Museum of Art) while wrestling with his father's overseas military duty; and the Chemical Brothers' "The Golden Path" (2003) concerns a 1970 office worker tantalized by the visions of freak-flag hippie life that break into his drab world. Darkness is always just around the corner in these fables: the ugliness of the unthinking mob in "Mono" and "Walking Tall," the brain death of white-collar life in "The Golden Path," and death itself in Modest Mouse's "Ocean Breathes Salty" (2004). Most surprising of all was the unexpected reversal of "Doesn't Remind Me," which begins as a humorous echo of *Rocky* (1976) and becomes, by its conclusion, a mournful story of loss, with the boy's father killed overseas, the yellow ribbon representing his military service tumbling to the ground at the moment his son exults over his victory in the ring. "Doesn't Remind Me's" child protagonist, enamored of a certain brand of stylized violence represented here by boxing and the model warplanes he enjoys flying, is unable to make the connections so clearly written on his mother's grief-wracked face about the relation between such exuberant pursuits and his father's unseen, presumably violent death.

The directors of Brooklyn-based video production company Waverly Films specialized in high-concept parody videos played straight. Jason Forrest's "Stepping Off" (2004), directed by Jon Watts, is a wicked satire of heavy-metal excess and pseudo-mystical claptrap. Starring laptop rocker Forrest as lead singer of a Led Zeppelin-esque hard-rock group, "Stepping Off" purports to be footage from his band's triumphant world tour. Fans clap, cry, and lose their cool, magic-making elves straight out of a Robert Plant lyric shoot off explosions, and the band plays Malmsteen Studio, Daltry Hall, and Halford Arena (each named for a god of Seventies rawk). "Stepping Off" teaches listeners to hear Forrest's otherwise unclassifiable single as pseudo-rock, a fake-metal video for a fake-metal song.

Advancing into the next decade after "Stepping Off," Armand Van Helden's "Into Your Eyes" (2005), directed by Benjamin Dickinson and Jeff Kaplan, borrows its guiding principle from John Carpenter's film *They Live* (1988), but hijacks its magical-sunglasses premise and twists it into a self-aware update of the 80s hair-metal video. A stereotypical rocker in a lumberjack shirt puts on a pair of sunglasses he's found and discovers that with them on, the world looks markedly different. Messages pop up on billboards imploring him to "Party" and "Move Your Feet," and, everywhere he looks, babes galore frolic. Slipping off his glasses, the fantasy world of sultry construction workers, handball players with come-hither stares, and grocery-store employees cavorting in bikinis recedes, replaced by drab, unassuming reality. Music here brightens up the gray-toned monotonousness of mundane life, but the nature of the fantasy is infectious, for better or worse; in the video's last shot, glasses firmly affixed, the protagonist looks into the mirror and, seeing a beautiful woman, shakes his/her ass. "Into Your Eyes" provides both the fantasy and a more objective, detached viewpoint that renders the fantasy utterly ridiculous. In both "Into Your Eyes" and "Stepping Off," parody kills its ostensible subject dead.

Also enamored of video cliché, but willing to push it to full-on excess, was British director Dougal Wilson, whose video for Benny Benassi's "Satisfaction" (2003) is a masterpiece of the cheesecake genre. Like an erotic Home Depot commercial, "Satisfaction" features scantily clad models testing out a variety of home-improvement tools. The models pound, drill, and screw, with Wilson emphasizing the sexual symbolism of each motion, providing close-ups of each point of entry. "Satisfaction" eroticizes manual labor, like an extension of the construction workers in "Into Your Eyes," but where Van Helden's video critiques the cliché, Benassi's shamelessly embraces it. Wilson's video for the Streets' "Fit But You Know It" (2004) takes the mundane thrust of Mike Skinner's shambling talk-raps and renders a lackadaisical world of East London streetscapes, beer-drinking, and hanging out, with Skinner flipping through a roll of snapshots that spring to life. Dizzee Rascal's "Dream" (2004) turns the grime MC into a kid-friendly marionette, leading his crew in some petty vandalism in their newfound home atop a baby-grand piano belonging to a prim-looking schoolteacher. Wilson's videos were absurd, but they knew it; their self-consciousness absolves them of all responsibility for their often-silly scenarios.

Roman Coppola (son of Francis, brother of Sofia) also looked to his occasional co-conspirator Jonze's culturally savvy, joshing sensibility as inspiration for his wickedly funny videos. Aping the format of instructional films, cooking shows, and the like, Coppola's video for Daft Punk's "Revolution 909" (1998) took inspiration from Jonze's woozy, left-field plotlines. A police officer pulls up to the scene of an illegal nightspot and, in attempting to sort out the crowd, zeroes in on one fresh-faced girl. Before he can collar her, he notices a reddish stain on his undershirt, and the video suddenly spins into another universe entirely, transporting us wholesale into an industrial film about the growing of tomatoes. A tiny tomato grows into full bud and is picked, collected, sprayed, and put in trays. The tomatoes are then delivered via truck to the local supermarket, where an old lady squeezes them, picks a handful, and sticks them in a pot in her kitchen.

The instructional film becomes a cooking show, and we are provided with instructions in how to prepare our new purchases—"Boil tomatoes for a few seconds," "peel away the skins," and so forth. Under the careful tutelage of this old-world Italian mother, the tomatoes become a tomato sauce for her pasta, carefully packed into her son the cop's lunch bag. As he snatches a hasty repast in the patrol car, a drop of the carefully prepared sauce falls on his shirt, and we are transported back to the present, where the cop is momentarily distracted by his newfound stain, giving the girl in his sights an opportunity to dash out of sight, and out of his clutches. "Revolution 909" is aesthetically adulterous, leaping between three discrete visual genres; it is also a gem of absurdism, a youth-culture variant on "for want of a nail, the shoe was lost" logical exaggeration.

Coppola was a charming raconteur, his videos playful and rarely serious. Air's "Playground Love" (2000), codirected with sister Sofia, is less polished than "Revolution 909," essentially a gag-reel version of *The Virgin Suicides* (1999), the film from whose soundtrack the song is taken. Zooming in on scenes from the film, "Playground Love" finds the inanimate objects that fill the frame aping the actions of their human masters, with the lovestruck teens' twin hunks of already-been-chewed gum lip-syncing the words to the song. Green Day's "Walking Contradiction" (1995) parodies rock-star excess, with Billie Joe, Mike Dirnt, and Tre Cool causing havoc six ways from Sunday by dint of their godlike self-absorption. Kids flip their bikes over, cars whiz through the air, movers drop grand pianos—all as a result of the band's monumental lack of regard for others. No matter what calamity befalls their neighbors, the boys of Green Day remain safely ensconced in their own personal bubbles.

Inspired by Jonze's twisted sense of humor, and Gondry's playful, childlike ethos, Garth Jennings (also known as Hammer & Tongs) made two of the more eye-catching videos of the era, Blur's "Coffee & TV" (1999) and Fatboy Slim's "Right Here, Right Now" (1999). The latter, roaming the same terrain as Pearl Jam's "Do the Evolution" (directed by Todd McFarlane and Kevin Altieri), is a four-minute history of the world, beginning 350 billion years in the past and concluding this afternoon. In it, a hyperspeed evolution plays itself out, with a one-celled organism becoming a fish becoming a larger fish becoming an amphibian becoming an ape becoming a Neanderthal becoming modern man.

A similar use of unusual point of view was on display in "Coffee & TV," a missing-persons story told from the perspective of a milk carton. Confronted by the sad faces of his human family, the milk carton, equipped with arms and legs, heads off into the big city in the hopes of tracking down their wayward son Damon. The metropolis is no place for a walking piece of cardboard, confronted as he is by runaway bicycles, flagrant milk drinkers, carton crumplers, and hungry toddlers, but he presses on, and after suffering a beating at the hands of some juvenile delinquents, nearly falling prey to the amorous attentions of Big Suzy, and watching his girlfriend, Lady Milk, cruelly crushed to death by a passerby, he makes his way to young Damon. Spotting his picture on the carton that has just taken a nose dive through his window, he picks it up and hops on a bus back to his family. After finishing the contents of the carton, he unthinkingly tosses Milk into the garbage. As mournful music plays, Milk sprouts wings as he ascends to heaven, with Lady Milk joining him along the way. "Coffee & TV" is a peppy parable of anthropomorphization, its whimsicality and vividly imagined point of view an expression of the faux-naïve style directors like Milk and Michel Gondry had established.

Faux naiveté became the order of the day, and animated videos ruled the roost in the indie-rock world, being cheap, idiosyncratic, and personal. Inspired by the example of outsider artists like Henry Darger, videos like Brendan Benson's "Cold Hands, Warm Heart" (2005), the Arcade Fire's "Laika" (2005), and Jose Gonzalez's "Stay in the Shade" (2005) are simplistic animated line drawings, looking more like the doodlings of a bored adolescent than a polished mainstream video.

As if to overcome their humble origins, many of these videos, and many indie videos in general, were unhealthily obsessed with violence and death. In "Cold Hands, Warm Heart," a genial-looking stick figure tries to commit suicide;

Interpol's "Evil" (2005), directed by Charlie White, features a haunted-looking puppet lip-syncing to the song while lying on a stretcher in the aftermath of a horrific car crash; Will Oldham and Matt Sweeney's "I Gave You" (2005) pans down from heaven to take in the shocked realization of a reckless driver that he has, in fact, killed someone. Death haunts these videos in a manner that could be read, in light of the increasingly hopeless news from Iraq, as political.

His work darker and more violence-besotted than the bulk of his contemporaries, British director Jonathan Glazer used the music-video medium as a short stopover on the way to *Sexy Beast* (2001) success, making only a handful of videos for Radiohead, UNKLE, Jamiroquai, and Massive Attack, among others. His video for the latter's "Karmacoma" (1995) reads in retrospect as a dry run for his feature debut, comprised of grubby gun-toting criminals joined by scary little girls out of *The Shining* (1980). Blur's "The Universal" (1995) takes its inspiration from another Kubrickian source, depositing lead singer Damon Albarn in *A Clockwork Orange*'s (1971) Korova Milk Bar.

Glazer's videos favored the abnormal and unsettling, making use of technological know-how to create disconcerting milieus. His video for Richard Ashcroft's "A Song for the Lovers" (2000) switches at will between mundane rock-star downtime and hints of mysterious *Shining*-like goings-on just beyond the frame. A shirtless Ashcroft dries his face, sits on the bed in his hotel suite, turns on a recording of his own song, and sings along, completely off-tune, as if "A Song for the Lovers" was mere background music, and Ashcroft just another shower warbler.

Ashcroft's bathroom routine is interrupted by thunderous banging at the door, and his lonesome dinner disturbed by the creeping sensation of lurking presences in his room, human or ghostly. Ashcroft pauses the song twice to check for noises, and after the second interruption, Glazer cuts to a disquieting shot from inside the bathroom, where the light, turned off by Ashcroft, is on again. Ashcroft slowly walks over to the bathroom, peers around the corner, the silence deafening, and . . . proceeds to urinate, as the camera tracks back out of the bathroom and the song returns for its final chorus. Glazer gets off on scaring us unnecessarily, deftly evoking the baseless jitters of unfamiliar surroundings.

Glazer's video for UNKLE's "Rabbit in Your Headlights" (1998) stars French actor Denis Lavant (*The Lovers on the Bridge*) as a homeless, deranged man walking through a tunnel, knocked over multiple times by speeding cars. After each impact, Lavant lays motionless on the asphalt, making us question whether he has survived the crash, before getting up once more. Looking steadily more bruised and battered as the video goes on, he somehow maintains his strength, perversely appearing to grow stronger after each collision. Finally grasping his own strength, he pauses, smiles to himself, and, anticipating

impact, extends his arms in a Christ-like pose. Smoke obscures the actual collision, but when it clears, it is Lavant walking away unscratched and the automo-
bile that is crumpled beyond recognition. The drivers of "Rabbit in Your
Headlights" are not merely negligent; they are malevolent, gleeful at the
prospect of hurting the helpless Lavant. Lavant is a representative of the abused
and downtrodden, growing ever-stronger, according to the video's calculation,
with every damage done to them.

Also dependent on the scare tactics of car-pedestrian collisions, with a similar reversal of fortune, Radiohead's "Karma Police" (1997) switches points of
view, putting us in the car with the perpetrators. Beginning with a shot of a car's
empty back seat, "Karma Police" pans forward until the camera peers straight
through the windshield. Setting forward, the car drives through an arid landscape of empty roads, fields, and telephone poles, pushing ahead until a tiny
white speck on the road grows into a running man. Lead singer Thom Yorke,
reclining in the car's back seat, gazes down into his lap as he sings, then leans
into the front seat, singing as if angrily lost in thought. The running man, in
close-up, is fat, old, unshaven, and hobbling, lurching awkwardly and eventually
falling to the ground. Crouching on the ground, he watches the car slowly, grue-
somely back up for the kill.

"Karma Police," like "Rabbit," never explains itself. Its hint of unspeakable
cruelty, echoing the malice of "Rabbit's" drivers, is broken by the helpless runner's discovering a line of dripping oil leading directly to the killer car. Finger-
ing a matchbook behind his back, he tosses a lit match into the oil and watches
the line of fire chase the car, its hood bursting into flame. The camera, trapped
back in the car, jerks around fruitlessly as flames engulf the windows, ending
with a pan backward that reverses the video's opening shot. This one reveals
Yorke to be no longer in the car, having vanished at some point. "Karma Police"
is an action film without justification or character, its choking air of creeping
evil an essential by-product of its lack of explanation.

The moving-room effect of Jamiroquai's "Virtual Insanity" (1996) stems
from locking down the camera and leaving the furniture free to slip and slide.
For most viewers, though, watching "Virtual Insanity" prompts a kind of wonder at its uncanny motion. Glazer's most famous video is devoid of the mias-
matic gloom of his other videos, possessed of a buoyancy and good humor
foreign to "Rabbit in Your Headlights" and "Karma Police." Lead singer Jay Kay
follows in Michael Jackson's magical footsteps, his dance moves switching
unpredictably between smooth and supernatural. Kay dances up to the camera,
then is conveyed smoothly toward the background, as if on a moving walkway.
Furniture suddenly slides forward and backward, to the left and the right, with
Kay's mincing steps deftly avoiding impact. Glazer keeps the malevolent touches

(creeping pools of blood, threatening crows) to a minimum, and "Virtual Insanity" is a paean to the power of the dance.

The cult favorite of the new generation of video directors (being one of the few filmmakers, along with Gondry, Jonze, Romanek, Anton Corbijn, and Glazer, and a handful of others, to merit their own greatest-hits DVDs), Chris Cunningham has only worked with a handful of big-name artists, preferring to concentrate his efforts on clips for electronica acts like Aphex Twin, Square-pusher, and Autechre. Cunningham's videos are tech-savvy mindfucks, occasionally indebted to genre filmmakers like Takashi Miike (whose fingerprints are all over Cunningham's video for Squarepusher's "Come on My Selector" [1998]), but primarily consisting of his own meld of the futuristic and the archaic, the sensuous and the disgusting. Cunningham's aesthetic dialectic makes it possible for him to be responsible for both the excruciating discomfort of Aphex Twin's "Windowlicker" (1999) and the purring machine-sex of Björk's "All Is Full of Love" (1999) (whose iPod-white gleam inspired another video in love with immaculate technology, the Postal Service's "Such Great Heights" [2003]).

It was repulsiveness, though, that made Cunningham's name. Working with artists not required to sell their images for public consumption, Cunningham had a field day twisting and distorting the star-making machine into unfamiliar, hideous shapes. For both of his collaborations with Aphex Twin (Richard D. James), "Come to Daddy" (1997) and "Windowlicker," Cunningham pastes James' head on woefully inappropriate bodies: a gang of youthful hoodlums in the former and swimsuit-clad party girls in the latter. Set in a grimy London housing project, and tinted a dull brown and gray, "Come to Daddy" vibrates with intimations of impending horror. Its faint air of overhanging menace intensifies when a television perched on a pile of garbage snaps on without warning, prompting a mangy, vicious-looking dog to bark furiously at it. The television reveals a distorted greenish image of a screaming mouth, a presence that summons, as if conjuring them up wholesale, a passel of little Aphexes (actually played by little people). They take the command to "come to daddy" as license to destroy, attacking a bystander in a nearby parking lot and roughhousing with each other. Cunningham has the song function as a malevolent nursery rhyme, egging the little criminals on to ever-greater acts of mayhem. As the mini-Richards skip together, the distorted heads on the TV screen become an emaciated, jelly-covered, full-grown body, which bursts through the television, echoing the famous scene from David Cronenberg's *Videodrome* (1983). Its bluish-white skin, oversized, distorted head, and fanged teeth make it a double of sorts to the mismatched children of destruction, all of whom share the distinction of being just realistic enough to be truly unsettling. Cunningham mixes and matches heads and bodies late in "Come to Daddy," putting James' head on the hatchling's body and gathering the frightening child-men around him as his own offspring.

Depending on how you look at it, "Windowlicker" is either significantly less disturbing or infinitely more so. Where "Come to Daddy" had been set in the nightmarish world of the housing projects, explicitly rendered as a foreboding locale straight out of a horror film, "Windowlicker" takes place in the (theoretically) more comforting realm of the hip-hop music video. Cunningham settles viewers into their surroundings with the comically overblown opening sequence of the video, which extends parody to a point of overwrought hysteria. Two stereotypical homeboys cruise the streets of Los Angeles in their car, their talk liberally peppered with profanity and stray libido. Spotting two women standing on a street corner, they pull up, introduce themselves, and are dissed mercilessly. The men and women exchange taunts back and forth to the point where it appears that, rather than watching a music video, we are seeing the accidental recording of a particularly pointless failed pick-up.

The cycle of boredom is suddenly broken by a comically oversized limousine, which knocks the men's minuscule coupe out of the way. The back window rolls down, and it is none other than James inside, summoning the women for his rolling party. The women appear frightened by his intimidating, scary smile, but they are convinced by his limber dance moves. Having already pulled the rug out from under the hip-hop video fantasy of easily accessible sex, Cunningham does it once more, patching together freakish she-males by pasting James' head on voluptuous female bodies clad in white bikinis. Cunningham's Aphex-women rut and grind in the back of the limo, poke their heads through the sunroof, and are filmed in Busby Berkeley-esque overhead shots, spinning their Aphex Twin logo umbrellas. By the end of the video, the horror-faces have grown even more disquieting, one particularly voluptuous body topped by a visage with giant buck teeth and broad, diseased-looking nose. As if to rub our faces in the ickiness of it all, "Windowlicker" ends with an ejaculatory spray of champagne raining down on the beautiful bodies and hideous faces alike as the women dance, shake their butts, and mash their breasts together. Not content with asexuality, "Windowlicker" is resolutely antisexual, turning sexuality into nightmarish fever dream. Cunningham's logic is utterly remorseless; he pursues the fiendish logic of his body-switching fetish to its bitter, unsavory end, both here and in "Come to Daddy."

Most of Cunningham's other videos are not quite so strange, but they do share an interest in the disturbing and the futuristic. Turning Madonna into a Goth goddess, "Frozen" (1998) flies along on its swooping desert crane shots, and the special effects that turn the singer's shawl into a flock of birds, and a black dog leaping at the screen. Madonna caresses the camera with her sideways glance, a deity of abandoned spaces, capable of strange magic in order to turn us all into her willing captives. Cunningham's video is practically mainstream, when viewed in the light of his other work, but "Frozen" nonetheless contains traces of the director's trademark mystic oddity, albeit a version heavily cleaned up for MTV consumption. Both Autechre's "Second Bad Vilbel" (1996) and Björk's "All Is Full of Love" feature robots at play, the former's fuzzy-looking androids easily trumped by the lesbian robot sex of the latter. Knowing how to play nice when he felt like it, "All Is Full of Love" was a kinder, gentler (although no less freakish) Cunningham.

While there would be no conclusion to the music video, no stirring finale to end the century-long show, one video from early 2006 attempts to summarize the entire history of televised musical performance in one five-minute clip. The Red Hot Chili Peppers' video for "Dani California" (directed by Tony Kaye) made the dizzying array of differing musical styles its star, leaping from Elvis to the Beatles to the present via a series of costume changes over the course of one television performance. Lead singer Anthony Kiedis and the other Chili Peppers undergo a marathon set of costume (and attitude) changes, leapfrogging from hip-shaking Elvis to suit-and-tie-and-hornrim-glasses-wearing Beatles impostors to acid-rock casualties to Funkadelic clones to glam androgynes to Goth burnouts to spandex-clad hair-metal rejects to (improbably) Nirvana circa *MTV Unplugged in New York* to their own long-sleeves-and-shorts aesthetic. Flipping through the pages of rock history, the Chili Peppers' video is a mash note to the stylistic adventurousness of the genre's wildly divergent wardrobe choices, even unfortunate selections like the blond fright wigs of the hair-metal bands. "Dani California" is not concerned with video, per se, but in its celebration of rock and roll's restless desire for the new, and its fond recollections of past incarnations, the video is like forty years of music video, from Elvis to Eminem, mashed up into one long song. Having long been pioneers in the music video, Red Hot Chili Peppers sum up an entire era of music video with "Dani California," clearing the tables for whatever might follow in the never-ending chain of shifting musical, cultural, and visual styles to which music video had paid such elaborate witness.

Afterword

I n the absence of MTV, the music video did not die; it merely mutated, clamping onto a new host: the Internet. Once solely the property of television programmers, music videos have become the province of bloggers, music websites, and Internet portals seeking new content. With the increase in high-speed Internet connections, it is now possible for home computer users to watch streaming video or download large music-video files. Yahoo, Google, and AOL are among the Internet titans with video services that put thousands of music videos a mere click or two away. YouTube and MySpace have both grown into Internet titans by virtue of their music-video holdings—YouTube's contributed by amateur collectors and band obsessives, MySpace's mostly posted by up-and-coming groups. Even MTV belatedly got into the act, adding a streaming-video program with much of their video library available for perusal.

The music video has gone from being centralized in the programming of two or three cable channels to being diffused all over the Internet, and what is lost in efficiency is made up for by the dazzling array of choices now available to music-video buffs. The Internet is now a twenty-four-hour music-video jukebox, with everything from the latest U2 video to obscure indie-rock clips available for viewing somewhere in the World Wide Web's wilds. In fact, indie rock and electronica videos thrive on the Internet, those genres' tech-savvy fans passing around links to their favorite acts' latest clips or posting them on their blogs. The music video has regained some of its underground, *samizdat* cachet, transmitted virally from one true believer to the next. It has also become a surprisingly central application in the new-media universe, played on computers, downloaded to cellphones, and purchased on DVDs. And with the latest generation of MP3 players (like the video iPod) capable of playing video in addition to audio, music videos are now just as portable as individual songs. Shunned from their original home, music videos have found a new home practically everywhere; and having lost their initial function as television fodder, videos have become impressively cheap, flexible, and omnipresent. Rather than killing them off, the cable channels' unceremonious dumping of music videos gave the form new life.

If this book had been written two or three years ago, any closing thoughts on the future of the music video would have been pessimistic in nature. The music video, having been so important to an earlier generation of music fans and culturally astute teenagers and young adults, had grown stale, made obsolete by digital culture and the ever-increasing puerility of youth-centric television. Music videos had apparently had their run and were now set to be consigned to the dustbin of history. Instead, music videos have been reborn, reanimated for the era of the Internet. While it seems unlikely that the video's splashy cultural moment will ever return, or that big-budget, blockbuster videos will make a comeback, the music video is alive and well. In the absence of much interest from MTV, VH1, and BET, the music video has become devoted more to breaking new bands or to targeting a particular constituency than maintaining the cultural dominance of a handful of superstars. In the late 1990s, when MTV first began turning its back on music videos, it was the moderately popular or up-and-coming band that was hit hardest, often barred by their labels from shooting videos. Now, the worm has turned, and the music video has become a far more receptive medium for the little guys out there than for the superstars. The music video has rediscovered democracy, dispersed to the four winds of the Internet. Music sites like Pitchfork and bloggers like Sasha Frere-Jones (music editor at *The New Yorker*) post links to videos, fan sites and MySpace pages offer exclusive clips, and sites like YouTube offer access to thousands of music videos past and present. YouTube in particular offers a glimpse of potential video nirvana—a single site at which all (or most) of music-video history is available with the click of a button. Music-video fans lament the difficulty of tracking down individual videos, particularly old or obscure clips, and the hope is that some day soon, one video site will obtain the necessary permissions to house a record label's entire video library. While that would make the task of future music-video scholars infinitely easier, it also is somehow entirely appropriate that so fragmentary a medium as the music video is scattered all across the Internet, entirely decentered and disorganized. For an art form dedicated to fleeting pleasures, momentary genius, and disposable triumphs, this only seems fair. And yet, the music video stands in a cultural position not dissimilar to that of the feature film prior to the success of the video-cassette recorder. Before the VCR, once a film disappeared from local theaters, it was gone for good, unless, like *Gone with the Wind* (1939) or some other blockbuster, it was occasionally trotted out for a re-release, or screened at a cinematheque or repertory theater. These were the rules of the game, until the VCR upended the

entire system, and the entirety of film history became available to home viewers. The same process holds true for music videos, whose back pages remain
partially blank, inaccessible to the curious and the devoted. Soon, though, the
music video archives will be wide open, and the work of sorting through its
treasures, by fans and scholars, will begin in earnest.

Top 100 Videos List

1. Guns N' Roses—Don't Cry/November Rain/Estranged (Andy Morahan)
2. Foo Fighters—Everlong (Michel Gondry)
3. Beastie Boys—Sabotage (Spike Jonze)
4. Replacements—Bastards of Young (Randy Skinner & Bill Pope)
5. Michael Jackson—Billie Jean (Steve Barron)
6. Johnny Cash—Hurt (Mark Romanek)
7. White Stripes—Fell in Love with a Girl (Michel Gondry)
8. Sinead O'Connor—Nothing Compares 2 U (John Maybury)
9. Madonna—Like a Prayer (Mary Lambert)
10. U2—One (Mark Pellington)
11. Duran Duran—Girls on Film (Godley & Creme)
12. Michael Jackson—Thriller (John Landis)
13. Bob Dylan—Subterranean Homesick Blues (D.A. Pennebaker)
14. Peter Gabriel—Sledgehammer (Stephen A. Johnson)
15. Nirvana—Smells Like Teen Spirit (Samuel Bayer)
16. Green Day—Wake Me Up When September Ends (Samuel Bayer)
17. Red Hot Chili Peppers—Californication (Jonathan Dayton & Valerie Faris)
18. Joy Division—Atmosphere (Anton Corbijn)
19. Fatboy Slim—Praise You (Spike Jonze)
20. Aerosmith—Cryin'/Amazing (Marty Callner)
21. Suicide—Frankie Teardrop (Paul Dougherty & Walter Robinson)
22. Daft Punk—Around the World (Michel Gondry)
23. Nine Inch Nails—Closer (Mark Romanek)
24. New Order—Perfect Kiss (Jonathan Demme)
25. R.E.M.—Everybody Hurts (Jake Scott)
26. Neil Young—This Note's for You (Julien Temple)
27. Pixies—Head On
28. R.E.M.—Losing My Religion (Tarsem)

29. Basement Jaxx—Cish Cash (Pleix)
30. Britney Spears—Toxic (Joseph Kahn)
31. Bruce Springsteen—Dancing in the Dark (Brian De Palma)
32. Dire Straits—Money for Nothing (Steve Barron)
33. Beatles—Can't Buy Me Love (Richard Lester)
34. A-Ha—Take On Me (Steve Barron)
35. Radiohead—Just (Jamie Thraves)
36. Audioslave—Cochise (Mark Romanek)
37. Queen—Bohemian Rhapsody (Bruce Gowers)
38. Talking Heads—Love for Sale (David Byrne & Melvin Sokolsky)
39. Sum 41—Hell Song (Marc Klasfeld)
40. Outkast—Hey Ya! (Bryan Barber)
41. Chris Isaak—Wicked Game (Herb Ritts)
42. Björk—Bachelorette (Michel Gondry)
43. Weezer—Buddy Holly (Spike Jonze)
44. UNKLE—Rabbit in Your Headlights (Jonathan Glazer)
45. Chemical Brothers—Out of Control (W.I.Z.)
46. Rentals—Friends of P. (Matt Sharp & Jason Russio)
47. X—Burning House of Love
48. Devo—Whip It (Gerald V. Casale)
49. Fountains of Wayne—Stacy's Mom (Chris Applebaum)
50. Metallica—One (Michael Salomon & Bill Pope)
51. Björk—It's Oh So Quiet (Spike Jonze)
52. Godley & Creme—Cry (Godley & Creme)
53. Grandmaster Flash and the Furious Five—The Message (Alvin Hartley)
54. LL Cool J—Mama Said Knock You Out (Paris Barclay)
55. Eminem—Without Me (Joseph Kahn)
56. Cars—You Might Think (Jeff Stein & Charlex)
57. Madonna—Ray of Light (Jonas Åkerlund)
58. Lisa Loeb—Stay (Ethan Hawke)
59. Beck—Deadweight (Spike Jonze)
60. Smashing Pumpkins—1979 (Jonathan Dayton & Valerie Faris)
61. Pearl Jam—Jeremy (Mark Pellington)
62. Howard Jones—The Prisoner (Danny Kleinman)
63. Michael Jackson—Earth Song (Nicholas Brandt)
64. Tool—Prison Sex (Adam Jones)
65. Daft Punk—Da Funk (Spike Jonze)
66. Foo Fighters—Big Me (Jesse Peretz)
67. Smashing Pumpkins—Tonight, Tonight (Jonathan Dayton & Valerie Faris)

68. Bruce Springsteen—Glory Days (John Sayles)
69. Nirvana—In Bloom (Kevin Kerslake)
70. Prince—Money Don't Matter 2 Night (Spike Lee)
71. Beck—Devil's Haircut (Mark Romanek)
72. Eurythmics—Beethoven (I Love to Listen To) (Sophie Muller)
73. A Tribe Called Quest—Scenario (Jim Swaffield)
74. David Bowie—Ashes to Ashes (David Mallet)
75. D'Angelo—Untitled (Paul Hunter)
76. Steriogram—Walkie Talkie Man (Michel Gondry)
77. Kanye West—All Falls Down (Chris Milk)
78. Captain Beefheart—Lick My Decals Off, Baby (Don Van Vliet)
79. Frankie Goes to Hollywood—Two Tribes (Godley & Creme)
80. Run-D.M.C.—Walk This Way (Jon Small)
81. Nirvana—Heart-Shaped Box (Anton Corbijn)
82. 2Pac & Dr. Dre—California Love (Hype Williams)
83. En Vogue—Free Your Mind (Mark Romanek)
84. Paul Simon—You Can Call Me Al (Gary Weis)
85. U2—Where the Streets Have No Name (Meiert Avis)
86. Radiohead—Karma Police (Jonathan Glazer)
87. Billy Idol—Cradle of Love (David Fincher)
88. Twisted Sister—We're Not Gonna Take It (Marty Callner)
89. Ryan Adams—New York, New York (James Minchin)
90. Guns N' Roses—Welcome to the Jungle (Nigel Dick)
91. Madonna—Borderline (Mary Lambert)
92. Pat Benatar—Love is a Battlefield (Bob Giraldi)
93. Golden Earring—Twilight Zone (Dick Maas)
94. Eminem—Mosh (Ian Inaba)
95. John Vanderslice—Pale Damage (Brent Chesanek)
96. Kinks—Come Dancing (Julien Temple)
97. Who—Happy Jack (Michael Lindsay-Hogg)
98. Missy Elliott—Work It (Dave Meyers)
99. Herbie Hancock—Rockit (Godley & Creme)
100. Scarface—On My Block (Marc Klasfeld)

Index